# MERE CREATURES

## A Study of Modern Fantasy Tales for Children

From the pen of Aesop to the studios of Walt Disney, animals have always had a powerful appeal as central characters in the stories most loved by children. In this study of ten twentieth-century classics of children's literature, Elliott Gose explores affinities between primitive stories and lore and contemporary fantasy tales, and demonstrates the literary art with which animal and other non-human characters are created.

Gose points out that important characters in many of the books are like the animal trickster figure in primitive myth. Toad in *The Wind in the Willows*, Charlotte in *Charlotte's Web*, and Bilbo Baggins in *The Hobbit*, among others, embody unsocialized traits that appeal to children in their undermining of conformity. Many of the stories concern a naïve hero who, without losing his innocent good nature, becomes knowledgeable and competent through an adventure that often follows the traditional quest pattern, culminating in the redefinition of the hero's individuality. Psychological integration is matched by social change: the hero brings back that 'animal energy' that revitalizes society.

Gose's study illustrates not only the timelessness of such characters in fantasy literature, but also their effectiveness in communicating profound psychological insights.

ELLIOTT GOSE is Professor of English, University of British Columbia. His earlier books include *The Transformation Process in Joyce's 'Ulysses'* and *The World of the Irish Wonder Tale*.

ELLIOTT GOSE

# MERE CREATURES

## A Study of Modern Fantasy Tales for Children

UNIVERSITY OF TORONTO PRESS
Toronto Buffalo London

© University of Toronto Press 1988
Toronto Buffalo London
Printed in Canada
ISBN 0-8020-5761-6 (cloth)
ISBN 0-8020-6674-7 (paper)

Printed on acid-free paper

---

**Canadian Cataloguing in Publication Data**

Gose, Elliott B., 1926–
Mere creatures

Includes bibliographical references and index.
ISBN 0-8020-5761-6 (bound). – ISBN 0-8020-6674-7 (pbk.)

1. Children's stories, English – History and criticism.
2. Animals in literature.   3. Fantasy in literature.
4. Children's stories – Psychological aspects.
I. Title.

PR888.F3G68 1988     823′.91′099282     C87-095255-2

---

Design: William Rueter RCA

This book has been published with the help of a grant from the Canadian
Federation for the Humanities, using funds provided by the Social Sciences and
Humanities Research Council of Canada.

This book is for
Kathy, Peter, and Sally

# Contents

PREFACE ix
ACKNOWLEDGMENTS xi

## PART ONE

Introduction 3
1 Darwin and Myth in the Nursery *Just So Stories* 17
2 Id, Ego, and Self *Winnie-the-Pooh* 29
3 The Emergence of the Trickster *The Wind in the Willows* 42
4 Love, Life, and Death *Charlotte's Web* 53
5 The Development of the Hero *The Jungle Book* 63

## PART TWO

Introduction 83
6 Newer Wonder Tales *The Wizard of Oz* and *Ozma of Oz* 90
7 Beyond Absurdity *The Mouse and His Child* 108
8 Epic Integration *Watership Down* 122
9 Archetypal Integration *Watership Down* 135
10 Crossing the Border *The Hobbit* 148
11 Conclusion 169

APPENDIX 183
NOTES 187
INDEX 195

# Preface

NIMAL TALES have a long history, reaching back to the origins of oral narrative. While most of the tales dealt with in this book include live animals as characters, in some the protagonists are stuffed animals, mechanical animals, or even imaginary beings. Whether modelled on live, inanimate, or imaginary creatures, such fictional characters derive their age-old appeal from the sense of connection they offer with a stratum of existence that may be lower and thus less than human but is also simply other and thus potentially more than human.

As the word *modern* suggests in the subtitle, I discuss in detail only tales written in the past one hundred years, although I connect some of them to ancient tales from the oral tradition. I have limited my analysis to ten works in the belief that I can best demonstrate their importance by a detailed appreciation of them. This decision has meant leaving out some stories that particular readers might have hoped or expected to find treated here. The use of animals in children's stories is broad and rich, and I don't pretend to cover all the variations, even in fantasy.

Those who want a survey can turn to Margaret Blount's energetic coverage in *Animal Land: The Creatures of Children's Fiction* (1974). For a literate discussion I recommend Roger Sale's often perceptive analysis of a number of animal fantasies in *Fairy Tales and After: From Snow White to E.B. White* (1978). A useful study of modern children's fantasy is Ann Swinfen's *In Defence of Fantasy* (1984). It includes cogent comment on animal fantasies, particularly in chapters 2 and 8.

It is only fair to alert the reader that for me the appreciation of fantasy includes a psychological dimension. I spell out in chapter 1 my belief in what D.W. Winnicott terms a sense of the self; C.G. Jung uses the same term as a goal in what he calls the individuation process; Bruno Bettelheim refers to a similar concept when he speaks of the integration process in a fairy-tale.[1] I shall be consistently calling attention to such processes in my discussion of the narratives dealt with in this book. But my aim will be not simply to impose a psychoanalytic schema on the books; rather I will be adapting some generalized findings of depth psychology, applied to fairy-tale and myth, to provide insight into the literary qualities of the books: their use of language, characterization, theme, and plot structure.

To conclude, let me say that I enjoy reading these authors, and took pleasure in writing this book. Emulating them, I have tried to write in a lively manner about books that I admire for their imaginative reasonance. Since I don't admire them all equally, I've also indicated my reservations. But mainly I have aimed to pass on enjoyment as well as some enlightenment to the reader of the chapters that follow.

# Acknowledgments

I WOULD LIKE to express my appreciation of the students in my children's literature classes over several years now. Their enthusiasm and willingness to take seriously the works discussed here helped to validate my own belief in the value of these tales. More specifically, I owe a debt to my friend, Nancy McMinn, and my wife, Kathy, for reading the manuscript with care as well as appreciation, and for numerous suggestions that have improved its style, content, and organization. I am grateful to the University of British Columbia for granting me study leave and providing me with grants for typing the manuscript.

For material quoted in this book I am indebted as follows: from *Winnie-the-Pooh* by A.A. Milne, copyright 1926 by E.P. Dutton, renewed 1954 by A.A. Milne, reprinted by permission of the publisher, E.P. Dutton, a division of NAL Penguin Inc, permission also granted by Methuen Children's Books; from *Charlotte's Web* by E.B. White, permission granted by Harper & Row; from *The Mouse and His Child* by Russell Hoban, permission granted by Harper & Row and by Faber and Faber; from *Watership Down*, by Richard Adams, copyright 1972 by Richard Adams, reprinted by permission of Macmillan Publishing Company, permission also requested of Rex Collings; from *The Hobbit* by J.R.R. Tolkien, copyright 1966 by J.R.R. Tolkien, reprinted by permission of Houghton Mifflin Company, permission also granted by Allen & Unwin; from *The Hero with a Thousand Faces* by Joseph Campbell, Bollingen Series XVII, copyright 1949, © 1976 renewed by Princeton University Press, diagram p 245 and excerpts reprinted by permission of Princeton University Press, permission also granted by Routledge & Kegan Paul.

# PART ONE

# Introduction

LL FICTION creates illusion, but the dominant fictional mode of our era, realism, attempts to play down the illusion by describing people, scenes, and actions that are in accord with our notion of how the environment functions, what really happens in life. Critics have noted how so-called realistic fiction can actually cater to our illusions about life, making improbable wish-fulfilment seem plausible; fantasy fiction goes even further and contravenes one of the key premisses in our conception of how the actual world functions. Thus my definition of fantasy is of a narrative that is based on the contradiction or calling in question of a natural law.

The stories dealt with in this book usually rest on the simple premiss that animals can think and talk the way we do. Because it is children's fantasy, the tale may also grant consciousness to stuffed animals, with the additional boon of their being able to speak to human beings, as in *Winnie-the-Pooh*. It may even animate mechanical toys, allowing them mobility within the limits of their machinery, as in *The Mouse and His Child*. Because Pooh and the mouse child are only modelled on animals, I have used the term *creatures* in my title, to include them and other humanized characters in the books we shall be considering.

In another kind of children's fantasy fiction, the author does not simply add an extra premiss or two to our already existing sense of the world. Rather he creates a population of creatures quite different from any we believe can exist – perhaps non-human creatures as in the hobbits and dwarves of Tolkien's Middle-earth, or a live scarecrow and a tin woodman as in the Oz books, or the prototypes of our present-day animals, as in the *Just So Stories*. Tolkien, Baum, and Kipling set their tales in lands far away from ours both in space and in time. The terrain and buildings in these lands are usually exotic, many of our natural laws are taken for granted, but some are replaced by the magical principle that words can take the place of actions. We can delight in the freedom (and the threat) that magic brings; like subjective fantasy (day-dream), it assumes that a wish can change the world.

In fact, fantasy fiction has its roots in day-dreams. Both offer an escape from the outside world. While both are narratives, fantasy fiction is usually free of the more egocentric characteristics of subjective fantasy. The self-indulgence of day-dream is replaced thematically by some element of adult responsibility, a sense of the internal and external conflicts that are part of life. Similarly, the vague setting of subjective fantasy is replaced in fantasy fiction by natural and social details that build up a recognizably fictional world and by a style that simultaneously pulls readers into the story and distances them from it.

In *Winnie-the-Pooh*, for instance, the tone and attitude of the narrator, especially in the introduction and conclusion that frame the stories, often encourage us to remember that this is a story about a stuffed bear that is his son's toy rather than drawing us in to share the fantasy of the bear's adventures. But the style and sensibility associated with Pooh, whose songs and day-dreams are so central, invite a suspension of disbelief that balances the distancing effect of the narrative voice. On another level, Pooh's childish greed and naïve openness, while ingratiating, are balanced by the events of the stories. There is a realism in the difficulties with which unfriendly nature and social decorum thwart Pooh's attempts to satisfy appetite, and in the internal conflicts he and Piglet have, as well as in their external conflicts with other creatures.

Despite this difference in premiss between fantasy fiction and realistic fiction, the two usually share a reliance on the conventions of literary realism. As W.R. Irwin has shown, the author of a fantasy tale often takes extra care in introducing us to the fantasy world, providing explanation or description to ensure the suspension of our disbelief.[1] Similarly Christine Brooke-Rose demonstrates that science fiction is a kind of fantasy that depends heavily on the conventions of literary realism to establish its alien worlds.[2] The same is true of animal fantasy: Richard Adams, for instance, sustains the heroic quest of his rabbits by a constant evocation of the English countryside, its plants, its geographical features, its weather, and its seasons. He also provides a realistic underpinning to his rabbits' primitive but humanized culture by frequent reference to actual rabbit physiology and habits (supported by an introductory reference to a volume of natural history, R.M. Lockley's *The Private Life of the Rabbit*).

Like Adams, most writers of fantasy fiction depend on a double appeal, to the reader's desire both to escape and to face reality. Most individuals experience difficulty in balancing interior feelings and exterior forces; fantasy fiction offers a temporary solution to its reader by decisively shifting the balance and focus toward the inward state. This shift by no means assures the bland escape of wish-fulfilment, however. Internal psychic conflict can be as important as conflict between the individual and an outside force. Most of the tales we shall consider present internal conflicts; although the drama comes from struggle with an opponent, this external conflict symbolizes or reflects an internal one.

Why do authors choose to write fantasy about non-human creatures? Animals that can speak provide a relief from everyday realities and routines. We are intrigued that an author has used imagination to create them. Yet since animals are presumed to live limited lives, narratives about them simplify the concerns of human society, streamlining the complexities of our culture to bring out essentials. Because animals express likes and dislikes without disguise, they can be used to lay bare the underpinnings of our complex social relations. The directness of their natures and their interactions may also be used to criticize human deviousness and lack of vitality, as Kipling does in *The Jungle Books*. Or the narrative gift of simplification may be used to reassure children, as Milne does in *Winnie-the-Pooh*, that they can cope with a demanding world.

Perhaps most important, an author who chooses to write about animals can project through them psychological concerns that his readers either cannot or do not wish to experience directly in human terms. Heroic fantasy is still written about human beings, of course. But a literary fantasy that chooses non-human creatures for its focus not only demands more of an imaginative leap; by that very fact it more easily ensures that many readers will be able to leave behind the internal moral censor that will otherwise cause some readers not to begin a similar tale with human characters. We have already seen that an author like Richard Adams, after his initial imaginative leap felt obliged to provide a wealth of realistic details to substantiate the world of *Watership Down*. But because he was writing about heroic animals, he also felt free to introduce a host of antiquated literary techniques, such as pretentious chapter epigraphs, epic similes, and other classical conventions. And these conventions are effective in describing the quest of these rabbits partly because readers have dropped their realistic expectation in order to become emotionally involved with a story about mere creatures.

As we shall discover in the second half of this study, other tales also make

good use of the quest, with its overtones of stagnation demanding renewal, of the need to encounter strange beings who offer important tests, of the search for meaning and value. This search may be as archaic as Bilbo's for a dragon-guarded treasure or as modern as that of the mouse and his child for meaning in the empty abstractions of verbal philosophy or in the death-dealings of physical nature. And the cast of creatures may also be as traditional as Tolkien's elves and goblins, or as contemporary as Hoban's dump rats and wind-up toys. In either case the tone and style is suited to the ambience of the characters, and the potential of their nature is mined for the theme. Bilbo's encounter with the trickster, Gollum, at the dark roots of a mountain is as important a test, and opportunity for psychic growth, as the mouse child's encounter with the void of infinite regress at the bottom of a winter pond. I shall provide more background on the quest, and its relation to the primitive shaman, in the introduction to part 2.

The rabbits who are Adams's epic heroes carry with them some of the vitality of the natural world from which man has separated, to his cost; in contrast, the gnomes who are L. Frank Baum's villains embody the crude aggression and greed of that world. Primitive story-tellers were also aware of, but projected onto animals, the dark side of humanity. Today, a writer like Russell Hoban may use shrews and weasels to embody the Darwinian search for satisfaction of the brute need for territory and food. *But Watership Down*, *The Wizard of Oz*, and *The Mouse and His Child* also offer a higher potential, the possibility of contact with an affirming spirit, with a cosmic level where the limitations of our time sense disappear. Such a belief is easier to entertain in our secular age if cast in the form of a fantasy with characters that are not human. The archetypal level is evident in Fiver's visions in *Watership Down*, the protective power of a kiss from the good Witch of the North in *The Wizard of Oz*, and the mechanical mouse's fortune, told in oracular fashion by a frog in *The Mouse and His Child*.

Thanks to Tolkien's success, recent authors feel able to write fantasies that have spiritual overtones and are openly intended for adults. But children are still the preferred audience, perhaps because their directness can be more readily counted on to match and appreciate that of the animals and other non-human characters in the creatures' heroic adventures. As we shall see presently, there seems to be a large community of interest among children, animals, and primitive adults. Humanity's fascination with animals goes far back in time. The pictures of animals on cave walls around the Mediterranean date from the ice-ages; one of the caves, Les Trois Frères, at Ariège in southwestern France, dates from the Middle Magdalenian period (approximately thirteen thousand years ago). In what is

termed its sanctuary, the cave contains pictures of two human figures, both male, both dressed in animal skins. One figure is surrounded by animals, mainly bison, but also horses and reindeer; the other, alone, is the Sorcerer, 'the only figure in this complex that is painted as well as engraved.'[3] Neither figure carries a weapon and both have the upraised foot of a dancer, suggesting their participation in a ceremony connecting both with the animal kingdom. Among primitive cultures, the world-wide phenomenon of totem identification of a clan with an animal indicates an even longer connection. Accepting some form of the theory of evolution makes it easy to speculate that there was a period in which humanity was growing apart from the other animals by developing speech and consciousness; it must then have begun to look back toward them as less than itself and yet part of the grand unconscious unity of nature from which humanity was separating itself. Depth psychology holds that one of the functions of dreams is to put us in touch with the animal level of ourselves, a substratum on which both our physical and psychic natures rest, though it is not usually present to consciousness. Animal figures in dreams often represent instincts that can be helpful if accepted, fearsome if denied. As Heinrich Zimmer put it, 'The interior animal asks to be accepted, permitted to live with us, as [a] somewhat queer, often puzzling companion. Though mute and obstinate, nevertheless it knows better than our conscious personalities, and would be known to know better if we could only learn to listen to its dimly audible voice. The voice is the voice and urge of instinct, and ... can effect our rescue from the impasses into which our conscious personalities will be ... conducting us.'[4] I look upon the tales we shall be studying as examples of the good that comes to an author – and then to his reader – when he is willing to listen to his animal voices, to dramatize their speech and actions, to elaborate them in a conscious framework that helps to bridge the gap between human and animal, conscious and unconscious, individual and species.

Tales about animals are part of a tradition probably as old as fiction itself. Many primitive tales focus on a mythological figure that takes different animal identities in different parts of the world and has been given the generic title of Trickster. In Europe, this figure appears in the medieval adventures of Reynard, a humanized fox developed from older folk-tales. In African tales, Trickster is a spider, Anansi, and a tortoise, but is best known to us as the hare or rabbit in stories brought to America by slaves and kept alive in the oral tradition of their new language. This animal trickster finally entered literature as Brer Rabbit, the protagonist of stories recorded for children by Joel Chandler Harris in the nineteenth century.[5]

One reason why blacks who were brought to America kept alive the Brer Rabbit tales is that they represented a model for survival. A slave who had no rights under an alien morality would find much to admire in a protagonist who outwits dominant predators through resourceful wit and amoral tricks. That such tales appeal to children is also understandable. They, too, are subject to beings who enforce arbitrary and difficult rules. Though part of the child looks up to adults and tries to emulate them, another part resists having to give up bodily pleasures that are socially taboo. Forced to repress natural desires, a child will readily sympathize with a vital character who evades such restrictions. In fact, as we shall discover when we follow the career of Toad in chapter 3, repressive rules are an encouragement to play-acting, to duplicity, deviousness, and lying, to the emergence of traits associated with the primitive trickster.

Among the American Indians, Trickster led a protean existence, as Raven on the Northwest Coast, Coyote on the Great Plains and in the Far West, and Hare in the Central Woodlands, as well as Spider, Blue Jay, Mink, Turtle, and Raccoon.[6] These tales were told both to instruct and to entertain. Because Trickster is a shamelessly amoral character, he does all the things that were taboo among the Indian tribes. Stories about him thus offer a disguised opportunity for vicarious enjoyment, an indulgence in forbidden pleasure in the guise of inculcating official values through negative examples.

Since we shall be encountering the trickster a number of times in the children's tales discussed in this book, it is worth investigating this figure in more detail. From the nature of the animals involved, we can note that, whether prey (like rabbit) or predator (like coyote), the trickster is usually a wild animal living by its wits, as demonstrated by its brief incursions as thief into the human world. The connection between animal and human is clear and constant in the activities of this figure. Just as in his animal form Trickster is often called Old Man, so when he appears in human form he interacts with animals as a peer, albeit a powerful and manipulative one. Especially in his human form, Trickster may be a culture hero of the tribe. The Northwest Coast version, Raven, brings light to human beings and rescues them from such threats as whales or floods. Usually, however, Trickster shows no set purpose, no fixed nature: as Paul Radin points out, he acts out of an 'impulse over which he has no control.'

The antiquity of Trickster is indicated by his being what Radin calls an 'inchoate being of undetermined proportions, a figure foreshadowing the shape of man.'[7] Carl Jung develops a similar insight: 'Radin's trickster cycle preserves the shadow in its pristine mythological form, and thus points back to a very much earlier stage of consciousness which existed before the birth of the myth, when the Indian was still groping about in a similar mental darkness. Only when his consciousness reached a higher level could he detach the earlier state from himself and objectify it ... to look back on a lower and inferior state.' The shadow to which Jung refers is what he calls a 'split-off personality' that 'stands in a complementary or compensatory relation to the ego personality.'[8] In individual psychology, the shadow is usually all those base attributes that society has taught us to grow beyond. Consciously we reject them, but unconsciously they represent a primal energy that needs an outlet. The shadow is connected with our animal nature.

It is a tribute to the psychic health and wholeness of the primitive Indian culture that, instead of repressing, it gave expression to this inferior state. Listening to these animal tales, the audience responded with 'laughter tempered by awe,' according to Radin. Even in our own culture, animal tales have an important and not entirely dissimilar function. Animated cartoons often feature trickster animal heroes: a mouse or a cat, a roadrunner or a coyote, a woodpecker or a rabbit. These creatures in their violence and amorality are a popular debasement of the trickster. Even in the more enlightened tales I shall be discussing, this primitive figure has a comparable vitality. We shall see a spider take on her immemorial role of trickster in *Charlotte's Web*; witness the process whereby a toad is forced into tricksterism in *The Wind in the Willows*; watch Bilbo learn the art of that craft from the arch-trickster, Gandolf, and from the ur-trickster, Gollum, in *The Hobbit*; and hear quintessential trickster tales in the adventures of El-ahrairah, tales that serve as models for the rabbits who must live by their wits in *Watership Down*. We shall also meet a number of tricksters in the *Just So Stories*.

One of the qualities associated with Trickster is playfulness; according to Radin, 'laughter, humor and irony permeate everything' he does. Far from being merely regressive and childish, humour and playfulness are closely allied to creativity. In fact, it has been argued that play is central to individual development and the origins of culture. Because play is clearly important in childhood and in animals, I propose to devote the rest of this introduction to a consideration of it.

Johan Huizinga in *Homo Ludens* traced all of man's important cultural manifestations to a sense of play. Although somewhat schematic, his case is nevertheless compelling. He developed two main characteristics of play: (1) it is done in free time away from the press of life's commitments; (2) having its own sphere as an interruption of ordinary life, play is only for fun, only pretend; in fact Huizinga pointed out that the word *illusion* 'means literally "in-play."' I would emphasize the parallel between these conditions and those of literature, which also creates illusion and offers the reader free time away from the press of living.

Huizinga demonstrated that poetry and drama, the two oldest forms of literature, began as play. Poetry 'lies beyond seriousness, on that more primitive and original level where the child, the animal, the savage and the seer belong, in the region of dream, enchantment, ecstasy, laughter.'[9] Focusing for the moment on the last four terms, I would suggest that, just as laughter frees our day consciousness from the burden of life as a serious business, so dreams compensate us for our conventionally unimaginative daytime activities. We shall return to ecstasy in the introduction to part 2.

Huizinga considered poetry to be intimately connected with myth. 'Working with images and the aid of imagination, myth tells the story of things that were supposed to have happened in primitive times.' The 'boundless exaggeration ... carefree inconsistencies and whimsical variations' of myth suggested to Huizinga that its sacredness is 'tinged with a certain element of humour,' its seriousness inextricably involved with the sense of play. (These two qualities are unified in primitive belief; only in the sphere of civilization are the playful and the earnest, the imaginary and the real, art and life separated.) When we come to the *Just So Stories*, we will discover how compatible are myth and humour, fused in that playfulness that can evoke the sacred in a child's story.

In his discussion of myth, Huizinga touched on one final element that is germane to this study. He believed that 'the play attitude must have been present before human culture or human speech existed, [and is] hence the ground on which personification and imagination work.' Play is in fact widespread among animals, and is not always mere preparation for adult activities such as stalking and fighting. Huizinga insisted that 'personification of gods and spirits in beast form' being 'one of the most important elements in archaic religious life,' we should imagine primitive man playing an animal in a manner both sacred and humorous, terrifying yet only a mime. We may thus infer 'that the play-sphere as we observe it in the child still embraces the savage's whole life.' Huizinga's connection of the primitive and the child mentality is a common one (though it is also disputed). It is a connection I have made and shall continue to make. Whether in child or primitive, Huizinga claimed, 'living myth knows no distinction between play and seriousness,' between laughter and terror.[10] Deriving pleasure from terror must be part of what causes people to read tales of terror. Movie horror shows present an even more involving form of fright, since there we actually see images of people caught up in threatening and terrifying situations. But the illusions that appear in fantasy written for children have a different premiss. Although they offer strong threats to the main characters, the convention is well established that no such danger will be fatal to the hero.

For a nearer approach to the psychic dimension of play, we cannot do better than turn to the work of D.W. Winnicott, a child therapist who expanded Freudian concepts to discover the crucial importance in a child's early development of transitional objects (such as cloth animals; he cites Winnie-the-Pooh). In a collection of essays titled *Playing and Reality*, Winnicott laid out a number of concepts relevant to this study. Like Huizinga he sees play as central: since 'the task of reality acceptance is never completed' and no one is ever completely 'free from the strain of relating inner and outer reality ... relief from this strain is provided by an intermediate area of experience ... which is not challenged.' Adults may 'lose' themselves in art or religion as a child does in play. In a summary halfway through the book, Winnicott clarifies what play is for a child: 'This area of playing is not inner psychic reality. It is outside the individual, but it is not the external world. Into this play area the child gathers objects or phenomena from external reality and uses these in the service of some sample derived from inner or personal reality ... In playing, the child manipulates external phenomena in the service of the dream and invests chosen external phenomena with dream meaning and feeling.'[11]

Winnicott's theory about playing as a bridge between inner and outer reality is well illustrated by Maurice Sendak's *Where the Wild Things Are*.[12] In this story, a boy named Max is sent to his room and there creates a fantasy world. Sendak's illustration shows Max with his eyes closed while the doorposts and bedposts turn into trees. Two panels later, Max is shown in a complete forest, and the text explains that the walls of the room have become the world. In Winnicott's formulation, 'in playing' Max has manipulated 'external phenomena [his room] in the service of the dream [his imagination].' The interesting question is why Max chooses to populate his fantasy with monsters.

Sendak's story begins in a situation closer to Winnicott's definition of where play takes place. Max is in his wolf costume, a child's sleeping suit specially fitted with pointed ears and a long bushy tail. We see him taking on the role of wolf and hear his mother complain, 'WILD THING!' Two of the ways Max shows his wildness are by chasing his dog with a fork in his hand and by shouting at his mother, 'I'LL EAT YOU UP!' For the latter he is sent to his room, supperless. Thus the story begins with play, Max's giving free rein to his aggressive, predatory impulses and finding that they are not appreciated. As Winnicott indicates, playing is not only 'inherently exciting,' it is also 'precarious' because it 'belongs to the interplay in the child's mind of that which is subjective (near-hallucination) and that which is objectively perceived (actual, or shared reality).'[13] Entering so strenuously into the subjective role of wild thing, Max has upset the 'precarious' balance by violating the social decorum of 'shared reality.' His excitement has generated a response from parental authority.

Deprived of shared reality, Max in his room indulges his imagination and journeys beyond the forest-bedroom as 'near-hallucination' into the far-fantasy world of the wild monsters. This transition is effected pictorially by a pirate boat named *Max*. Arrived in this subjective land, Max meets larger-than-life versions of those wild things he had acted and his mother had criticized. First he shows his mastery over them by 'the magic trick' of staring into their eyes 'without blinking once.' This act of dominance frightens them; they call him 'the most wild thing of all' and make him their king. Secure in his authority, Max calls for saturnalia: 'Let the wild rumpus start!' The next three double pages Sendak devotes to full-page illustrations without text. The first shows the creatures dancing to the full moon, though only Max in his wolf costume is howling. The second shows the creatures swinging from trees, presumably in honor of Max's actual simian descent (the other creatures look too heavy to be very lithe). In the third double page, Max rides on the back of the bull monster – a minotaur with human feet – eyes closed, his sceptre raised on high. Stopping the wild rumpus at this point, Max sends the wild things 'off to bed without their supper.' Having thus emulated his mother, he finds himself thinking of what she represents and realizes he is lonely for human love and food. He decides to go, deaf to the blandishments of the monsters: 'Oh please don't go – we'll eat you up – we love you so!' Despite their roaring and gnashing of teeth, Max sails back home where he finds his supper waiting for him on the table in his back-to-normal bedroom.

Having indulged his aggressive fantasy to the full in the three central panels, Max is able not only to return to shared reality, but to objectify the implication of these wild impulses. What he wants are food and love, both of which he was deprived of by his earlier wild conduct at home. The wild things offer him a version of both: 'We love you so – we'll eat you up.' Intuiting his need, they offer the closest they can, but it comes out like that play-threat of adults to children, 'I'm going to eat you up!'[14] The sublimated cannibalism of this mock threat may seem a joke to the adult who does it, but is enough to frighten any infant. Repetition may either neutralize the infant's fear or condition the child to enjoy the fear. Sendak has made this threat the very one that Max had used earlier against his mother. Having mastered, indulged, and then become satiated with his wild impulses, Max is finally able to take on the adult role and look at them from the outside, to balance what they lead to against something else he needs. He chooses to return to the real world because it offers the love and food that his emotions and body require if they are to mature.

I do not mean to suggest that constructive love and tame conformity are to replace indulgence in aggressive wild behaviour. But I would say that Max as child needs the support of love and food as a base from which playing can take place. Such play is, as Winnicott indicates, precarious. It tests limits. Going too far in the shared reality of the household, Max is isolated in his own room. Instead of sulking or indulging in self-pity, he lets his imagination go quite far in giving expression to his animal impulses once he has established dominance over them. Max's constructive use of his fantasy may be understood as part of a process suggested by Winnicott: 'The sense of loss itself can become a way of integrating one's self-experience.'[15] Deprived of human community, Max goes into himself, but what might be an opportunity for escape or revenge is converted into psychic integration.

To put it another way, fantasy is itself a testing of reality, of subjective reality. There are assertive impulses in the psyche. Max discovers the pleasure in dancing, howling, swinging from a branch. But he also discovers that such pleasures are insufficient. And he finally realizes that asserting can become threatening, when his own aggressive words, the ones for which his mother had isolated him, are played back to him in a different key. His return home is not a repudiation of the wild animals; his experience with them is central to the story; precisely because he experienced them so fully, Max is able to get a perspective on them and recognize love and sustenance as more basic.[16]

I have considered Sendak's story at some length not only because it allows us to see the psychological dimension of animal fantasy so clearly, but also because it contains some of the central themes that I shall be developing in the chapters ahead. Max as wolf chasing his dog suggests the conflict between the wild and the tame in animals, a theme that is touched on in all the books we shall consider. The appetite theme is also based on a contrast – between the threat of being devoured ('I'm going to eat you up!') and the appeal of eating (two of the three items on Max's supper tray are a glass of milk and a piece of three-layer cake). Because the two sides of the appetite theme involve the fear of death and the sustaining of life, we shall discover that it is important in most of the books to be considered in this study. Max's acting out the potential of his wolf costume and then being sent to his room illustrate another two-sided theme. Most obviously in *The Wind in the Willows*, but in other stories, too, we shall be meeting creatures like Toad, who act on their impulses, get isolated for it, but prove irrepressible – though Toad, like Max, is reintegrated into the community at the end. And finally, I shall investigate in the concluding chapter the importance of Winnicott's thesis that loss leads to gain. In most of the stories we shall discover that, like Max, the hero does experience loss, rejection, or isolation, and that it is as a consequence of such an experience that he is able to begin the psychic integration that leads to outward success.

The integrative nature of Winnicott's theory is clear. 'It is in playing and only in playing that the individual child or adult is able to be creative and to use the whole personality, and it is only in being creative that the individual discovers the self.' Whereas Winnicott deals with creativity as 'a universal' that 'belongs to being alive,'[17] I am interested not only in how the hero attains wholeness, but in how the reader shares that integrative process and how the author went through it in writing the book. The genesis of several of the books we shall be considering appears to have been connected with meeting children on their own ground. Milne borrowed the characters of an already existing play world shared by his son and his wife; Grahame, Tolkien, and Adams made up the first versions of *The Wind in the Willows*, *The Hobbit*, and *Watership Down* for their own children; and Kipling read his manuscript *Just So Stories* to a group of his own and other children.[18] Although these facts suggest that the tales will be appropriate for children, the creativity that went into them came from the authors. By letting their imaginations enter into an area where inner and outer may be fused, these authors enlisted 'external phenomena in the service of dream' and invested 'chosen external phenomena with dream meaning and feeling.' Being fantasies, their works more clearly announce their illusory nature than do conventional fictions. They thus boldly approximate themselves to the nature of play.

But by releasing his imagination into a fantasy realm, especially one inhabited by animals, the author serves notice that it is doubly removed from the external one, that the reader may lay down his or her defences and vicariously experience a gamut of feelings, some of which may normally be suppressed. Unlike play, of course, the situations will not be of the child's own creation; but he or she will often instinctively prefer and choose a tale because it fills a current psychological need.

All of the narratives I shall be dealing with offer at least that feeling of play that is liberating for the moment. Most of them also offer a sense of the possible re-formation of the world, of an integration that affirms the fullest scope for that sense of self that strives for realization, fulfilment, and creative power. My interest in these tales is thus clearly as much in the relevance of their themes for both children and adults as it is in the artistry with which the themes, the characters, the worlds are created. The reader is invited to share a world of imagination with the implicit offer that he or she may thereby come in contact with a potential that lies below the surface nature of each of us.

In the second half of this introduction, I have tried to connect animal and human through dream and play. But as already indicated, we shall be concerned in the chapters that follow not just with animals but also with other humanized creatures. Tolkien's hobbits, for instance, are the size of children, and live like human beings, in caves that Tolkien emphasizes are dry and comfortably furnished. Hobbits have only the slightest of animal characteristics – 'their feet grow natural leathery soles and thick warm brown hair'.[19] Their small size is in harmony with their natures, which are retiring rather than bellicose. Bilbo Baggins in particular is easily intimidated and is frequently made conscious of his suitability as a meal for some other more aggressive creature, such as a troll, a goblin, a wolf, or an eagle. This vulnerability enables a child easily to identify with him. A similar sense of inadequacy surrounds Pooh. A pre-school or primary school child would empathize with his difficulties in reading and in understanding long words. The limitations of the mechanical toys in *The Mouse and His Child* also suggest why a child might identify with them. But there are other reasons, too, why these less-than-human creatures would appeal to readers. The simplicity of nature of Pooh, Bilbo, and the mouse child is also attractive. None tries hard to hide his feelings (or is successful at it). Unlike an adult, none has developed the persona by which an outer appearance disguises inner reality. Working from the 'living core of the individual personality,' which Winnicott calls the self, all three heroes function to reassure the child that reality, despite its threats, does provide room for self-fulfilment. Since the stories about animals move toward the same positive resolution, we shall find in this reassurance a rationale for the importance of both animals and other subhuman creatures as protagonists of these tales.

In speaking of 'the wild things' in Sendak's tale, I referred to them as animals, creatures, and monsters. Although many of them have sharp claws and teeth, horns, and fuzzy bodies, they don't resemble any known species. But the point about them, as about a stuffed bear or even a metal mouse, is that they represent some aspect of the reader's psyche that is not openly acknowledged during daytime social interactions. Encouraged by these tales not to lose touch with the creature within, the child who reads or hears them is reassured that weakness may be acknowledged without shame, and assertiveness indulged without guilt, that both are natural and can be transformed into strengths as the child develops inner resources to meet the challenges of the outer world.

# 1

# Darwin and Myth in the Nursery

HE *JUST SO STORIES* were first read out by their author to an appreciative nursery audience, and one of their delights is the way Kipling indulges himself in child language. I can remember from my childhood the relish with which my brother and I would mouth the refrain from 'The Elephant's Child': 'Go to the banks of the great grey-green greasy Limpopo River.' I can also remember, less nostalgically, how in my enlightened adulthood I looked over the *Just So Stories* and decided that they really were not suited to mid-century children, thus depriving my son and daughter of the pleasure my parents had shared with us. My justification was twofold, that the tone was arch and the tales unscientific. Both points were true, but neither was on the mark. Herbert Read is, of course, correct in his otherwise appreciative introduction to a modern edition of the tales when he observes that 'the facetious is a dangerous style to adopt, even for children ... Such a style ... is *meant* to amuse; it has a design on us, it is not spontaneously funny.'[1] In 'How the Whale Got His Throat,' for instance, we are introduced to a 'single solitary shipwrecked Mariner, trailing his toes in the water. (He had his Mummy's leave to paddle, or else he never would have done it ...)' I would call the parenthetical sentence a facetious aside detrimental to the progress of the narrative. Or there is that turn-of the-century tic, the omitted prefix, which also disfigures *Ozma of Oz*: ''Member it wasn't the Low Veldt ... but the 'sclusively bare, hot, shiny High Veldt' ('How the Leopard Got His Spots'). But these blemishes are not numerous; for the most part, Kipling used language that still appeals to the 'Little Children' who were announced in the book's subtitle as its intended audience.

It is a book to be read aloud. The oral quality of the humour is well illustrated when the Crocodile first grabs the nose of the Elephant's Child.

'I think,' said the Crocodile – and he said it between his teeth, like this – 'I think today I will begin with Elephant's Child!' ...

The Elephant's Child was much annoyed, and he said, speaking through his nose, like this, 'Led go! You are hurtig be!'

Kipling then plays off the diminished speaking ability of these two against the verbosity of the Bi-Coloured-Python-Rock-Snake, which has the leisure of a mere observer. But in fact the snake does involve himself on the side of the Elephant's Child, as signalled by the following speech: 'Rash and inexperienced traveller, we will now seriously devote ourselves to a little high tension, because if we do not, it is my impression that yonder self-propelling man-of-war with the armour-plated upper deck ... will permanently vitiate your future career.' The contrast between his abstract elocution and the Elephant's Child's direct response to physical stimulus represents two poles of language that Kipling establishes in the stories. As we shall see, the tales are full of evocative descriptive phrases – as 'the Crocodile's musky-tusky mouth' – to which a child can respond immediately. But at the same time, Kipling as narrator includes phrases more in harmony with the Snake's vocabulary, such as 'Precission of the Equinoxes,' which makes playful use of words far beyond the grasp of a little child. Unlike educators who construct graded readers that never strain a child's presumed level of vocabulary, Kipling charms his young readers with long words, including place-names, which at first must be appreciated for their sound alone. In the discussion that follows, I shall be focusing on the ways he stimulates his young readers' active participation through sensuous words that invite oral savouring.

The style of these stories draws on those obvious resources of language that children and poets tend to favour: alliteration, rhyme, rhythm, and repetition. The alliteration is not merely piled on; 'great grey-green' may sound so, but when these words are capped by 'greasy,' the retraction of the lips can be held and relished. The sense of pulling-in that accompanies the saying of these words is immediately followed by an extrusion with 'Limpopo,' where the p's expel what has been taken in.

The rhyme is uninhibited. When the mariner is swallowed by the whale, or as Kipling comfortingly puts it, when he 'found himself truly inside the Whale's warm, dark, inside cupboards, he stumped and he jumped and he thumped and he bumped, and he pranced and he danced, and he banged and he clanged, and he hit and he bit, and he leaped and he creeped, and he prowled and he howled, and he hopped and he dropped, and he cried and he sighed, and he crawled and he bawled, and he stepped and he lepped, and he danced hornpipes where he shouldn't, and the Whale felt most unhappy indeed.' Good taste would demand that the rhymes stop long before they do, but both the developing narrative and the intended audience justify the eleven pairs. The story demands justification for a small man's being able to upset a great whale, and children always want more, if the rhymes have energy as these pairs do. The child hears a singsong that includes all the physical and oral actions that he or she either enjoys or has perhaps been deprived of enjoying by parental inhibitions and social rules. The mariner, in short, is a stand-in for the child (as Kipling suggested early on when he told us the mariner needed his mother's permission to paddle).

The rhythm is insistent. In 'The Sing-Song of Old Man Kangaroo,' Kipling imbues the narrative with the feel of the race that will cause the kangaroo to be transformed into his present shape. He employs a simple rhythm for the kangaroo: 'Still ran Kangaroo – Old Man Kangaroo. He ran through the ti-trees; he ran through the mulga; he ran through the long grass; he ran through the short grass; he ran through the Tropics of Capricorn and Cancer ...' Although this passage, like many others in the tale, certainly forces the reader into the monotonous cadence of a singsong, the final expansion of the rhythmic frame as the language wittily moves from concrete to abstract provides a nice closure (though it does not end the sentence). Kipling employs a longer verse and breath unit to capture the rhythm of Yellow-Dog Dingo, who is chasing Kangaroo: The first time it is 'Off ran Dingo – Yellow-Dog Dingo – always hungry, grinning like a coal-scuttle – ran after Kangaroo.' The second has a small variation: 'Still ran Dingo – Yellow-Dog Dingo – always hungry, grinning like a rat-trap, never getting nearer, never getting farther – ran after Kangaroo.' The third ends, 'and they came to the Wollgong River,' a more rhythmic conclusion than 'ran after Kangaroo.' But the fourth and fifth endings undercut the pronounced rhythm with a prosaic formula: 'Still ran Dingo – Yellow-Dog Dingo – very much bewildered, very much hungry, and wondering what in the world or out of it made Old Man Kangaroo hop.' Appropriate for a singsong, this undercutting is typical of Kipling's moving toward verse in this story and then coming back to prose. A similar tension is present in the development of the theme. The transformation of Kangaroo is accomplished not by the 'charms and incantations' he expected but by the monotonous singsong of the chase. Both Kangaroo and Dingo bring things down to earth after the chase by pleading hunger. As Dingo says, 'I've made him different from all other animals; but what may I have for my tea?' The narrative has in fact been dominated by a sense of the constraints of environment and of necessity: 'He ran till his hind legs ached. He had to!' The last three words are repeated five times during the chase, always as a climax – or anticlimax – to a rhythmic, poetic evocation of the race.

As hinted in the previous paragraph, rhythm and repetition are closely connected. The rhythms of the chase gain much of their effect by being repeated with variations. The same principle is at work in 'The Beginning of the Armadillos.' A jaguar meets a hedgehog and a tortoise and tries to remember his mother's instructions on the different means of dealing with each.

'When I meet a Hedgehog I am to drop him into the water and then he will uncoil, and when I meet a Tortoise I am to scoop him out of his shell with my paw ...'

'Are you sure of what Your Mummy told you?' said Stickly-Prickly Hedgehog. 'Are you quite sure? Perhaps she said that when you uncoil a Tortoise you must shell him out of the water with a scoop, and when you paw a Hedgehog you must drop him on the shell.'

Slow-and-Solid Tortoise adds to the confusion:

'Perhaps she said that when you water a Hedgehog you must drop him into your paw, and when you meet a Tortoise you must shell him till he uncoils.'

'I don't think it was at all like that,' said Painted Jaguar, but he felt a little puzzled; 'but, please, say it again more distinctly.'

'When you scoop water with your paw you uncoil it with a Hedgehog,' said Stickly-Prickly. 'Remember that, because it's important.'

'*But*,' said the Tortoise, 'when you paw your meat you drop it into a Tortoise with a scoop. Why can't you understand?'

Kipling dramatizes the child's attraction to nonsense, playing on the resources of language, mainly the ability of nouns to become verbs. After getting a paw full of painful hedgehog prickles, Jaguar evolves a rhyme to guide him the next time:

'Can't curl, but can swim –
Slow-Solid, that's him!
Curls up, but can't swim –
Stickly-Prickly, that's him!'

Unfortunately, this verse lacks the stability of a good mnemonic device. Hedgehog is able to reverse its meaning without altering its form:

'Can't curl, but can swim –
Stickly-Prickly, that's him!
Curls up, but can't swim –
Slow-Solid, that's him!'

The child who hears this story has reinforced in a comic way his or her own sense not only of the fun and games of language but also of its potential for confusion.

Listening to 'The Beginning of the Armadillos,' a child is encouraged to feel superior to the poor jaguar and applaud the clever prey who use their wits to escape the physically superior predator. It must have seemed quaint and conservative for a writer in 1902, at the height of the social acceptance of Darwin's theory of natural selection, to come out with a book based on fanciful explanations of how animals obtained their present shapes and appearances. Once offended by Kipling's strategy, I am now more charmed by his cheerful irrelevancies and the distortions of Darwinian themes: survival of the fittest (Old Man Kangaroo), evolution of forms ('How the Rhinoceros Got His Skin'), slight successive variation (the Elephant's Child), protective coloration ('How the Leopard Got His Spots'), and independent convergence of outer characteristics ('The Beginning of the Armadillos'). Just as science is said to provide the modern myths society gives its faith to, so Kipling may be seen as providing humorously didactic myths that explain our origin and nature. Although they absorb Darwinian motifs, these myths unashamedly go back to an animistic and magical vision of the universe, one appropriate to a child's way of seeing, as well as to the outlook of primitive man. In primitive myths and in fairy-tales animals take off their skins to reveal the basic under-shape as human; in these stories the rhinoceros takes off his skin, or the Ethiopian changes his, much to the excitement of his friend the leopard. In the Galapagos, Darwin observed that some finches had in isolation over centuries altered in shape to look like other birds. He inferred that this alteration allowed the finches to take advantage of food sources that are the prerogative of other birds anywhere but the Galapagos. Similarly the hedgehog and the tortoise converge toward the armadillo shape, though in Kipling's tale as a result of conscious choice and mutual aid.

Other pleasures of the *Just So Stories* are Kipling's illustrations and their explanations. The picture illustrating the evolutionary convergence of hedgehog and tortoise is delightful, with its polymorphous intertwining and its cosmic egg shape. Its boldly asserted pictorial premiss is underlined by Kipling's explanation: 'The snouty thing with the little eye ... is the

Armadillo that the Tortoise and the Hedgehog are going to turn into when they have finished bending' (what the tortoise learns) 'and swimming' (what the hedgehog learns). Both are converging from different directions toward a less vulnerable shape that is midway between their former ones.

In place of the natural laws that science had established in the nineteenth century to explain the evolution of species, Kipling offers a world of transformation based on desire and magic. Almost all the stories have overt magic in them. Besides the examples already offered, there is the camel given its hump by 'the Djinn in charge of All Deserts' after he sits down 'to think a Great Magic.' The Kangaroo is provided with sturdy legs and tail by 'the Big God Nqong,' but by means of physical exertion, as we have seen, not through charms and incantations. In 'The Cat That Walked by Himself,' the woman has a shoulder bone by which she three times makes a Singing Magic to draw to her three wild creatures out of the woods. And the most cosmogonic of all the tales, 'The Crab That Played with the Sea,' is full of magic.

This tale of the shaping of earth begins with a variation on the opening of two earlier tales: 'Before the High and Far-Off Times ... came the Time of the Very Beginnings; and that was in the days when the Eldest Magician was getting Things ready.' One of the actions of this omnipotent parent figure is to tell all the animals that they can 'come out and play.' All co-operate except the crab, who decides to 'play alone.' Like the camel and the cat, who were antisocial in earlier stories, the crab will have to pay for his aloofness, but what makes this story different, more powerful, is its context, which is a creation myth.

The Eldest Magician, with the initial aid of the elephant, cow, beaver, and turtle, creates in the North of this unshaped world the Himalayan Mountains, in the East the great Indian Desert, in the West the Everglades of Florida, and in the South the Malay Archipelago. Man, who lives in this archipelago, calls an imperfection to the attention of the Eldest Magician: the environment is disrupted by tidal movement because someone is 'playing with the Sea.' With the help of man's daughter, the Eldest Magician deduces that the someone is Pau Amma, the Crab, and that he is lodged at 'Pusat Tasek – the Heart of the Sea – where the great hollow is that leads down to the heart of the world, and in that hollow grows the Wonderful Tree, Pauh Janggi, that bears the magic twin-nuts.' Although he cannot make the crab obey him now, the Eldest Magician does coax him to emerge. 'He rose to the top of the sea in the moonlight. There was nobody in the world so big as Pau Amma ... One side of his great shell touched the beach at Sarawak; the other touched the beach at Pahang; and he was taller than the smoke of three volcanoes!' But when challenged to show his power as magician, Pau Amma can do nothing. The Eldest Magician then shows his power by causing the crab's shell to fall off. With this liability and the offer of three benefits, the crab finally agrees not to remain outside the social order.

The mythic level of the tale is emphasized by Kipling's two illustrations, especially the first. As glossed by Kipling, 'When the Man has done talking with the Eldest Magician he will walk in the Big Miz-Maze, because he has to. The mark on the stone under the Man's foot is a magic mark ... All this picture is Big Medicine and Strong Magic.' The Big Miz-Maze is, of course, outside the tale, but gives a strong sense of Kipling's characteristic prodigality – of which the illustrations and the end verses are further indications. It is a sense of a universe larger than the story, most obviously man's special relation to the creator. But on the margin of the tale proper is a sense of man's difficulties as he loses the larger picture and enters the maze in which his vision is limited by artificial walls (and in which he is cut off from primal nature). But there is also the sense of a talisman or guide. Man's right foot rests on a stone with 'a magic mark.' This mark is an ancient Indian symbol, the swastika. The word *swastika* means 'well-being' in Sanskrit. In 1905, of course, its associations with Naziism were far in the future; in fact, the arms of Kipling's cross run the other way from the German *Hakenkreuz*. I see it as a regularizing of the many-angled paths of the maze, thus a suggestion that there is a magic that can make sense out of the complexity of the social labyrinth. This myth is outside the child's tale, but not beyond Kipling's shaping imagination, which informs the animistic and magical universe created in this book.

Kipling constructed his stories to appeal to children's love not only of sounds, explanations, and magic, but also of mystery and trickery. Several of these tales make use of the trickster figure. He takes the traditional function of trickery as a prerogative of the weak and adapts it to a kind of fanciful Darwinism, making tricksters of those animals that are prey. Thus when the giraffe and the zebra move to the woods to escape the Ethiopian and the leopard, they develop protective colouring, camouflage. When the man and the leopard arrive at the forest, they can't find their former prey. The Ethiopian says, 'I can smell Giraffe, and I can hear Giraffe, but I can't see Giraffe.' The leopard makes the identical complaint about the zebra. At night the two predators manage to catch their respective prey by sound. Waiting for the morning light, they can finally see the altered appearance of the two. Leopard comments that the zebra ought to be 'a delicate greyish-fawn, and it ought to be Zebra; but it is covered all over with black and purple stripes. What in the world have you been doing to yourself, Zebra? ... How is it done?'

'Let us up,' said the Zebra, 'and we will show you.'

They let the Zebra and the Giraffe get up; and Zebra moved away to some little thorn-bushes where the sunlight fell all stripy, and Giraffe moved off to some tallish trees where the shadows fell all blotchy.

'Now watch,' said the Zebra and the Giraffe. 'This is the way it's done. One – two – three! And where's your breakfast?'

Tricked by their prey, the predators learn to adopt the same strategy, the Ethiopian becoming black 'for hiding in hollows and behind trees,' and then printing black spots with his fingers on the leopard. Thus both become equal in trickery with their prey. In two other tales we shall consider presently, the trickery also comes from the predator or superior figure.

Although the trickery in the leopard tale is the most overtly Darwinian in the *Just So Stories*, three others show a similar pattern. 'How the Whale Got His Throat' begins with the whale's tremendous appetite causing him to devour all the fish in the sea, 'till at last there was only one small fish left.' But he, being an astute fish, asks the whale if he has ever tasted man. No, says the whale, 'What is it like?' The small fish replies, 'Nice but nubbly.' In fact the mariner turns out to be nubbly with a vengeance. He fills the inside of the whale with bumps. If this characterization of man suggests that the small fish knows exactly what he is letting the whale in for, his subsequent warning to the whale makes it absolutely clear. The mariner, 'it is only fair to tell you, is a man of infinite-resource-and-sagacity.' The mariner shows his nubbliness by jumping up and down inside the whale, and his resourcefulness and wisdom when he makes a grating out of his raft and suspenders, a grating that keeps the whale from eating any more large fish, or men. The original trickster, the small astute fish, 'went and hid himself in the mud under the Door-sills of the Equator. He was afraid that the Whale might be angry with him.' But since the whale can now swallow only 'very, very small' fish, whereas the astute fish is merely small, he will at least be spared that fate. (Kipling tells us that the whale and the fish finally become good friends again, although he does so outside the story in the description of his final picture – another masterful mythological one of the Door-sills of the Equator, complete with its guardian giants and their impressive decorations on the door.)

The other tale about prey who evolve is, of course, 'The Beginning of the Armadillos.' As we saw in considering Kipling's use of repetition, the hedgehog and the tortoise are prey who trick the predator, the jaguar, into such confusion that they twice escape him. Their tricksterism is purely verbal the first time, as they mix up his maxim for dealing with each. The second time, they begin by more verbal obfuscation, but end by demonstrating the changed characteristics that each has acquired by emulating the other: 'Then they both curled themselves up and rolled round and round Painted Jaguar till his eyes turned truly cartwheels in his head.' Their trickery befuddles the jaguar not only verbally but viscerally. Told about this new beast, the jaguar's mother advises him to 'leave it alone.'

Two other tales link trickery with Darwinian changes, but in neither of them does the prey that evolves function as the trickster. As we saw in 'The Sing-Song of Old Man Kangaroo,' the Big God Nqong forces the evolution of Kangaroo by having him chased by the predator, Yellow-Dog Dingo. Kangaroo expects his wish – actually a demand – to be granted by effortless magic, and complains at the end that 'this is a practical joke.' He is referring to the somewhat grotesque hind legs and tail he has grown, but the whole experience can also be called a practical joke, a trick played on him by the god. For his temerity in demanding to be made different and 'popular and wonderfully run after,' Kangaroo receives the traditionally appropriate literal fulfilment of his desire.

In the remaining Darwinian tale, it is the predator who is the trickster. When the insatiable curiosity of the Elephant's Child finally leads him to the banks of the Limpopo River, he treads on what he thinks is 'a log of wood.' When it moves, he asks it politely if it has seen a crocodile. 'Come hither, Little One,' says the crocodile. Afraid of a spanking (which his relatives habitually give him when he asks questions), the Elephant's Child demurs. '"Come hither, Little One," said the Crocodile, "for I am the Crocodile," and he wept crocodile-tears to show it was quite true.' Then the Elephant's Child asks the question he has been wanting an answer to:

'Will you please tell me what you have for dinner?'
'Come hither, Little One,' said the Crocodile, 'and I'll whisper.'

Only when he has grabbed his prey does the crocodile answer that his dinner will be the Elephant's Child himself. In contrast to the tricks in the earlier stories, this one is only half successful. As with Old Man Kangaroo, the trick does result in a change to an improved shape of the one who is tricked. But unlike any of the other tales, in 'The Elephant's Child' the trick does not gain the trickster what he desires.

The trickster figure is only one among several characters that Kipling has adapted from the folk-tale. Two other such characters are the helper or ally, and the donor or provider. In 'The Elephant's Child,' there are two helpers, the Kolokolo bird and the python. The Kolokolo bird sends the Elephant's Child on his adventure. Because its advice was helpful, the bird is rewarded. When the Elephant's Child returns enlarged, as it were, from his adventure, he uses his trunk to spank all the relatives who had previously spanked him, but he treats the Kolokolo bird as a friend and ally.

A more ambiguous helper is the Bi-Coloured-Python-Rock-Snake, which spanks the Elephant's Child when they first meet. But after the Crocodile sinks his teeth into the nose of the Elephant's Child, the snake becomes an ally. First he helps keep the Elephant's Child from becoming the crocodile's dinner, and then when the Elephant's Child complains about his elongated nose, the snake points out to him its many advantages; he concludes by suggesting that his pupil use his trunk 'to spank people with.' In this way he also functions as does the donor in a fairy-tale. As analysed by Vladimir Propp, the donor provides the hero with some magical ability or object that the hero then uses to achieve his main objective in the tale.[2] Taking our cue from this pattern, we can see that the main – if covert – aim of the Elephant's Child is to get even with the adults who have invariably punished his natural curiosity. Only two creatures escape the Elephant's Child's punishment: the Kolokolo bird, which satisfied that curiosity, and the snake, which helped him convert the results of curiosity into personal power.

This tale seems to me to demonstrate well Kipling's mastery of narrative construction and of reader appeal. The tale develops a kind of character that is familiar in Kipling's stories for children as it is in primitive cultures: the child who is looked down on for his weakness develops strength and pays back those who have treated him as inferior. This pattern exists in tension with another in Kipling's tales, the need to force the isolated individual into a place in society. For denying the social compact, the camel is punished with a hump and the crab by being reduced to manageable size. In 'The Elephant's Child' an individual who wants to be part of the group is punished by all adults for asking questions, that is, for trying to communicate. But he refuses to be kept down, persists in questioning, suffers pain close to death for it, but emerges changed in shape and in nature, having learned the power of his trunk and the pleasures of aggressiveness. It is therefore appropriate that the adults be punished. The final resolution, however, is to have all the other elephants go get their noses stretched into trunks. 'When they came back nobody spanked anybody any more.'

'The Cat That Walked by Himself,' also makes interesting use of the trickster figure and the self-isolated title character. The story is based on an opposition between the wild and the domestic. Even man is wild to begin with, but woman prefers the dryness and comfort of a cave, and man comes to appreciate its advantages as well. The dramatic question in the story is whether any of the wild animals can be converted to such a life. When the woman makes a singing magic to draw them, the wild dog first decides to go and asks the cat to accompany him. The cat refuses, as he will do when asked by the other two animals. Having successfully enticed Wild Dog, Wild Horse, and Wild Cow into domesticity, the woman puts away her magic, claiming 'we have no more need of either friends or servants in our Cave.' She therefore refuses the cat's request to enter the cave in search of milk from the cow. As they discuss her decision, the woman promises that 'If ever I say one word in your praise, you may come into the Cave.' At the cat's prompting, she makes similar promises about the cat's sitting by the fire and having milk. These promises set the stage for the second part of the tale, in which the cat as trickster manipulates the woman into blessing him unknowingly. In the animism of this early time, each incident involves inanimate things showing volition: her first praise is answered by the skin that normally closes off the cave but falls down to allow the cat in; her second praise is answered by the fire puffing out smoke after which the cat sits by it; her third praise is answered by the milk pot, which cracks so the cat can lap up the spilled milk.

But the cat's victory is not complete. Though befriended by the woman and the child, it has still to make peace with the dog and the man. It makes a bargain with each but concludes each time with its refrain in the story, 'but *still* I am the cat who walks by himself, and all the places are alike to me.' Because of this reservation, both the dog and the man swear partial enmity to the cat. In working out this description of a cat's (supposed) actual place in the domestic ménage, Kipling invented a tale that illustrates another facet of the tension we have seen between the solitary individual and the social compact. The source of the compact, and of the magic that is its cement, is seen to be the woman. Of the wild creatures who at the beginning of the story walk 'by their wild lones,' only the cat remains true to his original condition. First two male animals, the dog and the horse, are domesticated, and especially attached to the man as hunter. But after the third animal, the cow, is domesticated, the cat is finally tempted to become tame, too, in order to have easy sustenance. It is as though the female magic that enticed the other three shifts from the woman to the only other female in the tale, the cow whose milk draws the cat. But because it is not proper magic, the cat can bargain. As trickster, he can try to retain some of his separateness, wildness, loneness. His doing so carries an explicit devaluing of domesticity, which earns him the enmity not only of the woman who started it all but of the first two converts, the dog and the man. This shift is psychologically appropriate: the cat's aloofness is a reminder of their former state, an affront to their having traded freedom for comfort. As at the end of 'The Elephant's Child,' a compromise is reached, a realistic one in which the price of the cat's freedom to roam is its being chased by the dog and the man, and the price of its comfort is catching mice and entertaining the baby, both limitations of freedom.

When we come to Kipling's earlier masterpiece, *The Jungle Book*, in chapter 5, we shall meet another variation on Darwinian motifs. In those stories for older children, we shall discover a diminution of trickery, as Kipling concentrated on the serious business of creating hero tales. He gained much in intensity by focusing on the conflicts of the thoroughly socialized human/animal world, but the single-mindedness of the heroes in those tales becomes an emblem of restricted possibilities when they are put alongside the polymorphous playfulness of the animals in the *Just So Stories*. Kipling's own playfulness in language and imagination is, as I have indicated, perhaps the most refreshing and characteristic quality of the stories. Like the Eldest Magician as he created the world, Kipling invites his animals to 'come out and play' in a fresh world full of mythic possibilities. To our delight, they do.

# 2

# Id, Ego, and Self

*INNIE-THE-POOH* offers the
child a sensuous world in which the appetites are not discouraged, a
protected world in which no serious mishap will occur. But we don't have to
look very far into the book to discover that it is not mere escapist literature.
Within the reassurance offered by its simple premiss that stuffed animals
have a life and nature of their own, each adventure functions as a testing of
physical and psychological realities from which the listening child can
learn. The first two chapters, for instance, are cautionary and deal quite
directly with the results of attempts at satisfying appetite.

Chapter 1 carefully inducts the young child into a world of toys
impervious to pain. The author-father talks to Christopher Robin about his
stuffed bear. The chapter is framed by Christopher Robin's dragging the
bear first down and finally up the stairs. The importance of this action
becomes evident at the end of the chapter. The father has finished telling
the tale of Pooh's attempts to get honey, attempts that end with his being
accidentally shot by Christopher Robin. The boy asks whether he hurt
Pooh, and the father reassures him. Then Christopher Robin goes upstairs,
dragging Winnie-the-Pooh *'bump, bump, bump'* behind him.[1] Several
implications are to be found in this juxtaposition of concerned inquiry and
unconcerned actions. First, the father can be seen as superior in comprehension to the child. (Here and at the beginning of the chapter and
elsewhere in the book, an adult may find the author too condescending.)
Second, the child can be seen as granting more credence to the story, in
which the bear speaks and acts on his own, than to reality, in which the
bear is only a soft, passive thing that the child can treat as he likes. Third,
the children who hear the story are reassured that, whatever happens or
threatens to happen in the stories, no real harm is going to come to any of

the actors. It is with the knowledge of such a cushion at the bottom that the young child can allow himself or herself to slide into the appetite-indulging and reality-testing adventures of Winnie-the-Pooh.

Although both Milne and Kipling provide reassurances to their young readers, Milne has inserted his into the very structure of his world, as well as into the relaxed pace of the action and the low-pressure interactions among most of the characters. Kipling, as we saw, aimed to attract his young readers through appealing sounds and rhythm, but the world into which they are introduced is quite a violent one of prey and predator. The relation between them is usually treated humorously rather than graphically, but the threat of death is there when the whale swallows the mariner, the crocodile grabs the elephant's child, the jaguar attacks the hedgehog, or the leopard catches the zebra. The immediacy is undercut somewhat by the action's taking place in various foreign countries and in 'High and Far-Off Times.' In contrast, Milne's forest is a recognizable environment, one in which children can easily imagine themselves. Its most violent action is a kidnapping, in which we accompany not the victim but one of the gang that has the tables turned on him. This chapter ends with the full integration of two aliens into the animal community.

But in the opening chapter such complex social interactions are still far-off. Pooh is propelled into adventure by his love of honey. Psychologically Pooh represents here the appetitive drive that relates everything to its needs. Having concluded that the bees are making honey just for him, he begins to climb the tree around which the bees are buzzing. This first attempt at satisfying appetite is frustrated when a branch breaks, and he falls into a gorse-bush. The second attempt is less direct, made with the help of Christopher Robin. Pooh uses camouflage to ascend with a blue balloon, to look like the sky, having himself rolled in the mud in order to look like a dark cloud. When the bees become anxious, Pooh allays their suspicion by having Christopher Robin walk under with an open umbrella, pretending it's going to rain. When a bee stings Pooh, he asks to be brought down, which Christopher Robin does by shooting at the balloon with his gun. His first shot misses the balloon but, as we saw, hits Pooh. The second shot is successful. Although Milne is discreet enough not to insert any overt moral into the tale, its cautionary nature is quite evident: an appetite unbridled is likely to bring more trouble than satisfaction, more pain than pleasure.

Pooh's attempts to disguise his aims are so transparent and the naïvety of them so appealing that we may feel the author heaps too many punishments on him. More interesting than Milne's conscious moral stance seems to me the unconscious dynamic apparent in the relations of the characters in the tales. Freud's three-part diagram of the psyche seems to me so far appropriate that we can see Pooh acting as the instinctive id (appetites and drives) and the author who constructs the plot functioning as a super-ego (the conscience as punisher). Christopher Robin, on such a reading, could be featured as the conscious ego, which tries to mediate between the other two parts of the psyche. He does have a greater reality sense, but in this tale is too easily manipulated by Pooh's need to fulfil his appetite. I think these attributions are neat and accurate as far as they go. Finally, however, they are limiting, and as we move into later adventures I shall introduce a less mechanical approach to the drama of the psyche as I see it in the book.

Chapter 2 offers another cautionary tale, one that gets its plot from Aesop's *Fables*: A hungry fox found some food left by a shepherd in a hollow tree; slipping in he ate until his stomach was so distended he could not get out. Another fox, hearing his cries of self-pity, suggested, 'Well, stay there until you are as thin as you were when you went in; then you'll get out quite easily.' This brief narrative illustrates the editor's contention that 'in a good fable the lesson is implicit in the narrative itself.'[2] His use of the word *lesson* is deliberate, since the word *moral* would imply higher concerns than this or many other animal fables warrant. In fact, this fable supports an even stricter observation made by Ben Edwin Perry, that the primary aim of a fable is often not even 'instructive but satirical.'[3] The second fox offers a solution, but it is one the first fox would be forced to follow in any case. Neither self-righteous nor really helpful, the second fox falls halfway between two more pronounced reactions that we shall see in Milne's adaptation of this fable situation.

The chapter begins with a bit of foreshadowing, Pooh doing his stoutness exercises in front of a mirror. He then goes out walking, sees a hole in a bank, and goes into a sequence of reasoning almost identical to the one that got him into his difficulty with the bees. He infers that Rabbit is in the hole and will provide him with food and a chance to show off his talent for humming. Although food, including honey, is again the main stimulator of appetite and then action, added to it is a naïve egoism, also hinted at in the presence of the mirror in the opening scene. This new theme plays its part in the story and distinguishes this chapter from the first. Pooh does find Rabbit inside the hole and is offered tea, on which he gorges himself. As a result, when he tries to get out of the hole, he can't, and when he tries to back into Rabbit's burrow again, he can't do that either. He is stuck, and Rabbit willingly lets him know it is from eating too much.

The lesson is overt, but enunciated by a character who does not have our sympathy. (Rabbit had tried to pretend he was not at home when Pooh first called and clearly wanted Pooh to leave before he actually tried to.) In fact, Milne is about to present us with a contrast between the responses of two characters whose attitudes represent the positive and negative poles of an important theme. The other character is Christopher Robin, who when he hears what has happened says, 'Silly old Bear.' He goes to Pooh and gently establishes that the greedy bear must go a week without food in order to get unstuck from the hole. But unlike Rabbit's recriminatory attitude, Christopher Robin's is positive and supportive. He offers to read to Pooh during this week of enforced slimming. Rabbit, meanwhile, deals with Pooh's other end, inside his burrow, in quite a different fashion, hanging his towels up to dry on Pooh's legs. While it is true that it would be pointless for Rabbit to read to Pooh's legs, it is also true, as we shall see, that Rabbit is the sort of person who treats others according to his own convenience. The humour of his using the legs as a towel rack illustrates Bergson's contention that the imposition of the mechanical upon the living is always comic. Pooh is demeaned, or to be exact, his subhuman physiology is emphasized. But the focus is less on him as stuffed toy than on him as id-driven and ego-centred child. After he has lived through the consequence of overeating, the story closes with an affirmation of his naïve egoism. He walks away humming, somehow still proud of himself.

The imaginativeness that Pooh showed in his plan for getting the bees' honey is evident again in chapter 3. The comedy of this adventure depends on Pooh's going in a circle as he tracks his own, and then his and Piglet's, paw marks. They decide that the big prints are those of a Woozle and the small ones those of a Wizzle. By the time there are four different sets of tracks, Piglet has become frightened and insists he has an important matter to attend to at home. He is then startled by Christopher Robin, who has been enjoying an overview of the whole tracking adventure from high in an oak tree. Piglet recognizes him, but instead of being reassured, still runs off home. Christopher Robin describes what he has seen in such a way that Pooh is able to reason out that he has been following his own tracks. The chapter concludes, as did the last one, with an affirmation of Pooh's essential nature. Although he claims, 'I am a Bear of No Brain at All,' Christopher Robin insists he is 'the Best Bear in All the World,' at which Pooh brightens up and goes home for lunch.

The introduction of Piglet in this chapter adds another dimension to the book's gradually emerging picture of basic psychological traits. Piglet is small, his name a diminutive; he is vulnerable, fearful. His psyche is so underdeveloped that when fear arises it can be allayed only by a retreat to his home. In contrast, Pooh wishes Christopher Robin would appear and is fully reassured when he does. By running home, Piglet escapes the immediate threat of Woozles but carries the fear with him. By remaining, Pooh discovers that the Woozle tracks are his own, that he has nothing to fear but his own imagination.

Freud contended that instinctual drives and naked emotions are basic, primary. D.W. Winnicott disagreed, believing that 'it is the self that must precede the self's use of instinct'; thus 'instinctual satisfaction,' though pressing and important, is not really primary. Winnicott's formulation of his sense of an individual's vital centre is important to our understanding not only of Pooh but of ourselves. 'The individual can come together and exist as a unit, not as a defence against anxiety but as an expression of I AM, I am alive, I am myself.'[4] The phrase 'defence against anxiety' can be illustrated from this adventure. At the point where anxiety appears, Pooh and Piglet believe they may be on the track of a number of Woozles. Pooh licks his hot nose to cool down his anxiety. But as Piglet finds when he emulates Pooh by licking his own nose, 'it brought very little comfort.' Piglet, who is usually unable to get beyond a search for relief from anxiety, then reverts to the one sure defence, the walls of his house. Pooh at this stage, though more advanced than Piglet, also looks outside himself for reassurance. But he looks to a person rather than an object, and to the qualities in that person. Schematically, I would contend that Christopher Robin stands for the self; he has an overview of the whole situation and is able to see that the two lower centres are frightening themselves. Pooh, in an advance over chapter 1, can be the developing ego, and Piglet can represent the fears of the id. From another point of view, of course, Pooh also contains all three of these facets of the psyche: he is driven by id appetites, he is developing that realistic sense of cause and effect by which the ego learns to manage the id, but most important he has that sense of 'I AM, I am alive, I am myself' that we shall see unfolding in future adventures and that can be clearly distinguished from mere ego assertiveness. (Pooh's modesty and empathy never desert him.)

Chapter 4 introduces two new characters, Eeyore, a gloomy, self-pitying anti-self, and Owl, a pompous, unperceptive word-monger. Meeting Eeyore, Pooh notices that his tail is missing. As Eeyore intensifies his guilt-inducing demands for pity, Pooh experiences a minor conflict, which provides the central theme of the chapter. Unable to think of anything helpful to say, he resolves to do something instead. He promises Eeyore he will go find his tail. His choice of commitment and action over soothing but unproductive words will carry Pooh through to success in his undertaking.

Characteristically, he begins by looking for help from someone with superior insight, in this case, Owl.

At Owl's door, Pooh is confronted with a puzzle that provides the reader with a first hint of just how helpful Owl will be. Owl has a knocker and a bell-pull, with confusing instructions for each. These instructions tell us that we are about to meet an intellectual game player. As with Eeyore, Pooh in his naïvety does not see through the game but nullifies its effect by calling out for Owl, who opens the door. Having told Owl of Eeyore's loss, Pooh waits for advice. The ensuing exchange is revealing: Owl says, 'The customary procedure in such cases is as follows.' Confused by these abstract words, Pooh again reveal his naïvety, asking, 'What does Crustimoney Proseedcake mean?'

Pooh's modesty balances his ignorance. But the nature of his misunderstanding is characteristic. Having just finished the long walk to Owl's home in the Hundred Acre Wood, Pooh is not only tired but hungry. He will soon hint that he would like some food (and will be ignored by Owl), but at this point he simply reduces Owl's abstractions to particulars, the kind of particulars that appeal to his sensuous nature. Psychologically, Pooh's reduction to concreteness of Owl's intellectualisms illustrates an observation of Freud's, that an infant takes pleasure in sounds themselves: 'He puts words together without regard to the condition that they should make sense, in order to obtain from them the pleasurable effect of rhythm or rhyme. Little by little he is forbidden this enjoyment, till all that remains permitted to him are significant combinations of words. But when he is older attempts still emerge at disregarding the restrictions.'[5] So Pooh, under stress, reverts to infantile understanding. But this regression, as the Freudian would view it, is actually Pooh's strength.

Having failed in his hints for food, Pooh attempts to rise to Owl's level, but cannot keep his attention on Owl's increasingly abstract words. When Pooh is finally allowed to leave, Owl proudly shows off his bell rope at the door. Since it reminds Pooh of something, he asks Owl how he came by it. When Owl responds that he pulled it off a bush, Pooh recognizes the rope as Eeyore's tail. Just as Owl's wordiness hides an insensitive nature, so Pooh's lack of intellect hides a perceptiveness that allows him to fulfil his pledge to Eeyore. After returning the tail, Pooh goes home to satisfy his appetite with 'a little snack of something' and to express his sense of self with a little verse, celebrating his achievement.

Chapter 5 continues from the Woozle chapter the tension between a desire for adventure and a feeling of fear. As in the earlier chapter, Pooh initiates the adventure, telling Piglet he has decided 'to catch a Heffalump.'

Piglet as before joins in, at first with interest and later with fear. During the discussion stage, they try to work out a plan to get the Heffalump into the trap they will dig. As in the first two chapters, appetite turns into the motivating force. Pooh asks Piglet how he would bait the trap if it were Pooh he was trying to catch. Piglet suggests honey, and Pooh's imagination is immediately transported into a scene in which he excitedly verbalizes sampling a jar of honey. Piglet finds it difficult to interrupt Pooh, whose reality sense has been overpowered by a fantasy of appetite indulgence.

Pooh goes home to bring a pot of honey as bait, taking a generous sample to verify that it really is honey. Having dug and baited the trap, he and Piglet return to their separate homes for the night. Pooh wakes late in the night and realizes he has donated his last honey jar to the Heffalump trap. Unable to get back to sleep, he goes to the trap and begins licking out the small amount of honey he left in the bottom of the jar. Meanwhile, Piglet has also awakened and begins to have anxious thoughts. Whereas Pooh had imagined a Heffalump eating his honey, Piglet worries that the Heffalump may eat pigs. He thinks of pretending to have a headache when it is time to go inspect the trap the next morning, but realizes he will have wasted half his day if there is no Heffalump there. So he decides to go while it is still dark to see if the trap has worked.

When he gets near the pit, Piglet hears a creature roaring inside; he runs off, crying, 'a Heffalump, a Horrible Heffalump!' As he continues, this cry for help gets distorted to 'a Herrible Hoffalump! Hoff, Hoff, a Hellible Horralump! Holl, Holl, a Hoffable Hellerump!' The seeming realization of his fears causes Piglet to lose control of meaningful language completely. Whereas Pooh earlier interpreted abstract words he had never heard before into concrete ones compatible with his experience and nature, Piglet begins with a statement whose meaning is clear, but under the stress of his emotion distorts it to comic confusion. The comedy comes partly from Piglet's loss of control. In Freud's view, each of us has experienced such a loss and is anxious not to repeat it, especially since society puts so strong a premium on keeping control, maintaining decorum. When we see someone else lose control, we feel superior. If our anxiety has been great enough the relief we feel can easily be expressed in laughter. As Freud put it, the listener to a joke 'laughs with the quota of physical energy which has become free through the lifting' of anxiety or inhibition.[6]

We need to look more closely at the comic meaning in Piglet's distortions. The first merely transposes two vowels: 'a Herrible Hoffalump.' The second becomes more scrambled, and gets more communicative: 'Hoff, Hoff, a Hellible Horralump.' Connecting 'Hell' with the pit they have dug is not difficult. The third is clearly Freudian – at least for those of us who ordered our reading glasses from a Viennese oculist: 'Holl, Holl, a Hoffable Hellarump!' Here in the climactic position, we find Hell given additional meaning by its connection with a taboo lower part of the anatomy. While not suggesting that Milne intended the effect, I am insisting it is there. As Freud emphasized, 'The joke will evade restrictions and open sources of pleasure that have become inaccessible' to consciousness.[7]

Piglet takes Christopher Robin to the trap, where they see a creature bumping its head against a tree root. Suddenly recognizing it as Pooh with his head stuck in a jar, Christopher Robin begins to laugh. He laughs because he gets the joke. That is, like a joke, the situation has kept Christopher Robin in suspense until the punch line when he sees the *double entendre* – roaring Heffalump equals Pooh with his head stuck in a honey jar. Since the surprise has involved anxiety, generated by Piglet's fear, we can understand why Milne describes Christopher Robin as laughing so hard. He is also laughing at Pooh as an example of Bergson's 'mechanical encrusted on the living.' By this reading, Pooh is the butt of the joke, an outcome consistent with the pattern of chapters 1 and 2: Pooh's appetite gets him into trouble. But there is more to the situation than that.

The outcome, though familiar, is different from our expectation. Pooh finally frees his head by breaking the jar. But rather than his being the butt of the joke, it is Piglet who feels ashamed and runs away. As Christopher Robin takes Pooh home to breakfast, he confesses his love of Pooh.

As before, Pooh's feeling of worth is reinforced by Christopher Robin, and he emerges from the experience with his sense of self intact. But Piglet feels humiliated and goes home with (as I take it) an actual headache to match the one he had earlier thought of using for an excuse. Or we could say he goes home with the headache Pooh has earned from smashing his head against a root to break the jar in which it is stuck. Piglet functions as a scapegoat, carrying off all the shame, while Christopher Robin and Pooh can rejoice in the release of tension that follows their earlier anxiety and restraint.

Yet rightly seen, Piglet's actions deserve praise, not shame. He it was who overcame fear to go to see if there were a Heffalump in the trap. Why is his courage not recognized? The answer, I think, also lies in Piglet. He is so defensive that he cannot laugh, at himself or another. It is his choice to run away, to opt for isolation instead of companionship. If he had been less ego-conscious, he could have begun by laughing at Pooh and ended by laughing at his own fear, a fear that was certainly not unwarranted. But he chooses retreat and pain. In the adventure we are about to turn to, he will again suffer but will finally be pushed to self-assertion.

Chapter 7 is the only chapter in the book in which overt hostility appears. The source of it is Rabbit, who wants the newcomers, Kanga and Roo, to leave and proposes to kidnap Roo to effect their departure. He involves Pooh and Piglet, but finds them poor planners, not really able to focus on his plot. Piglet even suggests that since Kanga is said to be somewhat fierce, the plot may not be sound. But Rabbit scorns Piglet's lack of courage and carries on with a plan to have Pooh distract Kanga while he stuffs Piglet in her pocket and takes Roo away. As in the Heffalump chapter, Piglet is the one who is shamed. His suffering begins immediately, as he is bounced around when Kanga hops away. Arriving home, she recognizes Piglet immediately, but decides to play her part in the deception by pretending that Piglet is Roo and treating him roughly while putting him to bed. Despite Piglet's best efforts to assert his own identity, Kanga persists in the pretence, giving him a (cold) bath, scrubbing him (hard), getting soap in his mouth, and finally telling her child that if he doesn't take his medicine, he will grow up to be 'small and weak like Piglet.'

At this point, Christopher Robin arrives with the news that Roo is enjoying himself at the house of Rabbit, who has become fond of him. But like Kanga, Christopher Robin refuses to recognize Piglet. He and Kanga play the game of who-is-it? While Kanga feeds Piglet the medicine, Christopher Robin decides he is a relative of Pooh's named Henry Pootel.

Pushed too far, Piglet finally takes action. As he has done twice before, he runs off home, but this time not in fear. When he is almost home, he rolls in the dust until he has resumed his old dirty colour again. This assertion of his own sense of his identity receives an implicit reward at the end of the chapter in the pairings that become a new part of the weekly routine: Kanga with Pooh, Roo with Rabbit, and Piglet with Christopher Robin. When Pooh gains a new mentor in the competent mother, Kanga, Piglet is able to take his place with Christopher Robin, an important advance over the end of the Heffalump episode.

As constant second fiddle to the more assertive Pooh, Piglet is a character that draws on the sympathies of many young children who have an older sibling. His repeated failure to rise to the challenges that Pooh always meets successfully is finally corrected in this episode. Even here, however, his attempt to play the trickster meets with initial failure. When his emulation of Roo is discarded, he cannot step straight back into his identity as Piglet. Instead he must undergo an aggressive undermining of his identity by both Christopher Robin and Kanga. He runs from this threat but erases the unaccepted new clean identity in favour of his old soiled one. We may speculate that there is an important difference between being unwashed and alone out of self-pity and actively choosing that condition.

Not only has Piglet gained recognition by Christopher Robin, we shall find in the next-to-last episode that he has become capable of creative action.

The three final chapters of the book provide respectively an impulsive act of modest heroism, a thoughtful and daring confirmation of it, and a concluding celebration of Pooh's full selfhood. If the chapter we have just considered represents a break in Pooh's development – as he goes along with an authoritative but mean-minded Rabbit – the chapter that follows it balances Roo's kidnapping by having Pooh save Roo's life. The goal of the adventure proposed by Christopher Robin is to find the North Pole. All the animals of the forest are collected and march off in a line behind Christopher Robin. When they stop for lunch, it comes out that none of them knows what the North Pole looks like. Then Roo falls in a stream, and most of the animals respond in their characteristic and unhelpful ways. But Pooh gets a pole and holds it over the water so that Roo can cling to it and climb out. Christopher Robin looks at the long stick Pooh has used and proclaims that Pooh has found the North Pole. He then plants it in the ground with a message to that effect tied to it. The expedition over, they all go back home. Thus Christopher Robin's pretend quest culminates in an actual crisis in which Pooh's down-to-earth nature again triumphs. The pole that he unthinkingly uses is then proclaimed as the goal of the quest. With the help of Christopher Robin, he has triumphed in reality and in imagination.

If unthinking action characterizes Pooh's quick response in chapter 8, cogitation and a plan precede his heroism in chapter 9. This chapter has the most literary structure of any in the book. It shifts point of view three times, the fourth being a return to the first. Each of the first three sections begins with the same event, rain that lasts for days. But we shall be keeping our attention on psychic development.

The first section is Piglet's. Isolated by the flooding caused by the downpour, he wishes for company but decides that since he is so small he, unlike any of his friends, 'can't do *anything*.' As the rain continues, Piglet finally asks himself what Christopher Robin would do. This reminds him of a story Christopher Robin told of a man on a desert island who had put a plea for help in a empty bottle and thrown it into the water. Piglet is inspired to do the same. His desire for company and his taking an initiative to be rescued are signs of Piglet's growth.

Pooh, meanwhile, has awakened from a long sleep to find his living room flooded. He takes ten jars of honey out on a limb of his house, and consumes all the honey over the next four days. Then, seeing a bottle floating near, he jumps in the water for it, hoping it contains honey. Instead, it actually contains Piglet's note, which disappoints Pooh until he makes out a *P* and decides it is intended for him. Wanting to get it to Christopher Robin to find out what it says, he comes up with an idea, to float on one of his empty honey jars. He names it *The Floating Bear.* Despite difficulties keeping his balance, he starts for Christopher Robin's house.

Christopher Robin has been marking the growing height of the water with sticks. After the rise on which he lives is turned into an island, he is visited by Owl, who converses in language so abstract that even Christopher Robin can't understand him. The boy is worried about Pooh, who suddenly appears. When Christopher Robin has read Piglet's message, he asks Owl to rescue Piglet. Owl declines: 'It is doubtful if the necessary dorsal muscles –' Christopher Robin interrupts to urge him at least to go reassure Piglet that help is coming. He concludes, 'Oh, don't *talk*, Owl, go on quick!' Left to plan the rescue, Christopher Robin and Pooh agree that the jar will not be adequate for two. Then Pooh comes up with a suggestion so unexpected and helpful that it leaves Christopher Robin open-mouthed. He suggests they use the boy's umbrella as a boat. And so they do.

In this chapter, both Piglet and Pooh become more mature and resourceful. Pooh outgrows the limitation that has also been his strong point through most of the book. As a Bear of Very Little Brain, he has allowed his appetite to get him in trouble, but he has also shown up Owl's hollow wisdom in finding Eeyore's tail. He has dreamed up a Woozle and tried to catch a Heffalump, two imaginative but unrealistic exercises. But he has acted instinctively to save Roo. Now, however, he has come up with two innovative insights, both of which he is able to execute successfully. His only remaining limitation is his inability to read, and that problem is addressed in the book's conclusion.

The final chapter contains the apotheosis of Pooh, as well as the exposure of Eeyore.[8] When Pooh hears about the party, he makes up a song in which two voices contend. One celebrates Pooh and the other tends not to know what all the fuss is about. One of the affirmative lines in the song is important: 'Well, Pooh was a Bear of Enormous Brain –' Since Pooh has throughout insisted the opposite, the exaggeration in the song represents a turning point. Because of his insight in seeing two objects as potential boats, Pooh must give up the stance of self-deprecation and accept the justice of Christopher Robin's naming the second boat *'The Brain of Pooh.'* This advance is validated by the present Pooh receives, 'a Special Pencil Case.' The box and its implements indicate that Pooh is ready to move beyond simple illiteracy to the world of reading and writing. We may fear that our hero will thereby lose the ability to take direct action. But taking

Christopher Robin as an example of the dispassionate (but active) self, we can see that this gift continues Pooh on the right path.

At the end of the tale, just before Pooh is dragged upstairs one last time, Christopher Robin asks whether Pooh's pencil case is better than his. The story-teller replies that it is 'just the same.' The author seems to be making two psychological points here. He is probably suggesting a connection – if not an identity – between Christopher Robin and Pooh. And he is certainly showing an awareness of that childish egoism that his son later quoted Milne as believing in.[9] But the passage also assumes that Christopher Robin's enforced socialization at school does not mean giving up the chief companion of his freer development in that make-believe world of animals where he first played out important feelings. His sense of limitation and potentiality, fear and confidence, gloom and joy find their integration in Pooh, who does not let the negative personae dominate, whose own positive responses are dependable and whose self-doubts have been resolved by the end.

*Winnie-the-Pooh* is a book full of acceptance, as we have seen; it is also full of integration, not just psychologically in Pooh, but in the happenings of its plot. All the animals are gathered together in the second chapter, to help free Pooh, in the eighth, when they go to discover the North Pole, and in the tenth, at the final party. Newcomers are integrated into the community. The pairings at the end of the chapter in which Kanga and Roo arrive in the forest provide benevolent links between Rabbit and Roo (aggressor and victim), Pooh and Kanga (the dreamy and the down-to-earth), and Christopher Robin and Piglet. This last pair, as indicated earlier, is in some ways the most important. Even the smallest and weakest, the most fearful and retreating of the individualized inhabitants of this world, even Piglet advances to a special relation with the support figure of the tales.

Christopher Robin is the authority who decides when to pull Pooh out of Rabbit's hole, the removed one who has an overview of the Woozle adventure, the involved one who sees through the supposed Heffalump, the trusted one who Kanga knows will ensure that no harm comes to Roo, the adventurous one who leads the North Pole expedition, the resourceful one whom Piglet, Owl and Pooh wish to join when the deluge comes, and the considerate and appreciative one who gives the party that draws them all together at the end. The party is in honour of Pooh, whose development of many of Christopher Robin's own traits the boy has been mainly concerned to support.

The party indulges the animal pleasure in eating and the social need for harmonious relations among diverse creatures. It thus reinforces the consistent import of the narrative, that both fearful and ignorant creatures can gain confidence and mastery. Pooh and Piglet function as the backward parts of the psyche. Their humorous adventures are the main focus of the episodes. But just out of the limelight is the human being who is really the concern of the tales, whose worries are exposed through the animal surrogates, whose strengths are implicitly emphasized by contrast with the protagonists' relative lack of competence. Christopher Robin makes room at the party table for all the animals – gloomy Eeyore, aggressive Rabbit, expressive Roo, competent Kanga, pontifical Owl, anxious Piglet, and a basically self-confident Pooh, who is now revealed as brainy. The covert reassurance to the child is both psychological and social: yes, impulses are sometimes contradictory and friends do sometimes disagree, but somehow they can be brought together in that integration that makes possible both outer relationships and inner growth.

# 3

# The Emergence of the Trickster

*HE WIND IN THE WILLOWS* contains two separate strands, both of which I liked as a child. I enjoyed the everyday experiences of Mole and Rat – not to mention their adventures – and the extravagant escapades of Toad. I didn't understand 'The Piper at the Gates of Dawn' and was bored by 'Wayfarers All'; later when as an adult I came to read the book to my children, I usually left out both. I now see how they fit in with a pattern, developed by Grahame, of impulsive action and its consequence, a pattern that emerges most clearly in the adventures of the irrepressible Toad. As a vital force in the book, Toad is a figure who displays many of the characteristics Carl Jung connected with the trickster as part of man's shadow side, those unsocialized elements so repulsive to consciousness, and so full of energy.

*The Wind in the Willows* is best read to children slightly older than those who will appreciate *Winnie-the-Pooh*. As Roger Sale rightly observes, Grahame's book 'has none of the superior tone that mars Milne's book ... It is *about* coziness, but it never seeks an uncomfortably cozy relation with its reader or listener.'[1] It is a world of comfortable houses and meals; although there is violence in it and the fear of violence, no one is killed or even maimed, reconciliation being effected after the melée at the end. Toad, like Pooh, is undaunted when his indulgence in sensuous delights brings him pain instead of pleasure. But Toad is not encouraged by a benevolent author or loving child. Rather, he is criticized and finally chastised by his friends for his escapades, a development that precipitates his change back into a trickster instead of forward toward a self. Although fraternal authority is exercised by Rat over Mole, the dominant authority is paternal, exercised by Badger, whose strength, isolation, and irritability make him a stern figure of awe. In taking over the conduct of Toad's life, he stands in *loco parentis*, having been a friend of Toad's father.

But the ultimate authority in this tale is Pan, the Piper at the Gates of Dawn, whose 'august Presence' inspires 'great Awe.'[2] To worship him, as Rat and Mole do, is to try to become one with the world of nature. In fact, however, the most characteristic conception of nature in this book is quite a civilized one. One of Grahame's extended similes describing autumn demonstrates this conception well: 'Nature's Grand Hotel has its Season, like the others. As the guests one by one pack, pay, and depart, and the seats at the *table-d'hôte* shrink pitifully at each succeeding meal; as suites of rooms are closed, carpets taken up, and waiters sent away; those boarders who are staying on, *en pension*, until the next year's full reopening, cannot help being somewhat affected by all these flittings and farewells.' As more than one commentator has noted, Grahame's animals are all too human. They wear clothes and own boats and picnic hampers. Their dwellings may appear to be holes or warrens, but the rooms inside have human furnishings. Toad Hall is indeed even externally a mansion. And Toad mingles with humans, being now large enough to drive an automobile, now small enough to be flung far off a barge by the woman steering it. Although these anomalies create no difficulty for most readers, they do suggest a lack of imaginative integration that means we must look elsewhere for the creative strength of the book.

More clearly than most children's books about animals, *The Wind in the Willows* is really about human beings, about the human psyche. The characteristic dynamic of the book is an oft-repeated impulsive psychic expansion, followed by a sense of fulfilment if the impetus comes from outside or by peril if it is a selfish impulse from within. The book begins with the most unalloyed of these impulses, Mole's abandoning spring cleaning underground, called by a 'spirit of divine discontent' to leave his 'dark and lowly little house' and burst out onto 'the warm grass of a great meadow.' His reward is to find a mentor, Rat, to induct him into the pleasures of spring on the river. As long as Mole follows Rat's lead, their days are passed in harmony with nature. But the two times Mole acts against Rat's explicit warning, things go badly. The first time he grabs the oars and overturns the boat. The second time, he sneaks off to visit Badger secretly and gets lost in the Wild Wood. Frightened by its eerie sounds and sights, 'in panic, he began to run ... aimlessly.' Finally 'he took refuge in a deep dark hollow of an old beech tree, which offered shelter, concealment – perhaps even safety, but who could tell?' There he is overcome by 'the darkest moment' of a field creature, 'the Terror of the Wild Wood,' until he is rescued by Rat.

Mole's fourth experience of this kind is more like his first leaving the underground and helps distinguish these two experiences from the boating and the Wild Wood ones. Out tramping with Rat one dark December eve, Mole experiences a 'summons' that takes him 'like an electric shock.' A 'mysterious' call reaches Mole, 'making him tingle through and through with its very familiar appeal.' Finally he is able to interpret what his senses are communicating to him: he is near the home that he left the previous spring. Unwilling to bother Rat with the feelings that accompany this recognition, Mole is dutifully trailing him toward his home, until a sob escapes him, and Rat finds out what has happened. Just as Rat originally introduced Mole to his home on the river, so he now insists that they go to Mole's home and there acts the host to an emotional and easily upset Mole.

On both the spring day and the December night, Mole received a summons from outside himself. Answering it, he had two positive experiences, one expanding into a new world, the other revalidating an old one. In contrast, his decision to row the boat and to enter the Wild Wood were both taken from an internal stimulus, and both brought him near death, though in each case he was saved by Rat.

The apotheosis of these positive external summons comes in 'The Piper at the Gates of Dawn.' In the boat looking for Otter's son, Portly, one 'short midsummer night,' Rat and Mole are startled to hear above the sound of the water what seems 'a sudden clear call from an actual articulate voice.' In a romantic setting of magical moonlight, they follow the call until Rat has a Keatsian perception: 'Now it passes on and I begin to lose it – the merry bubble and joy, the thin clear, happy call of the distant piping.' But rather than losing it, he follows 'the clear imperious summons' until he brings them to the piper, Pan himself, described in sensual detail. At his feet lies the lost child. When Pan disappears – from their memories as well as their sight – Rat and Mole have the consolation of discovering Portly.

Once again following a summons from outside results in a positive conclusion. This climactic incident makes it clear that mere good intentions will not achieve the conscious goal. Only when Rat and Mole follow the impersonal call of nature do they come unerringly to the personal goal they had temporarily forgotten. We may even reverse this insight: for an animal to follow personal inclination is to deny the animal god of nature. It is thus appropriate that Grahame has Mole feel explicit *panic* in the Wild Wood, the terror that comes to those who invade Pan's sphere in an improper spirit.

'Wayfarers All' presents the sad case of Rat, who in his autumn restlessness, and as an *alter ego* for his author, encounters a seafaring rat with earrings. With tales of his ulyssean adventures, this wayfarer holds

Rat 'bound, fascinated, powerless.' When the wayfarer leaves, he predicts that Rat will follow. 'I will linger, and look back; and at last I will surely see you coming, eager and light-hearted, with all the South in your face!' Hypnotized, Rat packs and is about to leave when Mole returns and recognizes that Rat is not himself. 'Grappling with him strongly he dragged him inside, threw him down, and held him. The Rat struggled desperately for a few moments, and then his strength seemed suddenly to leave him, and he lay still and exhausted, with closed eyes, trembling. Presently the Mole assisted him to rise and placed him in a chair, where he sat collapsed and shrunken into himself, his body shaken by a violent shivering, passing in time into an hysterical fit of dry sobbing.' It takes Rat a while to recover, but with Mole's encouragement he is writing a poem as the chapter ends.

This chapter seems to violate the Pan ethic that Grahame has carefully embedded in the rest of the book. An impulse comes to Rat not from any personal source but from outside, an impulse like that divine discontent that sent Mole on his way to wider horizons. Like Pan's pipes, the call promises enlarged experience. Is Mole right to stand in his friend's way? Isn't it a limitation for Rat that he should be writing poems about nature instead of fully experiencing it? It must be if Grahame is serious about his aim. In fact, as his biographer, Peter Green, demonstrates, he was ambivalent. He appreciated nature, but as indicated earlier his whole conception of animals and habitat is nature domesticated. The Wild Wood is a place to stay away from. Adventure is therefore something that both attracts and repels; it is dangerous and domesticity is safe. From this point of view, Mole is right to keep this odd couple together. But writing, for Rat and Grahame, thus becomes a substitute for a life that remains unlived.

Roger Sale is correct, I think, to conclude that for Grahame passion is 'the great enemy, because its dangers lie within us and can never be ruled out just by drawing a boundary.' He is also right to see Toad as a danger to Rat's domestic world because Toad is dominated by his passions. But I believe he is wrong to conclude that because it is 'the nature of passions to become repetitive,'[3] the adventures and further adventures become repetitive. Although Toad's adventures are not told with the refinement of the early chapters that Sale rightly admires, they have much more energy than those chapters. Each of these two strands of the book has its weaknesses: The domestic world of Rat and Mole can become over-sublimated and sentimental; the active world of Toad can descend to farce and slapstick. Green concludes that the adventures of Toad do represent that part of Grahame's bedtime stories for his son that he first committed to writing.[4] Their continuing appeal to children is indicative of their vitality.

Mary Ellmann sees Toad's psychology and destiny as growing out of his appearance: 'Toad is as he should be, all mouth, chest, belly and legs. Why is he alone involved in catastrophe after catastrophe? Because he has the long, drawn-down mouth designed to meet catastrophe. The chest is to swell when he boasts, the belly to fill out the washerwoman's dress ... each enthusiasm must be monomaniacal. Toad expands and shrinks according to his fortunes, as animals do even more perceptibly than men.'[5] As she and Green point out, Toad as aristocratic spendthrift plays a part in the socio-economic drama that is part of Grahame's theme. But these valid observations need another dimension to provide a fuller sense of the character. Toad is a child; to be more exact, Grahame has made him the kind of adult who has the means to indulge childish whims and appetites, and who insists on doing so. Lacking a grounded sense of reality, his ego is completely at the service of his id. His life is a series of enthusiasms and abandoned toys. His lack of a conscience and a sense of reality are highlighted, and compensated for, by Badger, the stern super-ego, and by Rat, the stable ego. Only after they take him in hand does the full nature of Toad reveal itself.

In chapter 2, 'The Open Road,' Rat and Mole go to visit Toad, expecting him to be still involved in boating. Toad soon disabuses them. 'O, pooh! boating!' Toad says in disgust. 'Silly boyish amusement. I've given that up *long* ago ... I've discovered the real thing,' namely the open road in a gypsy caravan. He talks Mole and a reluctant Rat into accompanying him on an overnight trip. The next day the trip is ruined by an automobile, 'advancing on them at incredible speed, while from out [of its] dust a faint "Poop-poop!" wailed like an uneasy animal in pain.' 'It was on them! The "poop-poop" rang with a brazen shout in their ears, they had a moment's glimpse of an interior of glittering plate-glass and rich morocco, and the magnificent motor-car, immense, breath-snatching, passionate, with its pilot tense and hugging his wheel, possessed all earth and air for the fraction of a second, flung an enveloping cloud of dust that blinded and enwrapped them utterly.' The horse bolts, and the caravan is wrecked. Rat is outraged and wants to report the car, but Toad sits in the middle of the road 'in a sort of a trance, a happy smile on his face, his eyes still fixed on the dusty wake of their destroyer,' at intervals faintly murmuring, 'Poop-poop!' His impressionable nature is taking on another enthusiasm. Shaken by Rat, he exclaims, 'Glorious, stirring sight! ... The poetry of motion! The *real* way to travel! The *only* way to travel! Here to-day – in next week tomorrow! Villages skipped, towns and cities jumped – always somebody else's horizon! O bliss! O poop-poop! O my!' His final epithets for the car sum up his new passion '– that swan, that sunbeam, that thunderbolt!' It is worth repeating Grahame's enthusiastic initial descriptions of the car since it comes so close to Toad's own: 'the magnificent motor-car, immense, breath-snatching, passionate.' However much Grahame consciously agreed with Rat and Badger in disapproving of Toad's new passion, as creative author he manages to share it. His empathy with Toad is responsible for the vitality of the adventures that follow from his hero's new enthusiasm.

In chapter 6, 'Mr. Toad,' Badger persuades Rat and Mole to force Toad out of this new passion. Badger is particularly offended by the costume Toad wears for driving, 'goggles, cap, gaiters,' an 'enormous overcoat' and 'gauntleted gloves' (the book appeared in 1908). Badger calls them 'those singularly hideous habiliments so dear to him, which transform him from a (comparatively) good-looking Toad into an Object.' With this excuse Badger proposes to treat Toad as an object. Rat says, 'We'll rescue the poor unhappy animal! We'll convert him!' And Badger does, for a few minutes. In a private room he lectures Toad, soon reducing him to tears. But when brought out to admit his past errors, Toad defies Badger and reaffirms the glory of his passion for motoring. He is thereupon locked in his room where he undergoes fits of excitement, spasms that are presumed to be withdrawal symptoms. 'When his violent paroxysms possessed him he would arrange bedroom chairs in rude resemblance of a motor-car and would crouch on the foremost of them, bent forward and staring fixedly ahead, making uncouth and ghastly noises, till the climax was reached, when, turning a complete somersault, he would lie prostrate amidst the ruins of the chairs.' Although these seizures eventually abate, Toad does not regain his former ebullience. Left one day in the care of common-sense Rat, Toad plays the role of dying animal so successfully that Rat is taken in and goes to get a doctor, not forgetting to lock Toad in. Toad immediately makes a rope of his sheets and leaves by the window.

This ability to act a part is intrinsic to Toad's nature, consonant not only with his susceptibility to the role of boat-, caravan-, or car-owner – and the costumes that go with them – but also with his responsiveness to others, his taking on from Badger, under pressure, the role of repentant prodigal. Toad's childish lack of 'character' – in Freudian terms, lack of a super-ego and a stable ego – causes him to take on the personality that gives immediate pleasure and avoids looming pain. Since all children have experienced the adult pressure to be responsible, or moral, or reasonable, and have been similarly tempted to evade these demands, the appeal of Toad to a child reader is all the more understandable. But we must note the difference between Toad's new role of deceiver and the old roles of enthusiast or penitent: he consciously chooses this role while the others spontaneously seemed to choose him. In fact, all are adopted under pressure, either of (exciting) stimuli or of another's (depressive) will.

He had earlier employed an extemporaneous verbal seduction of Mole: 'He played on the inexperienced Mole as on a harp. Naturally a voluble animal and always mastered by his imagination,' he easily communicates a sense of excitement to Mole. That vital imagination is tapped both more consciously and more deeply in the role he assumes for Rat.

This new role is that of the trickster, the archaic figure discussed in the introduction. Like the trickster in Jung's formulation, Toad has begun to play pranks; his attraction to costumes will soon move into transvestism as he shifts his shape from man to woman. Jung also speaks of the trickster's 'dual nature, half animal, half divine' and 'his exposure to all kinds of torture.'[6] In Toad's case, his trying to move into the human world will lead to imprisonment and the vivid threat of torture. What he does is steal a car in a mood that fits Jung's characterization of the trickster as divested of human consciousness and morality preparatory to taking on divine characteristics: 'As if in a dream, he pulled the lever and swung the car round the yard and out through the archway; and, as if in a dream, all sense of right and wrong, all fear of obvious consequences, seemed temporarily suspended. He increased his pace, and as the car devoured the street and leapt forth on the high road through the open country, he was only conscious that he was Toad once more, Toad at his best and highest, Toad the terror, the traffic-queller, the Lord of the lone trail, before whom all must give way or be smitten into nothingness and everlasting night.' Toad has moved from escaped animal to man in a car, to the powerful lord of creation and destruction. But in doing so he has involved himself in the pattern we saw earlier of impulsive expansion, to be followed either by confirmation or punishment.

Adopting Mary Ellmann's psychology of physiognomy, we could say that Toad's cycle is invariably inflation and then deflation. That cycle is strongly emphasized in this episode. Immediately after the passage quoted above, Grahame cuts to a courtroom with Toad in the dock, about to be 'loaded ... with chains, and dragged' away 'shrieking,' past 'mastiffs' straining 'at their leash' and pawing 'to get at him.' He is locked in the darkest and 'grimmest dungeon that lay in the heart of the innermost keep.' The whole scene is exaggerated, theatrical, straight out of a pantomime. Like a pantomime, it soon offers a transformation that will bring a happy ending. As in a fairy-tale where the daughter of the wicked magician aids the hero to escape, so the daughter of the jailer takes pity on Toad and effects the transformation that will provide him with a way out of prison. She proposes that Toad change clothes with her aunt, a washerwoman who comes regularly to the prison to collect laundry. After some resistance, Toad agrees. 'In return for his cash Toad received a cotton print gown, an apron, a shawl, and a rusty black bonnet.' Like Jung's trickster, whose 'undifferentiated ... consciousness' and amorphous nature allow him to 'turn himself into a woman,' Toad not only walks past the guards in female guise, but tricks the engine driver in the train station into letting a penniless washerwoman ride in his cab. This impersonation is given a severe test when Toad later begs a ride from a barge-woman. She pressures him into washing some of her clothes. After watching his bumbling efforts, she says, 'I thought you must be a humbug all along.' Toad drops his role to shout insults at her and gets thrown in the water for his temerity.

Stealing her horse, Toad once again begins the inflation process. He sings a variation of 'The British Grenadier' to express his revived conceit.

> 'The world has held great Heroes,
> As history-books have showed;
> But never a name to go down to fame
> Compared with that of Toad!'

... He sang as he walked, and he walked as he sang, and got more inflated every minute. But his pride was shortly to have a severe fall.

Approached by the people from whom he originally stole a car, Toad collapses in fear but is taken for a washerwoman and given a lift. As he revives, he persuades them to let him sit behind the wheel, and as he begins to drive the car he again starts to boast. They grapple with him, the car crashes, and Toad is thrown clear. As he walks away his ego again inflates, only to suffer immediate deflation when he sees he is pursued. In his final flight he falls in the river and find himself at Rat's door.

Although not yet free of the inflation/deflation cycle, Toad is relieved of his trickster role by his return.

At last he stood safe and sound in the hall, streaked with mud and weed ... dodgings and evasions were over, and he could lay aside a disguise that was unworthy of his position and wanted such a lot of living up to.

'O, Ratty!' he cried. 'I've been through such times since I saw you last, you can't think! Such trials, such sufferings, and all so nobly borne! Then such escapes, such disguises, such subterfuges, and all so cleverly planned and carried out! ... Humbugged everybody – made 'em all do exactly what I wanted!'

Here as earlier, Toad's boasting claims more than he has achieved. The word *humbug* reminds the reader that Toad was called exactly that by the barge woman when she saw through his disguise. Rat, as always, works to bring Toad down to earth. But Toad is still childishly irrepressible. 'While the Rat was talking so seriously, he kept saying to himself mutinously "But it *was* fun, though! Awful fun!" and making strange suppressed noises inside him, k-i-ck-ck-ck, and poop-p-p.' The vital but impressionable guiser is obviously still a part of him.

What brings Toad down to earth is Rat's news that Toad Hall has been taken over by stoats and weasels from the Wild Wood. 'Go on, Ratty ... tell me all ... I am an animal again. I can bear it.' For the time indeed, Toad has given up his aspirations to the human excitements of travel in machines, the godlike experience of power they offer. As usual he revives, however, and against Rat's advice makes a foray to try to reclaim the hall. Like Mole earlier, Toad returns to admit that Rat was right, his pride has led him astray.

In the last two chapters, Grahame makes explicit the parallels between Mole, as dutiful child, learning to mature, and Toad as regressive child, wilfully refusing to grow up. Paradoxically, this parallel is nowhere clearer than in Mole's taking on Toad's trickster role. Mole goes off on his own and returns very pleased with himself. '"I've been having such fun!" he began at once; "I've been getting a rise out of the stoats."' During Toad's foray, these same stoats had humiliated him. But Mole has gone disguised in Toad's washerwoman costume. He has played his part expertly and upset the stoats with exaggerated warnings of an attack. Toad's reaction is immediate: 'Oh, you silly ass, Mole! ... You've been and spoilt everything!' If Toad had done what Mole had just reported doing, Rat would undoubtedly have said the same, and the reader would agree he had put the stoats on their guard. But Badger backs Mole. Tricksterism has begun to be the mode of all the animals, only the others take it more seriously than Toad has done.

The grand trick that Badger plans to play is to sneak into the middle of the usurpers and give in to his destructive instincts. Like a true shadow figure, he will lead them through a dark tunnel that only he knows about and will carry 'a dark lantern' – one that can be closed to shut off its light. The tunnel leads under Toad Hall to a trapdoor in the pantry. There Grahame as author joins the four 'civilized' animals as –ironically – in the name of law and order, they act out their feral potential on the 'wild' animals.

What a squealing and a squeaking and a screeching filled the air! Well might the terrified weasels dive under the tables and spring madly up at the windows! Well might the ferrets rush wildly for the fireplace and get hopelessly jammed in the chimney! Well might tables and chairs be upset, and glass and china be sent crashing on the floor, in the *panic* of that terrible moment when the four Heroes strode wrathfully into the room! The mighty Badger, his whiskers bristling, his great cudgel whistling through the air; Mole, black and grim, brandishing his stick and shouting his awful war-cry, 'A Mole! A Mole!' Rat, desperate and determined, his belt bulging with weapons of every age and every variety; Toad, frenzied with excitement and injured pride, swollen to twice his ordinary size, leaping into the air and emitting Toad-whoops that chilled them to the marrow!

As a creature half human, half animal, Pan is a presiding deity appropriate to more chapters of the book than a casual reading might suggest. Here at the dramatic climax, Pan's dark side is assimilated to the trickster under whose aegis I have suggested all four avenging animals act. The congruence of these two subhuman figures should not surprise us. As Karl Kerenyi notes, Trickster represents 'a spirit of disorder, . an enemy of boundaries, a mighty life-spirit' that was well known to the Greeks. Kerenyi focuses on Hermes but mentions such sub-Olympians as the sileni, the satyrs and Priapus.[7] Pan is, of course, one of their number, his phallic nature as important as Trickster's. Although Grahame's disorder stops short of sexual orgy, it does include crossing boundaries between the sexes, as well as between the animal and human worlds, not to mention between the worlds of decorum and violence in the reclaiming of Toad Hall.

Only when violence is added to disguise and trickery is Pan super-imposed on Trickster. The panic that the stoats and weasels experience is an overriding fear that causes an irrational need to flee. The source of this fear is Badger, the one member of the foursome who lives in the Wild Wood, the only powerful and frightening member of the group. While Rat can be brave, it is a business-like, middle-class bravery based on the mastery of manufactured weapons. Mole, when found by Rat in the Wild Wood, lacked even bravery, but has matured since. Relatively helpless, like Toad, he too must resort to disguise and trickery. These qualities are finally approved by Badger, and appropriated by him in the surprise attack. The tricksterism of the weak and suppressed is assimilated to the panic-engendering aggressiveness of the strong and liberated, as Pan integrates Trickster.

As soon as the usurpers are routed, the agents of panic revert to their civilized personae, cleaning up the hall, posting a guard, pardoning those enemies who are captured and repentant, and telling Toad he must have a banquet to celebrate. 'It's expected of you – in fact it's the rule.' All trace of tricksterism leaves the four once they have extricated themselves from the incursion that upset the natural balance and made necessary such a reversion – or regression – to powerful animalism. Actually, Toad soon reverts if not to trickery at least to characteristic inflation as he plans to be continually in the spotlight at the banquet. But he is forestalled by his friends, and on the night of the banquet he appears to be a reformed creature, modestly underplaying his own part in the battle as he circulates among his guests. Many readers doubt the permanence of his change. But it makes sense if we see the tale ending with a stable balancing of its previously contending forces.

We need to remember how much of Toad's tricksterism the other three took on during the battle to regain Toad Hall. Mole, when disguised in Toad's washerwoman costume, is able to give in to impulse and upset those Wild Wooders who previously frightened him. Even Badger unbends from strict rectitude and employs dark, underground means in using the tunnel to surprise and savage his wild neighbours who have moved out of their natural sphere. If Toad's stable friends can, in effect, learn from him to regress toward their vital cores, it is only appropriate that Toad should finally absorb their lessons in self-control. The new balance resulting from this psychic exchange is certainly a dramatically appropriate stability, a final indication of the kind of unity Grahame achieved in *The Wind in the Willows*.

# 4

# Love, Life, and Death

ANY ANIMAL TALES deal with the difficulty of accepting death. None handles it with as fine a combination of tact and realism as *Charlotte's Web*. E.B. White announces the theme immediately, but with such humour and natural drama that the reader is not aware of any ulterior motive. Fern Arable's mother tells her at breakfast one morning that her father is going to kill the runt of his pig's new litter. Appalled, Fern runs out to stop him. Sobbing and yelling, 'This is a matter of life and death,' she overrides her father's admonition to control herself and persuades him to spare the pig.[1] The tale is in fact not only about life and death, but about the relative place of emotion and reason in a life lived under the threat of death. Fern gave an initial 'shriek' at her mother, which will be duplicated by Wilbur the runt pig when he is old enough to be told that his new owner intends to slaughter him. His gaining some control over his emotional reactions is an essential part of coming to terms with death, of gaining a certain control over it.

As early as chapter 9, we are told of Wilbur's love of life and the world around him. Just after this realization, when the fear of death comes back into his mind, he tells Charlotte that he doesn't want to die and then that he loves it in the barn. More important, when he hears the goslings go by, he listens to the sound 'with love in his heart.' Since the goslings are the most recently born members of the barn population, I infer that Wilbur has instinctively learned, not only that love can be received as an antidote – answer – to death, but also that love can be passed on to younger and even more vulnerable creatures. Part of White's point in connecting first a child and then a spider with his pig is that nurturing and love are not limited by the separation of species.

The development of a child's role as mother to a suckling animal has provided other authors with a whole book. But White has deeper concerns and disposes of this consequence of Fern's responsibility in his short second chapter. When spring comes, Fern builds a house outside for Wilbur and takes him for walks in a baby carriage. But time passes quickly, and by the end of the chapter, Fern's father is insisting that Wilbur has to be sold. On the understanding that she can visit the pig when she likes, Fern does sell him to her uncle, Homer Zuckerman, who lives down the road.

Thus Wilbur is introduced to a new life, and the book takes an unexpected turn.[2] Fern becomes a mere onlooker and gradually removes herself from the scene. Wilbur seeks love and finds it in Charlotte the spider. Why has White provided him with such an unlikely second surrogate mother? The shift from sow mother to little girl mother made sense, because Wilbur needed physical care somewhat as an infant would. Charlotte cannot provide such care, but then Wilbur no longer needs it. Already weaned, he is fed now on slops by Lurvy, the hired man. Although he does still need what we think of as the warmth of human love, Charlotte cannot provide that either. What she can offer is our surest indication of White's reasons for choosing to include her name in the title of his book.

Her incongruously small size makes Charlotte a potentially comic choice as mother to a pig. But White locates his humour elsewhere. I presume he was attracted to a spider as heroine for two main reasons: First, to further his plot, he needs a creature that can somehow communicate with humans. Since he chooses to use not spoken but written words for this bridge, a spider's ability to manipulate lines provided a possible agent. Second, to induct his child reader into the world of life and death he needs a creature intimately and obviously involved in this world. Charlotte with her web provides such an example, and seems to have had the paradoxical attraction to White of belonging to a class of insect that many people find repellent. By making this one spider helpful, White can reverse the emotional charge associated with the species, while dealing realistically with its habits. Charlotte not only gives Wilbur the details of wrapping up a fly for dinner; she admits that her way of life is messy but justifies it as necessary for her survival and maintains that it is useful to other species since she helps keep pests under control.

From the way White positions and characterizes Charlotte and the manner in which she treats Wilbur, I infer another aim he had in choosing her. Wilbur first hears her as a thin voice that allows him to locate her in a high corner of the barn entrance. No matter what happens, Charlotte will always remain above Wilbur, and will be a contrast to him in most respects. Where he is male, she is female; where he is heavy, she is light;

where he converses in grunts and squeals, she has a 'thin' voice. In addition, as White goes out of his way to emphasize in one chapter, while she can sail through the air, Wilbur must be content to remain solidly on the ground.

Like Christopher Robin's relation to Winnie-the-Pooh, Charlotte's to Wilbur is based on unconditional love. His boasts draw not a reprimand but her love. When a lamb offers him personal insults, she defends him. But her most important service to him is her attempt to mould him toward her own virtues. The contrast between their attitudes to his possible death provides the clue: whereas Wilbur trembles, Charlotte remains cool. She may not be able to offer warm mammalian love, but she can demonstrate the strength of a controlled, dispassionate approach to life. Her use of reason as her main tool is quite consonant with her nature, which White makes almost pedantic. (Her large vocabulary and her knowledge of Latin and natural history can sometimes present problems in narrative consistency.) These qualities stem symbolically from Charlotte's position above the passing scene. Although she, like the rest of us, must nourish her life on the death of other creatures, she has managed to find a vantage from which to observe the process coolly, though not passively.

Along with her acceptance of Wilbur's need for reassurance, Charlotte sees where he needs to develop. When he first learns he is being fed only to be slaughtered, she immediately promises to save him, but when this offer doesn't calm him, she finally tells him to stop crying. To ask a pig not to squeal when upset is to expect it to go against its nature. Yet just as Charlotte has triumphed over her death-dealing instincts in helping Wilbur remain alive, so we shall see her tutoring bear fruit later when he rises above his excitable porcine personality at a moment of crisis.

Charlotte also rises above her heritage as a spinner limited by instinct to orb webs when she weaves into her web the words that will eventually save Wilbur. Her ability to make this shift is presented by White as connected with her motives for spinning webs at all: 'If I can fool a bug ... I can surely fool a man.' Just as the bug is fooled by a web that can be seen through, so man will be fooled by a web that invites attention. Charlotte simply adapts her trickster's strategy to a new species. As trickster, the spider is, as we saw in the introduction, one of an archaic company. Anansi in Africa and Iktomi in North America were independently generated versions of the spider in this role. As recorded by Paul Radin, the Oglala Dakota told of Iktomi, who when condemned by God to this world where man will hate him, laughed and said he would dwell with birds and animals 'and talk with each in its own language; and ... would enjoy himself and make fools of mankind.'³ While not contending that White was influenced by this little-known tale, I would like to suggest that the surface parallels are indicative; though Charlotte acts out of benevolence instead of spite, she certainly displays trickster cunning in fooling human beings.

Charlotte's writing words that dupe the people in the story raises again the question of plausibility in the tale. Where a more 'professional' fantasy writer might gloss over the implications of her action, or provide a glib explanation, White chose to develop the point in a tangential chapter that introduces a mouthpiece for the author. Fern's mother goes to Dr Dorian because she is worried about her daughter's fantasy life. When she finally articulates her two questions, she asks whether the doctor understands how the words could appear in Charlotte's web and if he believes animals can talk. White had earlier validated Charlotte's belief that people were easily fooled by showing not only Zuckerman, but also the local minister and all the neighbours believing the message on the web. Dr Dorian's response implicitly both justifies their acceptance and criticizes their blowing up its (and their) importance. He claims that Charlotte's spinning a web in the first place is as much of a miracle as her spinning words. He confesses he doesn't understand either, but concludes that he won't let it worry him, a fairly explicit reaction to the anxiety of Fern's mother. To her second question he responds that since children pay better attention than adults, he is willing to believe Fern when she says the barn animals talk. We readers who have heard them do so are grateful for such an open-minded response. Yet I would have thought it more likely for an enlightened MD to say that though Fern is having fantasies it is only a stage that she can be expected to grow beyond. (In fact, he does suggest she will change – and predicts correctly how – but he never mentions or suggests Fern is involved in a fantasy.) In other words, White has articulated a mother's rational worry, by the standards of our world, and had them authoritatively answered, but by the standard of his own fantasy world. Surely a daring strategy!

Like Pooh, Wilbur moves from humble beginnings when only his need makes him lovable to a growth in capacity that makes him admirable in himself. Wilbur's growth is partly physical, but more important it is also psychological, again like Pooh's. What White tells us about the pig is what we noticed without being told about the bear: 'Wilbur was modest; fame did not spoil him.' The fame referred to has come to Wilbur as a result of Charlotte's messages: first SOME PIG, then TERRIFIC, and now RADIANT. These messages have changed Wilbur not only in the eyes of the world but in his own self-perception. When the second word is about to be written,

Wilbur protests that he's only average. Charlotte's response is that he is terrific as far as she's concerned. But when Charlotte is deciding on her third word, and expresses doubt whether Wilbur really is radiant, Wilbur responds that he *feels* radiant. This decides Charlotte. And White tells us that when each word is displayed, Wilbur tries to look like what it proclaims. And when Mrs Zuckerman gives him a buttermilk bath before they go to the fair, he feels not only happy but 'radiant.'

Charlotte's last two words are brought her by another important animal character, Templeton. A rat who cares only about his own welfare, he is entirely the opposite of Charlotte. Though a killer like Templeton, she is friendly and does care about others. Her uneasy partnership with Templeton not only provides the narrative with dramatic conflict but also enhances the thematic connection of extremes: life and death, love and selfishness, high thoughts and low appetites. Templeton and Wilbur share a dominance of appetite, symbolized by their sharing the contents of Wilbur's trough. Unprovided for, Templeton, like Charlotte, has to be a wily trickster. If his hiding the rotten egg is motivated by no more than a general belief that it may someday come in handy, when its exploding foils the attack on Charlotte of Fern's brother, Avery, Templeton is willing to take for himself the kind of credit that Charlotte will earn by specific actions on Wilbur's behalf.

The climax of Charlotte's plan comes at the county fair. If she can gain some sort of recognition for Wilbur there, a long life will be assured him. Templeton is asked to accompany them so he can supply a final word for Charlotte's web. He agrees to do so only when his appetite and his self-interest are appealed to. As the old sheep tells him, he will be able to gorge himself on all the 'disgusting leftover food' at the fair. His eyes blazing in anticipation, Templeton confesses he is tempted and then agrees to go. After they arrive and before he goes off for a night of overeating, Templeton brings back the last word Charlotte will put in her web, HUMBLE. And this final trick is again successful. Although the gross pig in the pen next to Wilbur wins a blue ribbon in the conventional competition, Charlotte's sign draws onlookers and sustains Wilbur's reputation; he is given a special prize.

White handles the scene in which Wilbur receives his medal from the judges as slapstick comedy. Since it is Wilbur's moment of triumph, we might ask why White chose to have Wilbur faint, Templeton bite his tail, Wilbur then revive with a scream of pain, Lurvy throw a bucket of water by mistake on Avery and Mr Zuckerman, and Avery then show off to the delight of the children in the audience. I think the answer lies in White's desire to put more value on private virtue than on public success. Wilbur's winning the prize is only a means to an end for him and Charlotte. White had earlier implied that Zuckerman's concern with his public position was demoralizing. The anticlimactic treatment of the climax is thus appropriate.

The reactions of Fern and Avery both contribute to White's intention. In a more conventional children's story Fern would have been sharing the spotlight with Wilbur, but White shows her finally making the change predicted by Dr Dorian from an interest in animals to an interest in boys. At the very moment when the family hears Wilbur publicly invited to the judges' stand, Fern chooses to go after Henry Fussy rather than accompany 'her' pig. Avery, on the other hand, has shown no interest in Wilbur previously. He has in fact been presented as a destructive boy, carrying around toy guns and dead trout, and trying to capture Charlotte. But now this aggressiveness is channeled into his comic performance in front of the fair-goers, pretending to shower, acting, as White says twice, like a clown; he redirects attention from Wilbur to himself. White presents this performance sympathetically, but we are in no doubt that it represents only a comic interlude in the serious action that led up to it and will lead to the still more serious events to follow.

The next chapter is titled 'Last Day.' In it Wilbur must face Charlotte's death, an event that will test how far he has incorporated the example and teaching of his mentor and surrogate mother. His immediate reaction to Charlotte's announcement that she is going to die is in the pig tradition: he writhes and cries. This emotional expressiveness does, however, represent an advance over Wilbur's earlier outbursts, which were charged with fear and pity only for himself. But Charlotte makes it clear that she does not want emotion expressed for her, any more than she did earlier for him. When Wilbur persists, Charlotte reasons with him why he must leave her. But even to accept her reasons will leave Wilbur split between necessity and desire. Out of his emotional turmoil comes thought, a plan such as Charlotte herself might have come up with, only instead of saving Charlotte it makes a substitution: Wilbur will take her egg sac back to the barn, so Charlotte's children can hatch there.

Wilbur's test is not over. It is one thing to want to take the egg sac; it is another to get it down from the ceiling where Charlotte has attached it. Wilbur realizes that only Templeton can accomplish this feat. He screams at Templeton, 'Pay attention.' Hearing Wilbur's plea for help, Templeton again demonstrates his lack of concern for others, asking what would be in it for him. Wilbur then makes what he thinks is his strongest plea: If

Templeton doesn't help, the pig will die of a broken heart. When Templeton mocks him, Wilbur loses control and screams at him, but Templeton only grins and recounts all he has already done for Wilbur. The crucial point has arrived. Wilbur's emotions and self-concern have failed to move the rat. Can he turn to his reason for an answer? Calling to mind Templeton's love of food, Wilbur promises always to let the rat have the first turn at his slop trough, if Templeton will rescue the egg sac. Templeton accepts the offer, secures the sac just in time, and the two animals are taken away in Wilbur's crate.

Soon the fairgrounds are deserted. The chapter ends with the private and poignant anticlimax of this section, Charlotte's death. The last sentence is 'No one was with her when she died.' Though understated as always, White's conclusion plays up the pathos of her situation, inviting the reader to feel it. Clearly White's teaching is less austere than Charlotte's.

Charlotte's death is of course not the end of the story; we are invited to focus instead on the birth of her children the following spring. Before that event, however, we are shown the fulfilment of Wilbur's bargain with Templeton. The rat grows enormous on his new diet. When warned he may be shortening his life, he accepts that consequence of his unlimited indulgence of his appetite. It is as though Templeton has taken on the role of glutton that has been traditionally associated with the domestic pig. But Wilbur, after being relieved of that role when Charlotte won him reprieve from premature death, has himself given up the appetite-dominated life that would lead him toward death. He has other concerns, mainly waiting for the eggs to hatch. When spring comes and the baby spiders appear, Wilbur reverts to his old emotional ways. 'Wilbur's heart pounded. He began to squeal. Then he raced in circles, kicking manure into the air. Then he turned a back flip.' As the spiders acknowledge him, Wilbur is very happy, for a few days. Then they take off in an updraft on their silk balloons. Feeling deserted, Wilbur cries himself to sleep. But when he wakes, he hears the same 'Salutations' with which Charlotte originally greeted him and realizes that three of her children have remained behind. They talk and exchange a pledge that Wilbur initiates: 'I pledge my friendship, forever and ever.' The last three words may sound a bit romantic, but even here Wilbur is following Charlotte's lead. She had suggested earlier that he might live forever. White certainly tells us that Wilbur lives to see many generations of spiders born in the barn. But he also lets us know that Zuckerman cares for Wilbur 'all the rest of his days,' an indication that Wilbur will live long and suffer only a natural death.

The book offers in its penultimate paragraph a last celebration of life in all its sensuous variety, ending with praise of 'the nearness of rats, the sameness of sheep, the love of spiders, the smell of manure, and the glory of everything.' Despite Wilbur's – and White's – appreciation of 'the glory of everything,' the reader will sense that the narrative contains more than the euphonious specifics that are offered as examples of this everything. 'The sameness of sheep,' for instance, does not do justice to the contrast between the snobbish lamb who rejected friendship with a smelly pig and the old sheep who first told Wilbur that cold weather is slaughtering time, and then twice helped enlist Templeton in the plan to save Wilbur. Nor does the 'nearness of rats' do justice to Templeton's part in the tale. I am not trying to suggest that White has fallen down here, merely that direct authorial contributions should be seen as only one strand among several that help render this book's complex statement about life.

At the centre of the book's action and its theme, I see Wilbur suspended, as in his initial abortive escape to freedom from the barn in chapter 3, between voices offering conflicting bits of advice. That time he chose to follow his appetite back to the pen. Although the coming of Charlotte puts an end to his dependence on strangers' opinions, the basic conflict remains – between his appetite, indulgence in which serves the aim of the farmer; his emotions, indulgence in which swing him from one extreme to another; and his intelligence, fostering of which gives him a more dependable ally in a crisis than either appetite or emotion. Yet Wilbur is not Charlotte, able to maintain always a high, composed attitude toward life and its problems. Nor is he Templeton, content with the satisfaction of a gourmand's short life. He is between these extremes, able to feel sympathy and empathy, subject to swings of emotion, but relying on reason when appropriate. His feelings are still strong even in the last chapter, where he expresses excitement when the eggs hatch, sorrow when the little spiders leave, and joy when three remain. Clearly we are right to respect White for not repressing these very human emotions.

Since Charlotte is so much against giving in to emotions, how are we to take her, finally? I find a clue in White's last sentence. Charlotte has been 'a true friend and a good writer.' This final witticism may hide an allusion to White's wife, also a writer, or it may contain an unintended reference to White himself. Certainly Charlotte is in many ways his spokesperson. (The reference to the Queensborough Bridge in chapter 9 would come more appropriately from White, who wrote a monograph about New York City, than from a country spider.) The word 'friend' also provides a link. Both the man and the spider claim that friendship is what binds Charlotte and Wilbur, but both demonstrate that love is an important part of friendship. Charlotte as writer is worth further consideration.

To humanity at large, Charlotte's first word is a miracle, in the sense that it violates nature dramatically and tempts people to use it for their own aggrandizement. On her last night, Charlotte produces two different works. She recreates the miracle in the web, with a new word to ensure Wilbur's triumph, but she also creates a sac filled with eggs and calls it first her masterpiece and then her *magnum opus*. Both these terms conventionally refer to art. White seems to be suggesting that all creation is one, whether applied to web or words, egg sac or silk balloon. The artist spins it out of herself or himself in isolation and darkness, to be appreciated by others during the day. One can perhaps begin to understand Charlotte's cool, detached view. Like the artist, she is the dispassionate designer who cannot order the parts properly if too attached to any one element. Yet like her author, she has put her art to the service of life and love, not by sentimentally pretending that death and selfishness don't exist, nor by cynically pretending that love is for suckers, life a mug's game. Just as White celebrates life, so Charlotte does in her decision to save Wilbur's, and in producing her sac full of eggs.

But to emphasize only Charlotte's creative and positive role in the tale is to fail to do justice to the complexity of her character. As we have noted, her life-affirming actions are imposed on a death-dealing nature. This paradox may be part of her mystery, but it is also part of her role as trickster. In this chapter and the last we have met two quite different kinds of trickster. The initial presentation of Toad offers little indication that he will be taking on that role. Charlotte, however, is a hereditary trickster, though her role in fooling her prey is seemingly passive, and allows White to develop the theme of alert patience, a human virtue. Even when Charlotte weaves words in her web, she has only to wait patiently for the gullible people to create their own illusion. Her means are not reprehensible, and her aim is unselfish. Toad, in contrast, uses a disguise he considers demeaning to escape prison and has totally selfish motives at every stage of his escape. In his frequent alternation of inflation and deflation, successful thief and pursued victim, Toad is much closer to the traditional trickster figure than Charlotte is.

Vital, energetic, adventurous, amoral, and unstable, Trickster is anarchic, a violator of the boundaries of nature and society. Suitably adapted to his part in a children's story, Toad meets these criteria, acting frenetically, lacking any centred purpose, outraging decorum and breaking taboos as he shifts his appearance from animal to human, from male to female. The result is a pattern of high drama and low comedy, of daring disguise and ignominious exposure.

Such a theatrical and mercurial conception was far from White's mind in characterizing Charlotte. Although physically less substantial than Toad, she is inherently more impressive. Initially mysterious yet reassuring, she is soon shown to possess an integrity that has no need of bluster or pretence. In her single-minded concern for Wilbur, she insists that each word in her web should accurately describe him. Because her trickster nature is associated with her ability to deal death, she is a figure to be taken seriously. White's transforming her into a life-saver transvalues the trickster role, a reversal not only of selfish to unselfish, amoral to moral, but of anarchy to order. Although Charlotte thus crosses the boundary from isolated trickster to organizer of the barnyard society, she retains many of her trickster functions in relation to human society. But even here the traditional role is modified, purged of its flamboyance. Charlotte is the hidden centre of trickery. In the drama she writes and directs, the human beings who are both audience and actors are unaware of her significance.

Charlotte simply provides people with an opportunity to expose their weaknesses. Although their gullibility in the story makes them ridiculous, they are shown to be doing the right thing – honouring a pig – for the wrong reason – believing the words in the web to be of supernatural origin. And the human climax of these mistaken notions is also appropriately off-centre: Wilbur is given a medal because he has attracted so many visitors to the fair. The slapstick comedy of the medal presentation again highlights these human shortcomings.

This climax is a fitting end to Charlotte's original realization that if she can trick insects with her web, she can also use it to fool humanity. Like the trickster in primitive tales, Charlotte is isolated from human society. His impulses lead him to actions that stand as a negative example to an audience that is committed to social propriety. But Charlotte has a different function. Although she fools human beings, her unselfish aim is to help a fellow creature. Rather than praising conformity, White invites us to laugh at people in groups and teaches us to value the private virtues of love and friendship, being helpful, and being reasonable.

When we meet the trickster as hero in *Watership Down*, we shall see that this figure can be adapted to display simultaneously the seemingly contradictory traits of Toad and Charlotte. El-ahrairah is not only an appetite-driven and compulsive trickster who threatens universal order; he is also the leader of a (rabbit) society, and he is willing to sacrifice himself to maintain it.

# 5

# The Development of the Hero

ISSIMILAR THOUGH *The Jungle Book* and *Charlotte's Web* are, they do have a generally similar narrative structure. In each a child enters the domain of some animals and is accepted by them. More important, in each this incursion causes a serious disruption of the previous stable pattern of relations among the animals and between them and man. The particular differences are, of course, more striking. One tale involves a girl, the other a boy; in one the animals are domestic, in the other, wild. In *Charlotte's Web*, Fern becomes a passive observer, and the focus shifts to the animals; in Mowgli's part of the *Jungle Books*, he is always both active and central. Fern's shifting her attention from the animal to the human world is easily accomplished, while Mowgli's split allegiance is emphasized by his growing up as an animal. The ease and reassurance offered by *Charlotte's Web* are entirely absent from *The Jungle Book*. Their wholly different tones can be illustrated by three lines of song from each. In her lullaby to Wilbur at one point, Charlotte sings, 'This is the hour when frogs and thrushes / Praise the world from the woods and rushes / Rest from care, my one and only.' In contrast, the epigraph to chapter 1 of *The Jungle Book* contains these lines from a jungle hunting song: 'This is the hour of pride and power / Talon and tush and claw. / Oh, hear the call! – Good hunting all.'[1] The hour is the same, the coming of night, but the anticipation is entirely different. Charlotte promises rest to a pig, while the hunting song incites wild animals to violence. Paired with *The Jungle Book*, *Charlotte's Web* may seem uneventful, though its tone is appropriate to domestic animals. Kipling's book does not contain as many details from an actually observed nature as White's; in fact, Kipling's realism borders on literary naturalism, as that deterministic doctrine had been developing out of the Darwinian code of the survival of the fittest in the late nineteenth century. Kipling's attunement to power relations leads him to emphasize natural laws. As James Harrison points out, 'it is law rather than freedom which seems to be the distinctive feature of Kipling's' jungle. In opposition to law, there is 'some manifestation of a life force which is as a rule youthful and vigorous ... its existence is a constant safeguard against the law becoming a mere dead letter.'[2] Mowgli is the life force in the first three tales of *The Jungle Book*, and his appearance begins a process of disruption that will not be satisfied until the jungle, through its animals, has interacted violently with the plains where the human village is.

The disruption begins one night when Father Wolf is waking to go out for his night's hunting. He is about 'to spring downhill when a little shadow with a bushy tail' crosses 'the threshold' and whines. It is Tabaqui the jackal, who 'runs about making mischief, and tells tales' – in short, a trickster somewhat feared by more powerful animals. He asks for a bone, and Father Wolf reluctantly extends hospitality to him, allowing him to enter and gnaw in the back of the cave. When finished the jackal praises the wolf-cubs, well knowing that 'there is nothing so unlucky as to compliment children to their faces.' Then 'rejoicing in the mischief' he has made, he tells them that the tiger, Shere Khan, will be hunting in their area. After the wolves complain at this breaking of 'Jungle Law,' the jackal is ordered out of the den. The violation of natural boundaries by both jackal and tiger foreshadows worse to follow.

Shere Khan unsuccessfully attacks some humans nearby, and a few minutes later an infant toddles into the cave and lies down with the wolf-cubs to suckle against Mother Wolf. When Shere Khan is led by the jackal to the wolf cave and demands the man cub, the wolves claim it as theirs and defy him. Mother Wolf even predicts that this cub will someday hunt Shere Khan. Too big to enter the den, the tiger leaves, after threatening to bring the matter up to the wolf-pack. This threat worries the wolves and provides Kipling with an opportunity to explain another Law of the Jungle, that when a wolf-cub becomes able to walk it must be taken to the Pack Council to be identified and given safe conduct by every member of the pack until it is grown. If there should be any dispute about admitting a cub to the pack, 'he must be spoken for by at least two members of the pack who are not his father and mother.' Shere Khan does claim the man cub; in the resulting dispute, no other wolf will speak for the boy. Yet he is spoken for, first by 'the only other creature who is allowed to speak at the Pack Council – Baloo, the sleepy brown bear who teaches the wolf cubs the Law of the Jungle.' He offers to teach the man cub, too. The second voice belongs to 'Bagheera, the Black Panther' who drops like 'a black shadow ... down into the circle.' He reminds the pack of an additional law that provides that the life of a doubtful cub may be bought, and he offers a fat bull he has killed not far away. The wolves gladly accept this offer, and the man cub, already named 'Mowgli the Frog,' is accepted. Shere Khan roars in frustration.

The force of the intruding tiger and jackal has been matched by the native bear and panther. Like Tabaqui, Bagheera is a shadow figure, but one who depends less on tricks than on power. 'He was as cunning as Tabaqui, as bold as a wild buffalo, and as reckless as the wounded elephant.' Baloo and Shere Khan are both more powerful than Bagheera, but neither is as effective because both are slower and somewhat lazy. The important difference between them is that the bear is a teacher of the Law, the tiger a breaker of it. Mowgli will be taught by Baloo how to obey and use the Law and by Bagheera how to develop his human cunning.

Bagheera is, in fact, the most complex of the animals in the story. He later tells Mowgli that he was born in captivity and ransomed the boy because of what he owed man. He learned 'the ways of men' so well that he has become 'more terrible in the Jungle than Shere Khan.' Because of this human connection, Bagheera is able to advise Mowgli to obtain some fire from a neighbouring village to use against Shere Khan at the next Pack Council.

Mowgli appropriates a pot of fire and finds he can light branches with it. He takes it to the council, where the pack calls in question first the fitness of Akela, the pack leader, and then Mowgli's membership. Just when it appears the majority of the pack will turn on the minority who support Mowgli, the boy steps forward and subdues all of them with a flaming branch. Then he speaks, first to accept exile (to go among men), second to save the life of Akela, deposed as leader, and third to shame Shere Khan by singeing his fur. He finally promises not to return without the tiger's hide. Immediately after this triumph, in which his power as a man becomes clear, Mowgli uncomprehendingly experiences another side of his human heritage: he sobs and tears run down his face. When he asks, 'Am I dying, Bagheera?' the black panther replies that they are only tears but that they do indicate he is a man. 'The Jungle is shut indeed to thee henceforward.' The boy then leaves for the village.

Mowgli and Shere Khan are equally disruptive forces in the wolf society they invade. Although powerful, the tiger is incompetent and selfish, a deliberate underminer of Jungle Law. Although weak, the boy learns competence and consideration, and tries to follow the jungle law. But his differences in appearance and nature are early apparent, as in his ability to stare down the wolves. Although these differences make inevitable his exile, the manner of his going is indicative. Not only does he show dominance over his enemy, he makes a vow that suggests the possibility of his return; just as Bagheera paid for Mowgli's entry with a bull, so Mowgli will in a sense pay for his own re-entry with the tiger's hide. He shows his humanity not only in his tears and his use of fire, but also in saving Akela. The old wolf has missed a kill, the traditional signal for his stepping down as leader and being killed. Mowgli allows the first but forbids the second, another act that leaves behind disruption. Because of his actions and Shere Khan's corruptions, the wolves will henceforth be without a leader.

The fulfilment of Mowgli's prediction comes to pass in 'Tiger, Tiger,' which begins when he goes off to join a village. He finds it barricaded against wild animals but is seen and brought before the village priest, whom Kipling portrays as all that is corrupt in established religion. Mowgli is given to Messua, who had lost a boy years before in the jungle. He learns the language easily, but when it comes to customs he refuses to recognize caste and is sent out to herd buffalo. At night he listens to Buldeo, the village hunter, tell tall tales of his experiences in the jungle. When Mowgli corrects his contention that Shere Khan is a ghost tiger, Buldeo says, 'If thou art so wise, better bring his hide to Khanhiwara for the Government has set a hundred rupees on his life.' This statement points toward the main action and conflict of the chapter.

In a traditional folk-tale, this statement would introduce the Impossible Task given the hero to fulfil. As we shall see when we come to 'The White Seal' and 'Toomai of the Elephants,' Kipling was aware just how useful such a task was in developing a plot and providing a theme for his stories. Its use in 'Tiger, Tiger' is not straightforward. Mowgli has already sworn to take the hide to the council rock. Buldeo's scornful suggestion shows the value a human hunter would put on the hide. Here as everywhere in this chapter, human values are shown as either material or superstitious and thus arbitrary, and finally empty. Jungle values are real because based on actual relations among creatures. In one sense, Mowgli will have a choice where to take the hide when he gets it. In another sense, we know all along that he will act on the values embodied in Jungle Law.

While herding buffalo, Mowgli keeps in touch with one of his wolf siblings, Grey Brother. One day the wolf reports meeting Tabaqui and killing him after the jackal has informed him that Shere Khan is sleeping with a full belly in a nearby ravine and plans to ambush Mowgli that evening. Grey Brother and Akela cut Mowgli's herd in two. Grey Brother takes the cows up the ravine until 'the sides are higher than Shere Khan can jump.' Akela and Mowgli take the bulls around to the head of the ravine.

That achieved, Mowgli pauses and calls to let Shere Khan know they are coming. Akela starts the bulls, which soon pick up the scent of the tiger. Then 'the torrent of black horns, foaming muzzles and staring eyes whirled down the ravine like boulders in flood time.' Hearing them, Shere Khan 'lumbered down the ravine ... heavy with his dinner and drink, willing to do anything rather than fight.' The natural force of the buffalo charge soon overtakes him and tramples him dead.

While Mowgli is skinning the ten-foot tiger, Buldeo appears and tries to appropriate the hide. 'Well, well, we will overlook thy letting the herd run off, and perhaps I will give thee one of the rupees of the reward when I have taken the skin to Khanhiwara.' Mowgli calls on Akela, who knocks down Buldeo and stands over him while Mowgli goes on skinning. Because of his belief in ghosts and sorcery, Buldeo takes Mowgli for a magician; he addresses the boy as 'Maharaj! Great King!' and asks to be released. When Mowgli agrees, the hunter flees to the village. There he interprets what has happened in terms of 'magic and enchantment,' upsetting the villagers. Thus when Mowgli tries to fulfil his human obligation by bringing home the buffalo herd, he is met with 'a shower of stones' and cries or 'Sorcerer! Wolf's brat! Jungle-demon!' As Akela comments, 'they are not unlike the pack, these brothers of thine.' Just as the pack was easily worked on by Shere Khan, so the villagers are by Buldeo. Just as the pack sacrifices a rational view of long-term good – of Mowgli as a pack member valuable because of his human abilities – so the villagers cannot see the long-term value of a herd boy who can rid them of a threat by virtue of his jungle allies and his human-animal cunning.

Mowgli, the little frog, has accomplished the Impossible Task; having killed the tiger, he will take its hide, not for a monetary reward as Buldeo suggested, but to the council rock where he will get greater value for it. It will demonstrate there the power of his word and of his actions. It will stand for his triumph over a disrupting force, a creature that violated the Law and exposed other jungle animals to danger because of its depredations against man. When Mowgli spreads the hide upon the Council Rock, Akela calls together the dispersed wolf-pack. Because they have been without a leader, some are lame from traps and bullets, some 'mangy from eating bad food, and many were missing.' Having answered their former leader's call and seeing this sign of Mowgli's prowess, they plead, 'Lead us again, O Akela. Lead us again, O Man-cub, for we be sick of this lawlessness, and we would be the Free People once more.' But Bagheera tells them why it cannot be: 'When ye are full-fed, the madness may come upon ye again.' Mowgli concludes, 'Man-Pack and Wolf-Pack have cast me out ... Now I will hunt alone in the jungle.' So he goes off with his four wolf brothers.

The wolves' pleas contain one of Kipling's key paradoxes, that true freedom lies within the law. But Bagheera's and Mowgli's responses carry the clear implication that men or animals in groups are subject to irrationality and corruption. As Harrison points out, 'the sternest upholder of the Law, and the only completely reliable animals ... are members of solitary species.' In contrast, 'social animals are all untrustworthy to some extent.'[3] When we look at the reasons for Mowgli's being ostracized from the wolf-pack and man-pack, we might also note something in his nature that is part of the cause. If he had not used his eyes and his fire so much to affirm his superiority, he might have been more accepted by the wolves. Clearly, it is partly pride that drives him away, when at the end of the first chapter he has broken Shere Khan's power and established his own. Similarly, if he had shown a more human reaction to Buldeo, he might have been welcome at the village rather than stoned. To say that he is too intent on skinning the tiger to have time to explain to an ignorant, superstitious, bullying hunter is simply to say that he lacks a social sense. Since Akela does obey him and exchange wolf talk with him, Buldeo has good reason to take Mowgli as a sorcerer. But Mowgli is obviously pleased to join the solitary species that keep the Law; he would rather not have to spend time on the difficulties of social interaction. In making this criticism I am not complaining about Mowgli's situation at the end; it is dramatic and provides a nice contrast to the integration scenes that have characterized the endings of the first four books we have looked at. But Kipling's negative portrayal of the villagers does seem to me over-harsh, almost a caricature. And Mowgli's retaliating by sending the buffalo charging into the village seems to me an action that bespeaks a slightly suspect need on the part of the author.[4] Like White, Kipling seems unfairly to hold those characters who live by a conventional reality sense culpable when they misunderstand actions following from the author's fantasy premiss.

Similarly, Mowgli's calling to Shere Khan is not, as one might expect, a chivalrous gesture to give his foe a fighting chance. He announces his own name and proclaims, 'it is time to come to the Council Rock!' He wants Shere Khan to know who is responsible and why he is being killed. But his plan has been worked out too well for Shere Khan to have any chance of escape. Even if the tiger had not indulged himself by filling his belly before he was to kill Mowgli, the sides of the ravine are still too steep for him to climb out. Shere Khan's other sin is cowardice: he was 'willing to do anything rather than fight.' But since we have just been told that 'no tiger can hope to stand' against 'the terrible charge of a buffalo herd,' he is displaying good sense in looking for an escape. My point is that Kipling has overloaded him with defects that are unnecessary to his fate. Unsavoury as his actions have always been, Shere Khan is reduced so far by the end that Mowgli's victory becomes less than it might have been.

'Kaa's Hunting' is marred by some of the same excess in punishment and character typing that we have seen in 'Tiger, Tiger,' but I find it in many ways the most satisfying of the Mowgli chapters. It is set during Mowgli's youth when he is still learning the Law of the Jungle from Baloo, who is pleased to be able to teach the boy more than the wolves are interested in learning. Mowgli learns 'the Stranger's Hunting Call' not only for mammals but for birds and snakes. Bagheera complains that Baloo's methods are too rough, and indeed Mowgli does resent the bear's cuffs. After Mowgli has shown off his vocal ability to Bagheera, he reveals that he has been approached by a troop of monkeys, the Bandar-log, who have filled him with inflated ideas of becoming their king. Hit by Baloo for his presumption, Mowgli admits that he talked with the Bandar-log because they took pity on him after a previous beating by Baloo. As his two mentors expose the pretentions, laziness, and irresponsibility of the monkey-people, it becomes clear that Baloo considers them so far outside the Law that he has never mentioned them to Mowgli. Bagheera chides his friend for this omission, and a chastened Mowgli promises to have nothing to do with the Bandar-log in future.

Then, while all three are settled into their midday sleep, Mowgli is kidnapped by the monkey-people, who have overheard the previous exchange. As they carry him 'through the tree-tops, twenty feet at a bound,' Mowgli begins to think how to escape. He sees a kite above the trees and gives the Master-Words of protection that he has just learned from Baloo. He then asks the bird to report his whereabouts to his friends.

As they follow on the ground, Baloo confesses to Bagheera that he is to blame for not having told Mowgli about the Bandar-log. He then decides that they need an ally feared by the monkey-people, Kaa the Rock Snake. Approaching cautiously they get his cooperation, and all three move toward the Cold Lairs where the kite has reported Mowgli to be. The Cold Lairs are the ruins of an ancient Indian city and palace, appropriated now by the Bandar-log, who are presented by Kipling as a low form of incipient humanity. There they boast of their abilities to Mowgli but are too disorganized even to bring him the food they promise. When Bagheera, the swiftest pursuer, arrives, the Bandar-log dump Mowgli into a summer-house from which he cannot escape. There he gives the Master-Word of protection again, this time in the snake tongue, thus keeping the cobras from biting him.

Because they outnumber the panther so overwhelmingly, the monkeys are willing to attack Bagheera, who is soon in trouble. Realizing this, Mowgli calls to him to make for the water tank, where he gains a needed respite. Then Baloo arrives and begins hitting the monkeys. Though more powerful than Bagheera, he is soon hard pressed, too. Meanwhile Kaa, who arrived before Baloo, has got himself well positioned for action. He comes to Baloo's rescue, and as soon as the Bandar-log recognize him they flee in panic. As they retreat Kaa speaks 'one loud hissing word,' and they halt in silence. Kaa then frees Mowgli from the summer-house. After Mowgli has thanked him according to the protocol of the Jungle, Kaa praises him and suggests that the three leave, for 'what follows it is not well that thou should'st see.' Up to this point Kaa's immense physical power has been emphasized, 'the driving blow of his head backed by all the strength and weight of his body,' like a 'battering-ram ... weighing nearly half a ton driven by a cool, quiet mind living in the handle of it.' But impressive as is this side of Kaa, there are others.

Part Trickster, 'old Kaa ... could make himself look so like a dead branch or a rotten stump that the wisest were deceived, till the branch caught them.' Not only had no monkey 'ever come alive out of his hug,' 'none of them could look him in the face.' This third aspect of Kaa's power is different from Mowgli's. Animals can look at the boy, but even Bagheera has to drop his eyes after half a minute of trying to return Mowgli's stare. Kaa's power is far stronger, an hypnotic power used for ritual purposes. When the moon sets, Kaa ensures there is enough light for his captive audience to see him and begins 'the Dance of the Hunger of Kaa,' weaving his body into innumerable shapes, 'never resting, never hurrying, and never stopping his low humming song.' When the dance ends, Kaa suggests to the monkeys that they cannot 'stir hand or foot without my order'; they repeat his words in mesmerized affirmation. When he commands them to advance one step forward toward the creature they fear most, not only do all the monkeys advance, but Baloo and Bagheera do, too. Only Mowgli is unaffected, and when he lays his hands on his friends, 'The two great beasts started as though they had been waked from a dream. "Keep thy hand on my shoulder," Bagheera whispered. "Keep it there, or I must go back – must go back to Kaa."' So strong is the spell of the Rock Snake.

Once they are away Bagheera admits that Kaa 'knows more than we ... In a little time, had I stayed, I should have walked down his throat.' Baloo responds, 'Many will walk by that road before the moon rises again.' Kaa's power in this scene is equalled only by the power of Kipling's imaginative conception and description. He compellingly evokes our atavistic response to the strength and sinuousness of the snake, its contact with earth, its deceptive ability to blend into the background, but above all its peristaltic ability to pull in alive its mammalian prey. Kaa's throat as a dark road down which even Bagheera must walk is a conception that taps that primordial descent into darkness that both repels and attracts humanity.

Yet we must note that Mowgli is impervious to the spell. We are told that he does not 'know anything of a python's powers of fascination.' Presumably this is a human trait and separates Mowgli from the other animals. As readers we feel conscious relief at his immunity, glad that only lower species are lured to destruction, but our relief itself can tell us how deeply we have felt the fascination thus denied. We will have other opportunities to confront the descent into darkness in looking at the remaining chapters of *The Jungle Book.*

'Kaa's Hunting' ends with an anticlimax. Once free of the snake's spell, Bagheera's attention shifts to Mowgli as the cause of his recent difficulties. Even more than the pain he has suffered, he resents the cost in honour. Not only did he have to seek refuge in the water tank, on the advice of a cub, but fearing that Kaa might have abandoned them, 'in despair' he had recourse to the 'Snake's Call for protection.' Kaa twits him about this call for help after he has the Bandar-log under control. Added to this shame is Bagheera's sense of having been 'made as stupid as little birds by the Hunger-Dance.' In need of a scapegoat, Bagheera decides that Mowgli must be punished, since it all came of his 'playing with the Bandar-log.' He has forgotten that he had earlier correctly put the blame on Baloo, who had accepted it, for not forbidding Mowgli to play with the monkey people. He has also forgotten that Mowgli not only directed him to the water tank but saved him from walking down the dark road of Kaa's inside. Yet Mowgli and Baloo, instead of pointing out these facts to him, agree that the boy must be punished for breaking the Law. Bagheera then gives 'half-a-dozen love-taps,' which Kipling claims constitute a 'severe' beating for 'a seven-year-old boy' such as Mowgli.

As at the end of 'Tiger, Tiger,' I find here the author's extra-literary imperative overpowering his otherwise acute sense of cause and effect. If any punishment should be given, it should be to Baloo, who has failed to include a key lesson in a jungle education. And if the adventure teaches any lesson, it should be to Bagheera, who needs to learn that the proper way to deal with a lapse from his high sense of power and honour is to look into himself rather than look outside for a scapegoat. Unfortunately, he will not learn that lesson, seemingly because his creator does not understand it.

Kipling presents a more positive rendering of the actual descent down the dark road into archaic night in 'Toomai of the Elephants,' one of two tales we shall look at from the other half of *The Jungle Book*. This story is about Kala Nag, an old elephant who has served the Indian government for forty-seven years. Toomai's great grandfather had helped catch and train Kala Nag for the Afghan War, his grandfather had taken him to the Abyssinian War, but his father is only a mahout, first in timber hauling and now in capturing and taming wild elephants. The broad conflict in this tale is between wildness and tameness – a variation on the theme of conflicting wildness and domesticity that we saw in 'The Cat That Walked by Himself.' Kala Nag was transferred from civilized timber hauling to chasing and subduing other elephants in the mountains after 'he half killed an insubordinate young elephant who was shirking his fair share of the work.' Violence and justice are again connected with wildness. Little Toomai likes the mountains and the excitement of the stockade where the wild elephants are collected. His father prefers the well-regulated life of the plains. He tells his son, 'I am getting old, and I do not love wild elephants. Give me brick elephant-lines, one stall to each elephant, and big stumps to tie them to safely ... Next week the catching is over, and we of the plains are sent back to our stations. Then we will march on smooth roads, and forget all this hunting.' Before many nights have passed Little Toomai and Kala Nag will together follow a far rougher and wilder road.

Being young, Little Toomai has fantasies; he imagines Kala Nag bought by a rich rajah. 'Then thou wilt have nothing to do but to carry gold earrings in thy ears, and a gold howdah on thy back, and a red cloth covered with gold on thy sides, and walk at the head of the processions of the King. Then I shall sit on thy neck, O Kala Nag, with a silver ankus, and men will run before us with golden sticks, crying, "Room for the King's elephant!" That will be good, Kala Nag, but not so good as this hunting in the jungles.' This dream of ease is in fact more appropriate to Big Toomai; the honour that actually comes will be more closely connected with hunting in the wild jungle than parading in the tame city.

Before the newly caught elephants are taken down to the plains, Petersen Sahib, the English head of all the elephant-catching operations, appears at the hill station. He overhears Machua Appa, the head tracker from the hill tribe, lament the imminent departure of Little Toomai, so different from the other plains people. Singled out by Petersen, Little Toomai has Kala Nag lift him up level with the sahib, who is on his elephant, Pudmini. After joking with him, Petersen gives Little Toomai four annas, tells him he may in time 'become a hunter,' and gently warns him to stay out of the wild elephant stockade, or Keddah, where he had recently risked his life.

'Must I never go there, Sahib?' asked Little Toomai, with a big gasp.

'Yes.' Petersen Sahib smiled again. 'When thou hast seen the elephants dance. That is the proper time. Come to me when thou hast seen the elephants dance, and then I will let thee go into all the Keddahs.'

There was another roar of laughter, for that is an old joke among elephant-catchers, and it means just never. There are great cleared flat places hidden away in the forest that are called elephants' ball-rooms, but even these are only found by accident, and no man has ever seen the elephants dance.

Little Toomai has just been given the Impossible Task, and the remainder of the story details how he fulfils the conditions laid down.

Immediately after this interview the elephants march off, down out of the hills. At camp that night Little Toomai, in front of Kala Nag, beats a small drum for a long time, thinking on 'the great honour' Petersen has shown him. Then he goes to sleep beside Kala Nag. During the night, the elephants are so restless that Big Toomai takes off Kala Nag's chain to shackle more securely one of the new elephants, counting on Kala Nag's remaining safe as he had before under similar circumstances. But shortly thereafter, Little Toomai wakes to see Kala Nag leaving the camp. He calls to be taken and the elephant lifts the boy onto his neck.

At first Kala Nag moves without sound. In the dark of their march through the jungle, Toomai can hear other animals. Then the elephant begins to go down into a valley, noisily, as he 'ploughed out his pathway.' Toomai becomes aware of other elephants and decides that they are going to the elephant's dance. 'All the mist about him seemed to be full of rolling, wavy shadows.' The dark shapes have made an elephant road, a 'path ... six feet wide' that Kala Nag can now follow. Finally they come to 'an irregular space of some three or four acres' of ground 'trampled down as hard as a brick floor.' The moon shines in this cleared area, showing 'white wood' and white flowers, but the elephants' 'shadows were inky black.' They crowd into the open space, 'chucking and gurgling,' talking 'in their own tongue.' When a cloud comes over the moon, Toomai sits 'in black darkness ... all alone in the dark.'

Then an elephant trumpets, and 'a dull booming noise' begins. Kala Nag starts lifting up 'one fore-foot and then the other,' as the sound grows. 'The elephants were stamping all together now, and it sounded like a war-drum beaten at the mouth of a cave.' Both the sound and the jarring vibration run through the boy as the elephants enlarge their natural compound. Finally dawn comes, and the booming stops 'with the first ray, as though the light had been an order.' Tired and weak, Toomai asks Kala Nag to accompany Pudmini, who is also there, back to Petersen's camp, since it is closer than his own. When they arrive there, Toomai announces he has seen the elephant dance, and Petersen Sahib and Machua Appa follow the trail to the compound to verify his claim.

That night there is a feast in the hill camp. 'Little Toomai was the hero of it all; and the big brown elephant-catchers, the trackers and drivers and ropers, and the men who know all the secrets of breaking the wildest elephants, passed him from one to the other, and they marked his forehead with blood from the breast of a newly killed jungle-cock, to show that he was a forester, initiated and free of all the jungles.' Then Machua Appa announces that the boy has earned a new name, 'Toomai of the Elephants, as his great-grandfather was called before him. What never man has seen he has seen through the long night, and the favour of the elephant-folk and of the Gods of the Jungles is with him. He shall become a great tracker.' Then he commands the elephants present to salute the initiate and calls out himself. 'And at that last wild yell the whole line flung up their trunks till the tips touched their foreheads, and broke out into the full salute, the crashing trumpet-peal that only the Viceroy of India hears – the Salaam-ut of the Keddah. But it was all for the sake of Little Toomai.' The boy's early dream of glory has been surpassed. Instead of accompanying Kala Nag 'at the head of the processions of the King,' he has ridden the elephant through its powerful dance and has himself received 'the full salute' of the camp elephants. Because of his daring, the weakening lineage he was born to is invigorated, as he receives the name of the great grandfather who originally named Kala Nag. More, he is made one with the hill people, the trackers, those who follow wild ways, the favoured of Petersen Sahib.

The process by which he has earned this destiny can be paralleled to the process by which the Bandar-log enter Kaa. Toomai also goes on a dark road where he is frightened and mesmerized. Although he feels 'all alone in the dark,' he goes not to destruction but to self-fulfilment. He is taken by a creature as powerful as the Rock Snake. (Kipling tells us early on that Kala Nag means 'Black Snake.') In both cases the descent into darkness is connected with archaic forces, in Toomai's especially with the shadow side of the elephant, a night world of primordial ritual that is unknown to those who live only by day.

Just as his initial fantasy of taking part in a rajah's procession finds its double fulfilment in the ride to the elephant dance ground and the salute of the Keddah, so his beating the drum while thinking 'of the great honour' shown him by Petersen's gift of four annas finds its fulfilment first in the powerful booming of the elephants' 'war-drum' stamping out of their dance ground and then in the supreme honour rendered him at the end. Although the early fantasy and the drum beating both demonstrate a little boy's limited understanding, they also show his vital impulse that the events of the story confirm and celebrate.

Kala Nag's position is more ambiguous. On the one hand he is included in Machua Appa's reference to 'my lord the elephant,' a noble, possibly divine species. The animals' power is so great that Machua Appa admits 'the ways of elephants are beyond the wit of any man, black or white, to fathom.' But he also speaks truth when he addresses the elephants of the Keddah as 'my lords in chains.' Man may not understand elephants, but he is able to keep them captive. And the chains are not merely physical. Pudmini snapped hers to join the dance, and Kala Nag could have. Kipling's point in not having him chained is precisely that Big Toomai knows he can trust the elephant not to try to escape. Kala Nag's going to the elephant dance does not invalidate this expectation: both he and Pudmini return to captivity.

Kala Nag is particularly interesting because he is wilder than most of the other tame elephants. Shifted from plains duty to the hills, he there uses his aggressiveness to take on 'the biggest and wildest tusker of the mob' of newly captured elephants and 'hammer him and hustle him into quiet.' His aggression is thus in the service of order. His subduing a tusker is the first step in taming the wild. His having earlier 'half killed an insubordinate young elephant who was shirking his fair share of the work' shows Kala Nag's sense of justice and commitment to man's work ethic. Although – or because – Kala Nag uses his wildness in the service of taming others, he does not lose touch with it, as his going to the elephant dance shows.

The story thus contains a kind of balance. Kala Nag, the lord in chains, accepts servitude, yet keeps his vitality alive. Men are in danger of becoming too tame, wanting only smooth roads on the plain, as Big Toomai does. He desires a life of routine and fears his son's being singled out, sure it will be for punishment rather than praise. But Little Toomai has some of the vitality of the wild in him; with the encouragement of Petersen, who realizes his order must include that vitality, and the final confirmation of Machua Appa, who is intimate with the elephants, Toomai comes to identify with the wild. The central agent is, however, Kala Nag. Without the closeness of Little Toomai to him, without the elephant's responding to the boy, the initiation would never have occurred. The boy who desires to exchange the safety of civilization in which he was born for the danger and liveliness of hill life is paired with the elephant that has channelled into man's disciplined ways the vitality of nature where it was born. Together they go down a dark road in the jungle, mingle with shadows, and return to the day world of humanity's work revitalized, with a bond so strong that the boy becomes Toomai of the Elephants.

The image of the descent into darkness also appears as part of the pattern of confirmation of the hero in two other stories in *The Jungle Book*. In 'Rikki-Tiki-Tavi' the mongoose is pitted against a pair of cobras, Nag and his mate, Nagaina. At the end of the story when Nagaina flees, the mongoose pursues and bites onto her tail as she goes down her hole. 'It was dark in the hole ... He held on savagely, and stuck out his feet to act as brakes on the dark slope.' He emerges victorious and, like Toomai, is publicly celebrated for his heroism in ridding the garden of poisonous snakes. The pattern of descent into darkness is neatly varied here, as the mongoose goes, not down the dark road of death inside the snake, but with the snake down a dark tunnel that could as well lead to his death as to hers. ('It might open out and give Nagaina room to turn and strike at him.') In the lonely darkness, he faces death and triumphs. Since his actions are consciously aimed at protecting the English family that had saved him as a baby, the theme of wildness in the service of tameness is present again.

A variation of that theme is also evident in the last story I shall discuss, 'The White Seal'; more clearly, however, this tale offers a paradigm of the development of the hero. One of its climaxes includes a descent into darkness. Like 'Kaa's Hunting,' 'The White Seal' is about lessons and learning. Like Mowgli and the Elephant's Child, the young seal is curious and adventurous, unable to settle into the conventions of his species. Although being white makes him seem different, it is more a sign of his specialness than a reason for other seals' rejecting him. His early learning is like that of any seal, how to swim around the nursery on the Aleutian island where he was born, how to play, what predators to stay clear of. When the seals go south in the fall, he learns about living on the open sea, how to fish and tell when the weather is about to change. When the seals return to the Aleutians, the curiosity of the white seal leads him on an expedition that will shape his life for the next six years.

The seal, Kotick, follows two men and the herd of his playmates that they are driving inland to slaughter. The men don't include him because he is white and they are superstitious. They are upset by his following them, 'the first time a seal has come to the killing grounds alone.' But they go ahead with the clubbing and skinning of the other seals. Kotick is horrified and rushes back to the beach; there he gives the news to the first creature he meets, a sea lion that already knows all about it. 'You must have seen old Kerick polishing off a drove. He's done that for thirty years.' But Kotick refuses to accept this terrible fact, and the sea lion unthinkingly, like Petersen Sahib, sets him the Impossible Task: 'If you seals will come here year after year, of course the men get to know of it, and unless you can find an island where no men ever come, you will always be driven.' When Kotick asks whether there is such an island, the sea lion sends him to 'old Sea Vitch,' the Walrus. Also unable to answer, Sea Vitch in turn sends him to search for an animal Kotick has never seen, Sea Cow. With no interest or co-operation from the other seals, Kotick spends the next five years exploring, looking for Sea Cow or for a safe haven for seals.

He roams the Pacific, finding many islands, but none unvisited by men. Ready to give up after his fifth year of searching, Kotick meets an old seal who says, 'Try once more. I am the last of the Lost Rookery of Masafuera, and in the days when men killed us by the hundred thousand there was a story on the beaches that some day a white seal would come out of the north and lead the seal people to a quiet place.' This legend gives Kotick renewed hope. Back at the Aleutian island that summer, he resists his mother's request that he marry, saying, 'It is always the seventh wave that gets farthest up the beach.' He has just turned seven. He goes west and meets a herd of huge creatures, bigger than walrus but unaggressive, in fact completely silent and unresponsive. Kotick realizes they must be sea cows. Even though they seem stupid and will never answer his question in words, Kotick sticks with them. They finally stop grazing and begin to travel north but so slowly that Kotick's patience is sorely tried. Then 'one night they sank through the shiny water' and 'began to swim quickly.' Surprised, Kotick follows as they head 'for a cliff by the shore – a cliff that ran into deep water.' They plunge down twenty fathoms and enter 'a dark hole at the foot' of the cliff. 'It was a long, long swim, and Kotick badly wanted fresh air before he was out of the dark tunnel that they led him through.' They have brought him to a beach where men never come; at one end, 'a line of bars and shoals and rocks ... would never let a ship come within six miles of the beach.'

Full of his good news, Kotick returns to the Aleutians only to find the seals unwilling to accompany him. 'You can't come from no one knows where and order us off like this. Remember we've been fighting for our nurseries, and that's a thing you never did.' Finally Kotick is forced to fight the seals. 'I've found you the island where you'll be safe, but unless your heads are

dragged off your silly necks you won't believe. I'm going to teach you now.'
Large and in good condition, Kotick beats every seal who offers resistance
until finally they agree to follow him. In the process, Kotick has been
transformed. 'He was not a white seal any more, but red from head to tail'
from the wounds he has received.

Like Rikki-Tiki-Tavi, Kotick has followed a creature larger than himself
into a dark hole and has returned triumphant. Rather than facing death
directly, however, Kotick has, like Toomai, experienced a part of the world
no creature of his species has ever seen before. Also like Toomai, when he
returns to his own kind he undergoes a blood initiation that validates
his lonely discovery in darkness. But whereas Toomai's is a positive
acceptance, Kotick's is not; he must fight for recognition. In the process the
whiteness that has set him apart as pure and special is submerged, at least
temporarily, in the red wounds of his animality. He who has held himself
above fighting and mating finally proves himself in a grand battle and
afterward chooses a female.

At the beginning of the tale, Kotick's inner specialness, his curiosity,
sends him to a traumatic experience from which he emerge alive only
because of his outer specialness, his white coat. Like a true culture hero, he
responds to the challenge with energy and discipline. Even so, he might
never have made his sixth attempt had he not met the old seal who informed
him that his success had been foretold, his destiny assured if he kept faith.
With this higher vision, Kotick is able to fend off the pressure of his species
nature, resist society and domesticity for one last heroic expedition on his
own. At the point where his ability to be patient is tried to the utmost, he
sticks by his quest and is allowed to be active again, following his helpers to
the goal.

Like the quintessential fairy-tale hero, Kotick passes three tests. In the
first or preliminary test he wins from the walrus the information that will
allow him to recognize the main test. In that main test he meets the sea
cows and is able to stay with them until they lead him through darkness to
the fulfilment of his quest. He faces the third, additional or confirming, test
when he returns to his people and must prove publicly what he achieved
privately, that he is heroic and has found a treasure.[5] This test means
teaching others in a short time what he has learned over six years. The
lesson involves violence, as it so often does in Kipling. But unlike Mowgli's
at the end of Kaa's hunting, this lesson involves more than the protagonist's
suffering. In 'teaching' the others, aggressively forcing them to follow him,
Kotick is also entering their way of life.

Like the initiate in primitive initiation rituals, Kotick has a reciprocal relation with his social group. The initiate returns from nature bearing a vitality that the tribe needs, but he is himself in need of socializing, of being integrated back into its ways. The grand battle on the beach serves both ends. As at the end of 'Toomai of the Elephants,' there is a balancing of conflicting forces: solitariness and society, heroic searching and domestic mating, an idyllic haven secure from slaughter and beaches filled with male seals battling for their territory. The hero's task is fulfilled when he reinvigorates the group. From the stagnation that may result from a thoughtless acceptance of the habits of his species, his vitality brings into being a new harmony. At his best here, Kipling uses animals to demonstrate the necessity of wildness and discipline in attaining such an integration.

# PART TWO

# Introduction

I N DISCUSSING 'Toomai of the Elephants' and 'The White Seal' at the end of the last chapter, I touched on the quest narrative and the initiation ritual, two archaic patterns that have been found around the world. Since the remaining tales in this study are all quest narratives, we need to consider the background of the quest before moving on to them. Evidence from primitive tribes in Asia and the Americas suggests that the quest has its origins in dreams and in visions; through them the solitary individual attempts to move beyond the established daytime practices of the tribe into the world of spirit, and to return with the invigoration of an initiate who has been isolated and then reborn. The quester may gain the supernatural power of a confirmed hunter or warrior, the special plant knowledge of a curer, or continuing aid from an animal helper such as a shaman usually has.

These options are hardly available in our tradition. To attain the civilized culture in which we live, society has had to make the universe secular, to certify the religious leader, the curer, and the warrior on their intellectual mastery or technical competence rather than recognizing their individual experience of internal or spiritual mastery. We are all well aware of the gains that accompanied this process: increased objectivity, public knowledge, and domination of the environment. We may be less aware of the loss: subjective spirituality, private certainty, and a series of connections with the natural and supernatural as a continuum.

The initiation quest that validated that connection still moves both adults and children today. For instance, the books we are considering make available a gain in self-confidence and self-reliance to the young reader who follows Toomai, Dorothy, or the Mouse Child on their undoubting quests into areas that adults fear to enter or simply don't believe in. If the child reader feels weaker than other children or otherwise set apart from them, such tales offer the assurance that sources of strength will develop. The child who senses inner power can also take heart from the perseverance of the White Seal and Fiver, who are true to their visions of a future reality. Similarly, young readers who either doubt or look forward to an ability to be authoritative find there is hope in the increasing confidence displayed by Bilbo and Hazel.

The child will probably be pulled into a tale by the simple excitement of heroes facing a series of adventures. Behind the excitement lie not only the reassurances I have mentioned but patterns and depths of which the child – and sometimes the author – is unaware. These quest patterns offer vicarious rewards comparable to those of tribal myths and visionary adventures. In *The Way of the Shaman*, the anthropologist Michael Harner tells how he went to the Ecuadorian Andes to study a tribe, was inducted into the shamanic process, discovered its efficacy, and returned to the United States to teach it to others. The fascination of Harner's book lies in its ability to explain the gain of letting go the reality sense of our culture under conditions that allow its replacement by a psychic process from the primitive world. In his spirit quest, the shaman hopes to gain a guardian spirit who is most often a 'power animal.'[1] Harner relates this animal to Indian myths of men or women who marry animals, or totem poles that trace clan lineage back to an animal ancestor. Such myths and totems testify to the universal primitive belief in the kinship of humans and animals. This universality suggests that that sense of kinship has psychic roots deep in the imagination of humanity.

Mircea Eliade elaborates on this animal-human connection in his thorough comparative study, *Shamanism: Archaic Techniques of Ecstasy*. He notes how frequently shamans in many cultures use animal voices, masks, and costumes, and he sees these attributes as indications that the shaman is trying to regain what humanity lost when it separated itself from the other animals. 'While preparing for his ecstasy and during it, the shaman abolishes the present human condition and, for the time being, recovers the situation as it was at the beginning. Friendship with animals, knowledge of their language, transformation into an animal are so many signs that the shaman has re-established the "paradisal" situation lost at the dawn of time.' Eliade finds this aim particularly clear in Siberian cultures.

The animal that the shaman 'reanimates' is his alter ego, his most powerful helping spirit ... he sings of his exemplary model, the primordial animal that is the origin of his tribe. In mythical times every member of the tribe could turn into an animal, that is, he was able to share in the condition of the ancestor. In our day such intimate relations with mythical ancestors are the prerogative only of shamans ...

In numerous traditions the mythical theriomorphic ancestor lives in the subterranean world.[2]

The shaman's entry into a dark lower world introduces a theme that we will meet in each of the tales yet to be considered. In *Watership Down*, we shall discover that Adams consciously draws on the shamanic quest in developing one of Fiver's visionary experiences.

Eliade suggests that the shaman's quest is often the model for the descent to the underworld found in myths and epics: 'Several of the most famous journeys to the underworld, undertaken to learn the fate of men after death, are "shamanic" in structure, in the sense that they employ the ecstatic techniques of shamans. All this is not without importance for an understanding of the "origins" of epic literature.'[3] In this view epics are late public versions of the quest, perhaps taken from shamanic tradition, perhaps based on a myth or ritual which originated in shamanic quests that had become standardized through cultural tradition. Any theory on the origins of such traditions must be speculative; I favour Eliade's position with its implication that the tribal beliefs and forms that influenced later religion and literature had their origin in individual experience, in the 'archaic techniques of ecstasy' that use unconscious dreams and semi-conscious visions as their vehicle.

In the shaman's quest we can find both the animal *alter ego*, which is the main focus of this study, and the descent into the underworld, which will be a key event in the narratives to be discussed in the chapters that follow. In addition to the archaic patterns and character types that are shared by the modern narrative quests we shall be investigating, there is the crucial facing of darkness, the void, the disintegration that is associated with the underworld descent. The quest pattern has been analysed by several prominent commentators in this century. Eliade provides many examples but only a brief 'schema of initiation: descent to the lower regions followed by ascent to the sky, where the Supreme Being grants shamanic power.'[4] Elsewhere he adds that death and symbolic resurrection are key events in this shamanic initiation and that dismemberment is a frequent and painful part of the vision quest.

A fuller version of the quest pattern is offered by Joseph Campbell in his wide-ranging study, *The Hero with a Thousand Faces*. In three central chapters, Departure, Initiation, and Return, he lays out the steps he has abstracted from a study of myth, folk-tale, epic, romance, and religion. The quest begins with a call to adventure, after which the hero usually gains a helper. Then he comes to what Campbell calls the threshold of adventure.[5] Crossing this threshold is difficult and may take a variety of forms, such as a battle with a dragon, a sea journey by night, dismemberment, or descent into the belly of a whale. It is followed by tests that the hero will pass, usually with the aid of more helpers. Then the hero reaches the goal of his quest and confronts his destiny, which will take one of three forms: a woman he must win, a man he must challenge, or a treasure he must obtain. There follows the return, which may occur as a flight and pursuit. At the threshold of return there is another struggle, from which the hero may be rescued by a helper. The quest will usually end with the woman brought back as bride or with a public display of the treasure.

Earlier than Campbell, Carl Jung had outlined a similar version of this quest. *In Symbols of Transformation*, first published in 1912, Jung traced the hero's quest with a wealth of mythological and philosophical, literary, and religious material to develop his theory of archetypes. From a psychoanalytic perspective, he saw the hero as symbolizing an aspect of the individual that is stuck in its present situation and needs to regress into the lower realms of consciousness with the aim of revitalizing the personality. Part of the quest may take place in what Jung called the personal unconscious, the area of repressed feelings discovered by Freud. Here the hero will meet a shadow figure, often in the form of an animal – as we saw in looking at the trickster in the introduction to part 1. But below this level of the personal unconscious is another, more profound and dynamic – the impersonal or collective unconscious, containing basic forms shared by all mankind. These manifest themselves in the figures Jung called archetypes, figures that the hero must confront successfully if he is to return and be renewed. The shadow is an archetype: it has its origin in the collective unconscious, although it is often associated with repression in the personal unconscious. As our amoral animal nature, the shadow is a figure that provides continuity with humanity's past and is thus able to lead the hero down into the primordial realm.

Jung focused in *Symbols of Transformation* on another archetype, the anima, that image of the female that is buried deep in a man's nature and will be projected on women he meets, in different forms depending on his age and attitude: she may be the mother to whom he looks for succour, the mate that he wishes to marry, or the old woman to whom he turns for advice. Each of these also has a negative form. Jung used the story of Hiawatha for his model and showed how the Indian hero is sustained by a mother-figure, his grandmother, Nokomis. Since Longfellow's source for *Hiawatha* was an Indian Trickster cycle, its hero quest pattern has all the more relevance to the tales we shall be considering.

Hiawatha is sent on a quest by Nokomis to avenge the death of his mother, killed long before by his father, Mudjekeewis, the West Wind. Travelling west in his canoe, Hiawatha combats Mudjekeewis. In Jung's view, 'Hiawatha is fighting the typical battle of the hero for rebirth on the Western Sea. The fight is with the father, who is the obstacle barring the way to the goal.' Overpowered, Mudjekeewis grants Hiawatha part of his own divine nature. In providing this gift, he functions as another important archetype, the wise old man, a figure Jung defined as 'a personification of meaning and spirit.'[6] On his return, Hiawatha meets another incarnation of both the anima and the wise old man, in Minnehaha and her father. As anima, Minnehaha is the beautiful potential mate whom Hiawatha determines to win. As wise old man, her father, the arrowsmith, again stands between the hero and his goal, forcing Hiawatha to call up all his intelligence and spirit to win her. Successful, he returns with her to his world. In psychological terms, the individual has been reinvigorated by the bond with his feminine nature and by gaining boons from two father-figures.

Among several other encounters that have been left out in this telling, Hiawatha experiences the descent into darkness and disintegration. In a characteristic North American Indian myth – with a shamanic background – Hiawatha challenges a monstrous fish, is swallowed, and descends into its dark interior; there he smites its heart, killing it to emerge victorious. Through Jonah and the whale, this motif is well-known to Western culture; it is found in fact throughout the world. In the Christian mystic tradition, which shares some elements with the shamanic one, this experience has been described as the dark night of the soul that St John of the Cross found a necessary prelude to union with God. The continuing validity on a personal psychological level of this process is suggested by its appearance in the nineteenth-century writings of Søren Kierkegaard, whose experience of the void was a basis for modern existentialism.

In the twentieth century the best-known exponent of existentialism is Jean-Paul Sartre, one of whose books is titled *Being and Nothingness*. Sartre insists that no authentic response to life is possible until one faces the anxiety caused by realizing that the universe is void of meaning. This emphasis on an internal darkness that flows from the inevitable in-coherence of existence helped shape the theatre of the absurd, the dominant dramatic mode of the fifties and sixties. Unlikely as must seem any connection between such heavyweight material and a child's story, in 1972 the two came together in an unrecognized classic, Russell Hoban's *The Mouse and His Child*. In chapter 7, 'Beyond Absurdity,' we shall accompany the title characters of this book in a descent to the dark bottom of a winter pond, where they are spared being physically swallowed by the monstrous C. Serpentina, only to be engulfed by his pretentious and overpowering philosophy of nothingness. Facing this threat, the mouse child will, in true shamanic and heroic style, journey with a helper into the heart of the void and there affirm his own existence; grasping the secret of life, he will return across the threshold of the pond and ascend into the light of spring, reborn.

The other tales at which we shall be looking tend not to be so self-consciously contemporaneous and at the same time archaic as *The Mouse and His Child*. As far as I can determine, J.R.R. Tolkien was unaware of the writings of Jung when he wrote *The Hobbit* in 1937. Yet Jung's theory of archetypes fits it well. Although the anima is not personified in Tolkien's tale, both the shadow and the wise old man play vital roles in it. And the pattern of descent into darkness with a threat of being devoured, followed by a successful emergence, is constantly repeated there.

Since Richard Adams draws on *The Hero with a Thousand Faces* for one of his chapter epigraphs in *Watership Down*, we can expect that he is writing from a conscious knowledge of the initiation quest pattern that has such a strong literary and psychological resonance. In fact, we could easily apply Campbell's version of the quest pattern to Adams's tale. I have found that the pattern fits the several discrete adventures into which the book naturally divides: the events leading up to the arrival at the down, the expedition to Nuthanger Farm, Bigwig's experience in Efrafa, and El-ahrairah's epic journey to the dark realm of the Black Rabbit of Inlé. Each includes a call to adventure, a threshold struggle, a descent into darkness, a treasure to be won, and another threshold struggle as part of the return. Rather than demonstrate this pattern in the two chapters devoted to *Watership Down*, I have provided an appendix that applies Campbell's schema to part of the novel.

Keeping alive animal vitality and trickster energy appears as a central theme in *Watership Down*. As is appropriate to a primitive world, dream and vision are important means of guidance and foreseeing, with Fiver's initial vision of destruction starting the series of quests that make up the tale. Later, Fiver as a seer has a demonstrably shamanic experience. As we shall discover in the next chapter, *The Wizard of Oz* lacks such high-powered happenings, but it does offer a quest. So does *Ozma of Oz*, which features a descent into darkness, the threat of immobilization there, and an ascent back to light and life. Moreover, the animal helper in *Ozma* is a trickster, who emerges as the powerful saviour of the questers.

# 6

# Newer Wonder Tales

N HIS INTRODUCTION to the first
edition of *The Wizard of Oz* (1900), L. Frank Baum set out the program that
he claimed motivated him to create his story: since 'every healthy youngster
has a wholesome and instinctive love for stories fantastic, marvelous and
manifestly unreal,' we moderns can appreciate why fairy-tales appeal to
them. But in the twentieth century we need 'newer "wonder tales" in which
the stereotyped genie, dwarf and fairy are eliminated, together with all the
horrible and blood-curdling incident[s].' The 'modern child seeks only
entertainment in its wonder-tales and gladly dispenses with all disagreeable incidents.' However, Baum did not eliminate all disagreeable
incidents in his books. Although he dispensed with most stereotyped
other-world figures, he did keep witches in addition to his own individually
characterized ones. But he also kept many of the devices and motifs of the
old form, thus making true his claim to offer in *The Wizard of Oz* 'a
modernized fairy tale.'[1]

Unlike most of the books considered in this study, *The Wizard of Oz* has
a human being as its central character. Of course Mowgli was human, too,
but he grew up among animals as one of them. In Baum's tale, the animals
are, in contrast, definitely subordinate to Dorothy in a human society. The
book does, however, contain a large and varied assortment of creatures:
winged monkeys, talking mice, and a deadly composite animal, the
Kalidah. It also contains two wicked witches who are clearly not human.
One of them dries up and blows away; the other is simply dissolved by
water. After we take a preliminary look at Dorothy's pet dog, Toto, my
focus will be on the three creatures who support the heroine – the
Scarecrow, the Tin Woodman, and the Cowardly Lion – who take on the
role of animal helpers in a traditional fairy-tale.

Whereas Dorothy's three helpers have affinities with animals that enact comparable roles in fairy-tales, the relation of Toto to Dorothy is anomalous. He functions as her shadow, dumb and instinctive, unsocialized, an important initiator of adventures. To begin with, we might note that though Toto encounters myriad talking animals in the magical land of Oz, he himself does not gain the power of speech there. Yet inferior as he remains, he plays a crucial part in each stage of Dorothy's quest. First, he initiates the adventure by hiding under the bed after Dorothy's aunt has called her to the cyclone cellar; as a result the cyclone carries him and Dorothy away in the house. Second, when they return to the Emerald City to request their reward for destroying the Wicked Witch of the West, Toto knocks over the screen that hides the Wizard of Oz, thus exposing him as a timid little man who has to explain the illusions by which he has intimidated Dorothy and her helpers. Finally, Toto causes Dorothy to miss the balloon flight by which the Wizard proposes to carry her back home. An important result, as we shall see, is that she must then find her own means of return.

Besides his initiating role in these three important turning points, Toto on two other occasions is either the cause of or the model for aggressive actions by Dorothy. Early in her trip to the Emerald City, when Toto is threatened by the Lion, Dorothy strikes the beast on the nose and thus exposes its cowardice. Then when Dorothy is enslaved by the Wicked Witch of the West, Toto shows that the Witch is both vulnerable and non-human by biting her on the leg shortly before Dorothy dissolves her with a bucket of water. Like Dorothy, Toto is small and fearful, but also like her, he insists on asserting himself. As a non-verbal animal, Toto stands for an uncivilized part of Dorothy, the amoral shadow side that exposes the illusions and vulnerability of coercive authority and propels the conforming child into adventures and actions that her social consciousness would not consider or approve.

Toto's atavistic behaviour is quite unlike the conscious helpfulness of the Scarecrow and Tin Woodman, and even of the Cowardly Lion. As commentators on the fairy-tale have argued, however, such helpful creatures are also an aspect of the hero they aid. As Max Lüthi comments, 'man is in contact with nature, which accepts his assistance and in turn comes to his aid.' But he also indicates that, like Toto, 'the helping animal in the fairytale can embody unconscious forces within us.'[2] Heinrich Zimmer describes the animal side of the human more pointedly. 'Helpful animals' are 'symbolic figures' that 'embody and represent the instinctive forces of our nature, as distinguished from the higher human qualities of intellect, reason, will power.' When a human being like Dorothy rides on an animal like the Cowardly Lion, it represents the assimilation of the 'instinctive impulses of [her] composite being.'[3] Specifically, when the Lion shows himself no coward by jumping over the chasm with Dorothy on his back, he demonstrates a bravery that she gains for use in her climactic confrontation with the Wicked Witch of the West.

But as Lüthi indicates, it is not a one-way relationship. Not only does the animal bring practical help and emotional enhancement to the human being; it also often gains from the relationship. 'The animals can be viewed as forces within the soul of the individual which at first are in need of assistance but finally unfold and develop.' Certainly, 'lower natures are to be transformed into higher ones, but this does not take place without suffering and sacrifice – and cruelty.'[4] In the initial battle against the Wicked Witch of the West, the witch triumphs and cruelly destroys the Scarecrow and the Woodman; they can be shaped anew only after Dorothy has defeated the witch. The Lion also suffers. He is caged and starved by the witch until liberated by Dorothy, and earlier undergoes an even more significant ordeal. He invades a field of poppies whose poisonous fumes put him into a deep sleep that will become permanent if he is not removed. The Tin Woodman concludes, 'He is much too heavy to lift. We must leave him here to sleep on forever.' Fortunately, however, they find a way to rescue him.

The rescue of the Lion follows a typical fairy-tale pattern. The Tin Woodman has killed a wildcat that was pursuing a mouse. The animal thus spared turns out to be the queen of the mice, who pledges aid in case of future need. Unlike the situation in the usual fairy-tale, the need emerges immediately. The Scarecrow comes up with a plan for rescuing the Lion: the Woodman makes a wheeled platform, which the mice then pull out of the poppy field. This sequence is based on the tale type of the Grateful Animals,[5] represented in the Grimm collection by 'The White Snake' and 'The Queen Bee.' In both a kind-hearted young man spares lowly creatures (eg. ants, fish, birds), which vow to repay him and do when he is later faced with the difficult tasks assigned by the princess he wants to marry. Unlike the mice in *The Wizard of Oz*, these fairy-tale grateful creatures appear in a sequence of three, their abilities matched to the three tests set by the princess.

Whereas the grateful animals do only one specific task, the helpful animal accompanies and aids the hero through all his adventures. Dorothy gains three helpers at the beginning of her trip to the Emerald City, rescuing first the Scarecrow and then the Tin Woodman from immobility. She is of course aided by them at a number of points in her subsequent adventures. In contrast to a fairy-tale like 'The Golden Bird,' in which the prince constantly disregards the warning of his helper, the fox, not to do certain things, *The Wizard of Oz* provides a heroine who always listens to her helpers. Whereas the prince must constantly be rescued from a series of mishaps he brings on himself, Dorothy is helped through a series of dangers that are an inevitable part of her quest.

An important development in Baum's tale is that at the climax of her quest, Dorothy must rescue all three of her helpers. As we shall see, in defeating the Wicked Witch of the West, Dorothy takes on the role of the reasonable, good-hearted, and ultimately courageous heroine, Gretel, who in the Grimm tale thus rescues her brother, Hansel. Considering the qualities Dorothy shows, we could say that she, like the hero of some fairy-tales, seems to absorb into herself the virtues of her animal helpers.[6] Baum has complicated each helper's key quality by having it appear initially as its opposite, but most readers notice that the brainless Scarecrow resourcefully thinks up a number of helpful solutions, that the heartless Woodman has very tender feelings, and that the Cowardly Lion is always brave in defence of his friends.

*The Wizard of Oz* introduces its reader to a different kind of fantasy world from most of those we have so far considered. Rather than an alteration of the observable world by one or two fantasy premisses, Baum's tale presents an entirely different world, operating on different laws. In that world animals can of course think and speak as in fantasies already discussed, but even more important, the scientific laws of nature have given way there to the rules of magic. At the beginning of the tale, Dorothy is kissed by the good Witch of the North and told that the mark left on her forehead will protect her from harm during her sojourn in Oz. Magic objects and spells may occur, it is true, in a narrative facsimile of our world, but in Oz we enter a world whose very foundation rests on magic.

When a Kansas cyclone drops Dorothy's house down on top of the Wicked Witch of the East, we know what sort of world we have entered. The good Witch of the North immediately appears to plant the protective kiss. The Munchkins' praise of Dorothy for having set them free from bondage to the wicked witch also helps take the horror out of what might be a 'blood-curdling incident.' Although the witch is conveniently covered by the house, Baum does need to have her feet stick out. When Dorothy sees them she gives 'a little cry of fright.' The body of the witch soon evaporates, but her silver shoes remain. When the good witch tells Dorothy to put them on, the girl does so willingly, showing as little squeamishness at wearing a dead witch's shoes as a fairy-tale heroine would in accepting the gift she had earned by some act of violence.

After having gained her three helpful creatures and having overcome with their aid the obstacles on her way to their goal, Dorothy arrives in the Emerald City and seeks an audience with the Wizard of Oz. In fact, each of the four travellers has a request, and to each the Wizard gives the same reply: He will grant their wishes when they have killed the Wicked Witch of the West. They embark on the second part of the quest, which is filled with more danger than the first because the witch knows they are coming and sends her fierce helpers against them. First comes a great pack of wolves, which the Tin Woodman is able to slay with his axe. Second is a large flock of crows, whose necks the Scarecrow twists until all are dead. Third is a swarm of bees. Scattering the straw stuffing of the Scarecrow over the vulnerable creatures to camouflage and protect them, the Tin Woodman again faces the foe alone. The bees waste their stings on his metal body and die. Finally, the witch uses her magic gold cap to call on the Winged Monkeys. Ordered to destroy Dorothy, the Scarecrow, and the Tin Woodman, and to bring the Cowardly Lion to her alive, the Monkeys obey, except in the case of Dorothy. Because of the mark of the kiss on her forehead they cannot destroy her but must instead bring her back with the lion.

Like Hansel and Gretel in the witch's power, the Lion is caged and Dorothy forced to serve as kitchen-maid. Instead of fattening the Lion to eat, however, the witch tries to starve him into submission, but fails, for Dorothy feeds him at night. Also like Gretel, Dorothy finally kills the witch, though by accident rather than design. The witch, knowing the silver shoes contain magical power, manages to steal one. When she refuses to return it, Dorothy in her anger throws a bucket of water on her. The witch literally dissolves. Her subjects the Winkies are overjoyed to be free. They gladly find and then re-stuff the Scarecrow and repair the Tin Woodman, whom they ask to become their emperor. But for the moment the four comrades are more concerned to get what the Wizard has promised them for succeeding in their quest.

They encounter more difficulties on their way back to the Emerald City, but these are overcome when Dorothy learns that the golden hat she took from the witch's cupboard will allow her to call the Winged Monkeys three times. Transported to the Emerald City by the Monkeys, the travellers are at first denied access to the Wizard; finally admitted, they discover that he is not a real wizard at all, only an illusionist who, like Dorothy, came to Oz from the United States. When the questers demand their rewards, he gives the

Scarecrow brains made out of bran filled with pins and needles, the Tin Woodman a red-silk, sawdust-filled heart, and the Cowardly Lion a brew that will give him courage. Speaking for his author, the Wizard is quite overt in his moral. To the Lion he says, 'Courage is always inside one; so that this [liquid] really cannot be called courage until you have swallowed it.' To himself afterward, he says, 'How can I help being a humbug ... when all these people make me do things everybody knows can't be done?' This is a good moral for our world, but a poor one for Baum's. Not only his readers but more important his characters have experienced the kind of magic that does things 'everybody knows can't be done.' The issue is even clearer in his next thought. It was easy to make the three creatures happy 'because they imagined I could do anything. But it will take more than imagination' to fulfil the promise to Dorothy of sending her back home to Kansas.

The Wizard sets to work with Dorothy to build a balloon to pass over the deadly desert that protects Oz from the outside world. Following the laws of our world, they make something that works and carries the Wizard away. It would have carried Dorothy too, except she was trying to catch Toto when the balloon broke loose from its moorings. The natural laws of our world having failed her, she is advised to have recourse to the magic laws of Oz. With her three helpers, she goes south to find the only witch she has not met, Glinda the Good.

On the way, the Woodman again helps out with his axe, chopping off the limbs of some trees that repel anyone trying to enter the forest they protect. In another forest they meet a huge gathering of growling wild animals. The Lion discovers they are quarrelling over who should rule them. They ask him to be the King of Beasts and he accepts. Now all three helpers have become rulers, the Wizard having appointed the Scarecrow to take his place before he left.

Once the four arrive in Glinda's country, the good witch tells Dorothy that her silver shoes have the power to transport her wherever she wants; the girl then uses them to return home. In other words, magic does easily what the Wizard's practical knowledge did only imperfectly. Imagination overcomes natural law, in an epitome of the premiss and process of fantasy.

Another way of understanding the importance of this final section of the novel is to note how it fits into the three-part structure of the fairy-tale. Dorothy passes the preliminary test involuntarily when her house drops on the Wicked Witch of the East. For that liberating act, she is rewarded by the praise of the Munchkins, the kiss of the good Witch of the North, and the silver shoes of the dead witch. As is traditional, the powers won in the preliminary test are used in passing the main test. Dorothy's main test is confronting the Wicked Witch of the West. The protective kiss safeguards her from destruction, and an argument over one of the silver shoes provides the occasion for her unpremeditated elimination of the Witch.

The supplementary test is the one in which the hero, after returning to society, is there recognized and rewarded as the victor in the main test. Dorothy's reward should come from the Wizard, but as we have seen she does not gain it immediately, but must embark on a further quest, travelling to the kingdom of Glinda, the good Witch of the South. Besides rounding out the quaternity of female powers from which Dorothy draws strength, this additional quest results in her being rewarded with the knowledge that she has already obtained on her own the ability to return home. The power of the shoes gained from the first witch is fully revealed by Glinda, the fourth witch. The public recognition that normally accompanies the supplementary test is extended not to Dorothy but to her three helpers. As we have seen, the Tin Woodman became emperor of the Winkies after she passed the main test, the Scarecrow was proclaimed ruler of Oz by the Wizard at the point where Dorothy should have been recognized and rewarded for destroying the Wicked Witch of the West, and the Cowardly Lion became king of the beasts as a result of cunning bravery during the successful quest to reach Glinda's castle. The helpers thus function as obvious surrogates in gaining the recognition won by the successful hero at different stages of a fairy-tale.

If we examine the dynamics of Baum's world from yet another point of view, we notice that power in Oz is unequally divided between males and females. In fact, the four witches of Oz have among them all the power, not only for evil but for good. In her successive encounters with them, Dorothy gains power from each. Her helpers are all male, but when she finds them they are also mere creatures: the Scarecrow is lucid but lacking in starch, unable on his post to frighten away crows; the Woodman is so tender-hearted he is apt to rust himself with his own tears; the Lion is a confessed coward, also prone to tears. This sexual differentiation is just as obvious in the next two Oz books.[7]

Taking the Wizard and Dorothy as two aliens set down in Oz, we may contrast their reactions. When he first arrived, the Wizard tried to confront evil, but was defeated by the Wicked Witch of the West, and then took a defensive stance in the palace, completely cut off from the life of the Emerald City he claimed to rule. In contrast, Dorothy, on her entry into Oz, has the good fortune to kill the Wicked Witch of the East, an act that brings her the protective kiss and silver shoes. But her treatment of the shoes and the gold cap indicates that the basis of her good luck is her saving innocence. She sees them as practical clothing and has to be told in each case what their magical power is. Even then her use of them is to solve problems, not to gain power like a witch, or the appearance of power like the Wizard.

The two bad witches are the most powerful forces in Oz, yet Dorothy triumphs over both. In fact, she is implicated in the death of both. She acts assertively, I would say aggressively, but certainly not violently. Just as the first witch evaporates, so the second dissolves, but into a brown 'shapeless mass' that Dorothy disposes of by throwing another bucket of water over it and sweeping 'it all out the door.' Baum's portrayal of the witch as less than human, hardly organic, preserves Dorothy's blameless nature. Similarly, he treats the recovery of the silver shoe as a mere housekeeping problem. 'She cleaned it and dried it with a cloth, and put it on her foot again.' The combination of her anger, bravery, and matter-of-factness in this incident epitomizes the qualities that carry her through the adventure.

More important than Dorothy's relation to the witches is her relation to her three comrades. She responds helpfully first to the plight of the Scarecrow, who wants to escape a tedious life stuck on a pole, and next to that of a rusted mechanical figure. Both, of course, repay her kindness. The third creature is in a different category. Not only is the Cowardly Lion flesh and blood, he is aggressive, striking down both the scarecrow and the woodman. But after Dorothy strikes and reprimands him, she finds him tractable, willing to confess his cowardice. This same aggressiveness appears later when Dorothy throws water on the witch in righteous anger over the theft of her shoe. Her friendliness and assertiveness are both in contrast to the Wizard. He is more like the lion when Dorothy first meets him, loud and threatening but frightened behind the façade.

When Dorothy leaves Oz each of the three helpers will become the ruler of an important domain there. From this point of view she has been the catalyst for enabling limp intelligence, immobilized feelings, and unsure wildness to gain the confidence that precedes autonomy. Of course it is the Wizard who officially gives the Scarecrow his brains, the Tin Woodman his heart, and the Cowardly Lion his courage, but the ruler will not act until they have eliminated the evil that has isolated him. Even then the gift does not come from him, since, as he points out, each already had what he asked for. Certainly each had it potentially, but none was in a position to recognize it, to act on it, and to test it, until Dorothy rescued the first two and co-opted the third for her quest. Her modest determination, friendliness, and ability to express justified anger are the key qualities in the liberation of the forces the helpers represent.

When we meet Dorothy in the third book of the series, she is older, her relation to her new helpers therefore somewhat different. The issue of male-female power is, however, very similar.

II

In *Ozma of Oz*, Dorothy makes a sea voyage to Fairyland, carried by an ocean storm to the kingdom of Ev – just across the deadly desert from Oz. She is not only older now but more self-conscious in her actions. She first realizes she is in a magic land again when the hen with which she shares a chicken coop on the ocean begins to talk. The hen claims that its name is Bill, but since it has just laid an egg, Dorothy renames her Billina. Although allowing the name, the hen refuses to keep within the tidy bounds of feminine propriety that the girl tries to impose.

Like Toto in *The Wizard of Oz*, Billina functions in this book as the instinctive animal nature that, if not ignored or suppressed, can lead Dorothy to success in the important adventures ahead. More individualized than Toto, the hen can talk and is consistently aggressive. Not only conscious but cunning, she emerges as a wily trickster, a powerful representative of the amoral shadow archetype. As a special example of the fairy-tale helpful creature, she turns out to have almost as much right to the title of heroine as Dorothy herself.

After the storm at sea, Dorothy is awakened to a new day, and a new life in Fairyland, by Billina's proud cackling. Since her eggs will function as a potent weapon at the climax of the tale, this introduction can be taken as a portent of female power. But the beginning is commonplace enough. Dorothy says she is hungry, and Billina offers her a fresh egg. Dorothy refuses because she has no way of cooking it. The hen soon admits to being hungry, too; when Dorothy suggests she eat the egg, Billina shows the first sign of that aggressiveness that is so notably a part of her character and that will become crucial to the success of the quest. '"Do you take me for a cannibal?" cried the hen, indignantly. "I do not know what I have said or done that leads you to insult me!"'[8] Like Alice with the creatures of Wonderland, Dorothy is being made aware that animals also have personalities and sensibilities.

Billina has more to teach Dorothy. When she looks on the beach for ants, sand bugs or small crabs to eat, it is Dorothy's turn to be shocked. '"Eat live things ... you ought to be 'shamed of yourself!" Billina makes the perfect riposte: "Live things are much fresher and more wholesome than dead things, and you humans eat all sorts of dead creatures."' When Dorothy denies this, Billina cites 'lambs and sheep and cows and pigs and even chickens.' Dorothy tries to slip out with an illogical truth:

> 'But we cook 'm,' said Dorothy, triumphantly.
> 'What difference does that make?'
> 'A good deal,' said the girl, in a graver tone. 'I can't just 'splain the differ'rence, but it's there. And, anyhow, we never eat such dreadful things as *bugs*.'
> 'But you eat the chickens that eat the bugs,' retorted the yellow hen, with an odd cackle. 'So you are just as bad as we chickens are.'
> This made Dorothy thoughtful. What Billina said was true enough, and it almost took away her appetite for breakfast.

The creature has unsettled the human on a tender subject.

As Billina keeps pecking in the sand, she and Dorothy get into a new argument that leads to an important discovery. In Baum's augmented fairy-tale pattern, the initial helper provides the heroine with a magical object that facilitates the quest. Billina 'stubs her bill' on what she claims is a piece of metal. When Dorothy says it is probably a rock, Billina proves the accuracy of her sense by uncovering a gold key. Dorothy puts it in her pocket and, of course, soon finds a use for it.

The two walk inland, and the still-hungry Dorothy finds two unusual trees, one growing 'square paper boxes,' and the other 'even more wonderful, for it bore quantities of tin dinner-pails.' She picks one of each and finds in them a solution to the dilemma in which Billina's argument about food has left her. Each edible item in the containers has 'a separate stem' by which it has grown in the box, which is in turn attached to the tree. In the lunch box is, among other delicacies, a ham sandwich, in the dinner pail turkey and tongue. Dorothy has discovered an answer to the guilt of the carnivore: meat grown by a tree.

The girl has broken an unstated interdiction, however. Immediately they are attacked by creatures who claim proprietary rights to the trees. As usual, the result is immediate difficulty and long-term gain. The creatures are Wheelers. Instead of hands and feet, they have wheels and go on all fours like animals. Fortunately, Dorothy and Billina are able to run to a nearby rocky hill where the creatures cannot follow. Although the Wheelers can talk and write – in the sand – they are portrayed as less than human. At one point they curl themselves up 'like big dogs' and try to fool Dorothy by pretending to be asleep.

At the top of the hill Billina spies in the rock a minute crack that outlines a door. Dorothy sees what might be a keyhole, tries Billina's key, and is faced with her second helper, Tik-Tok, a mechanical man. Once she winds up his thought and speech mechanisms, he explains how he came to be there. The former king of Ev had him made. In a fit of passion, the king then sold his wife and ten children to the Nome King, but regretting his action, locked up Tik-Tok, put the key in his pocket, and drowned himself in the sea. Told about the Wheelers, Tik-Tok asks Dorothy to wind up his action mechanism so he can protect her. As he points out, because the creatures lack hands and feet, they can hurt only with their heads. Using the tin dinner pail, he subdues them easily, captures their leader, and turns him into a temporary third helper, a guide to the palace of Ev.

At the palace Billina twice shows her aggressive nature. First she intimidates the maid, who tries to keep her out, by flying at and then past her to join Dorothy. Later, relegated to the chicken yard, she wins a fight with a rooster who tries to 'lord it over' her. When Dorothy remonstrates, Billina says, 'Do you think I'd let that speckled villain of a rooster ... claim to run this chicken house, as long as I'm able to peck and scratch? Not if my name is Bill!' Dorothy tries to reprove her: 'It isn't Bill, it's Billina; and you're talking slang.' But the hen is unrepentant, proud to have lived up to her name.

When Dorothy and her helpers are ushered into the palace, they meet Princess Langwidere, a self-absorbed woman who became ruler when her uncle drowned himself and left no other successor. Her peculiarity is that she has thirty heads, which she changes as her vanity motivates her. On this day, unfortunately, she wears her most hot-tempered head. Offended by Dorothy's unwillingness to trade her head for one the princess no longer wants, Langwidere has the girl imprisoned in a tower. Tik-Tok tries to protect his mistress but his action mechanism runs down.

From her tower, Dorothy spots something moving across the desert. It is Ozma come to rescue the Ev family from the Nome King. (In *The Land of Oz*, the second book in the series, Ozma has been found and set upon the throne as rightful ruler of Oz, the Scarecrow gladly abdicating to be her helper.) Now she has brought a twenty-seven-man army, plus the Scarecrow, the Tin Woodman, and the Cowardly Lion, not to mention her own live saw-horse and a new creature, the Hungry Tiger, who, paired with the Lion, draws Ozma's chariot. Princess Langwidere agrees to Dorothy's release and wishes Ozma well in freeing her aunt and family; she herself finds ruling a bore.

The Hungry Tiger continues the appetite theme. His name contains an ambiguity that reflects the paradox of his nature: is he always feeding or always hungry? We discover that he would love to eat fat babies, or plump hens like Billina, but his conscience won't let him. 'No, hungry I was born, and hungry I shall die.' When Dorothy then pets him and calls him a good tiger, he contradicts her. 'I am a good beast, perhaps, but a disgracefully bad tiger. For it is in the nature of tigers to be cruel and ferocious.' He appears to be another in Baum's menagerie of emasculated males. Yet Baum makes him a threatening figure:

At one time Dorothy found the little maid Nanda crouching in terror in a corner, with the Hungry Tiger standing before her.
'You certainly look delicious,' the beast was saying. 'Will you kindly give me permission to eat you?'
'No, no, no!' cried the maid in reply.

Like a trickster on the borderline between animal appetite and human restraint, he lets her go when she promises him a huge meal. He consumes another such meal in the Nome Kingdom, and a third that finally fills him in Oz at the end of the story. But in between he is still intimidating. To Dorothy, when they are approaching the Nome Kingdom, he says, 'If he makes hash of you I'll willingly eat you for breakfast tomorrow morning.' His ambivalence is thus maintained until the very end.

Dorothy's rescue ends the first part of the book; it is mainly a prelude to Ozma's quest, which Dorothy joins, accompanied by her two new helpers. There are evident, though not extensive, parallels between the two parts of the book. Just as Dorothy and Billina earlier faced a rock that she had to open if she was to find Tik-Tok and be able to move on, so in the second half their quest is halted by a rock wall that only Dorothy can open. Similarly, just as her early foes, the Wheelers, are borderline creatures, moving between rational speech and 'wild cries' that indicate their animal nature, so her later antagonist, the Nome King, can argue rationally but when pressed will roar 'like a savage beast' (thus revealing his kinship with the Hungry Tiger). In each case Dorothy is rescued by one of her helpers – by Tik-Tok from the Wheelers, by Billina from the Nome King. The climactic threat in both halves is also the same, alienation of self, as a creature with one of Langwidere's heads in the first part, as an ornament in the Nome King's palace in the second.

The Nome King, like the Wicked Witch of the West, is a non-human creature with clearly human traits. As the evil antagonist, he is all the more interesting for being a more complex character than the witch. He is 'Ruler of the Underground World' and uses his thousands of Nomes to mine precious metals and gems. We are told that he resents all who live above ground because so many have invaded his territory to steal his riches. He has set up barriers to keep such visitors away from his kingdom. The main obstacle the expedition meets on its journey there is a mechanical giant; not a sentient creature, it nevertheless pounds the path with a huge mallet. Because the valley is steep and narrow, there is no other approach to the 'Underground World.' The Scarecrow thinks up the solution. 'Each time the mallet lifted ... there was a moment when the path ... was free.' So all they have to do is 'run under the hammer, one at a time,' at that moment.

But a new obstacle faces them when the path ends. Unlike Dorothy and Billina earlier, they have no key to unlock the rock wall through which they must pass. Tik-Tok suggests they call on the Nome King to open it. When Ozma's demand produces no results, Tik-Tok points out that the Nome King is not to be commanded on his own territory. Ozma is willing to request the king, but when this is not efficacious, she refuses to demean herself by entreating him. Dorothy offers to plead and is successful.

They are soon in the presence of the king, who reminds Dorothy of St Nick: 'A little fat man,' he seems 'kindly and good humored' and really does 'shake like jelly' when he laughs. His true nature – closer to that of Old Nick – is suggested by his picking up a live coal in his fingers to light his pipe and by his hard bargaining with Ozma. To her contention that he holds the family of Ev prisoner, he blandly points out that they are his legal slaves. He also denies that he cheated the king in the bargain. 'I gave him the long life, all right; but he destroyed it.' If an accident or another person had taken the king's life, then there might be cause for grievance. When Ozma accuses him of treating the royal family cruelly, he responds that he dislikes cruelty; seeing the delicacy of his royal slaves, he has transformed them into ornaments in his palace. 'Instead of being obliged to labor, they merely decorate my apartments,' unconscious of any ill-usage. When Ozma cannot out-argue him, she threatens force. He laughs and shows her his huge army assembled in a vast cave.

Realizing that the king is invincible, the Scarecrow suggests they wheedle him. The king approves: 'I'm so kind-hearted that I cannot stand coaxing or wheedling.' He finally offers them a bargain. There being eleven enchanted members of the Ev family, each person in the expedition may enter his inner palace and touch eleven objects, saying the word 'Ev.' At each correct guess, the object will again become human. If, however, no guess is correct, the person touching will become transformed, too. Counselled not to accept the offer, Ozma decides it would be 'weak and cowardly' to pull back from the very object of her quest. She accepts, goes into the palace, and discovers how full it is of ornaments and furniture. After her last guess, Baum tells us there is a new object in the palace.

The Nome King kindly adds one additional guess for each new person transformed. The Tin Woodman is the next unsuccessful entrant. The twenty-six officers and one private of Ozma's army follow him; all are transformed.

At this point the Nome King halts the game to get some sleep. Dorothy, the three humanized creatures and, the three beasts of burden all go off to their bedrooms. Then Dorothy realizes that Billina is missing. Billina has fallen asleep under the Nome King's throne but is wakened by an argument between the king and his chief steward, an argument that reveals that the king's power resides in his magic belt. In her hiding place she also learns that the royal family of Ev are all purple ornaments, Ozma and her army green ones.

The next morning, the king reveals how much enjoyment he gets out of the game. Tik-Tok takes his turn first and Dorothy next. She happens to touch a purple kitten, which is transformed into the prince Evring. Meanwhile Billina has begun to cackle. When the Nome King discovers that she has just laid her morning egg he is unnaturally upset: 'Eggs belong only to the outside world – to the world on the earth's surface, where you come from. Here, in my underground kingdom they are rank poison.' The Scarecrow offers to keep this egg along with one he collected earlier, but Billina first makes the Nome King promise to let her have a chance in the palace, too. Her request is granted, after the Scarecrow is unsuccessful.

Once in the rooms, Billina takes her time, 'curious to behold all the magnificence of this underground palace.' Her sharp hen's eye spots all the remaining ten purple ornaments, and she begins transforming them. First the queen, then her nine children appear. Then Billina turns her attention to the green ornaments, and is able to transform all the Oz group except the Tin Woodman.

Each time Billina guesses correctly a bell rings in the throne room, and the more often the bell rings the more angry the Nome King becomes. His true nature emerges when Dorothy begins to laugh; the sound drives him nearly frantic and he roars 'at her like a wild beast.' When Billina appears he announces that the rescuers are his prisoners. She reminds him of the bargain. He responds like a trickster: 'I said you might leave the palace in safety ... and so you may, but you cannot leave my dominions. You are my prisoners, and I will hurl you all into my underground dungeons.'

The Nome King thus symbolically takes over the devouring threat that the Hungry Tiger has represented previously. Not desiring the upper earth creatures as food, the king has converted them into inanimate objects, treasures in his domain. But his destructive intent was and is apparent. For instance, when a general refused to enter the ornament palace, the Nome King threatened to 'throw him into one of my fiery furnaces.' The contestants in his deadly game must enter the Nome King's inner sanctum where most become ornaments. But Billina has subverted and reversed this process, bringing out the lifeless objects as live people.

Ozma orders her army to battle the Nome warriors, but the officers refuse, pleading heart trouble. The private does attack but is quickly disarmed. Meanwhile Billina has been whispering in the ear of the Scarecrow. He now pulls an egg out of his pocket and throws it at the Nome King. It breaks, covering 'his face and beard with its sticky contents.'

'Help, help!' screamed the King, clawing with his fingers at the egg, in a struggle to remove it.

'An egg! An egg! Run for your lives!' shouted the captain of the Nomes, in a voice of horror.

Billina then turns to Dorothy and urges her to unbuckle the Nome King's belt. She does and puts it on.

Unaware of his loss, the Nome King has regained his presence of mind and begun a transformation spell, but his steward tells him why it is not working.

The Nome King clapped his hand to his waist, and his rock colored face turned white as chalk. 'It's gone,' he cried, helplessly. 'It's gone, and I am ruined!'

Dorothy now stepped forward and said: 'Royal Ozma, and you, Queen of Ev, I welcome you and your people back to the land of the living. Billina has saved you from your troubles, and now we will leave this drea'ful place, and return to Ev.'

While her comrades cheer, the Nome King creeps back onto his throne like 'a whipped dog.' But he recovers and offers them safe exit from the Underground Kingdom in return for his belt. Although he tells Dorothy she doesn't know how to use it, when she commands the door to the passage outside to open, it does. The only thing the belt cannot do is discover the Tin Woodman when Dorothy goes back into the palace. As they leave the Nome Kingdom, the king makes one more attempt to stop them, sending an army along the passage after them. Dorothy turns the front ranks into eggs and the others turn and run.

Once the escapees are away from the underground country, they enter, as Dorothy promised, into 'the land of the living.' 'They began to pass ... trees, in which birds were singing; and the breeze that was wafted to them from the farms of Ev was spicy with flowers and new-mown hay; and the sunshine fell full upon them, to warm them and drive away from their bodies the chill and dampness of the underground kingdom of the Nomes.' They have indeed left a lifeless kingdom. The Nomes are 'rock colored' and even their food is mineral. The coffee offered Dorothy there is 'made of a richly flavored clay, browned in the furnaces and then ground fine ... not at all muddy.' Not only do the Nomes spend their time and energy on non-living materials – mining gems, smelting, and working metals – the Nome King's pride is in his collection of artefacts. He can think of no better use for living things than turning them into ornaments. The fact that eggs are poison to the Nome King and his warriors is also indicative, not to say symbolic. Eggs are seeds of life, and the Nomes clearly abhor life as we know it, passed in the fructifying warmth of the sun. Such images of light and dark, warm and cold, not only play a large part in *Ozma of Oz* but, as we shall see in the next four chapters, are frequently associated with the kind of quest we are concerned with.

The source of this new life is, of course, Billina, the yellow hen who lays yellow-yolked eggs. Besides being creative, she is also a trickster, who cunningly uses information overheard by chance, and when the contest rules are broken knows how to employ surprise and force to achieve her goal. More like a general than a conventional helper, she directs the Scarecrow and Dorothy in their separate assaults on the Nome King. In combining creativity and aggression – laying an egg and using it as a weapon – she integrates the two sides of herself whose separation was indicated by her two names: Billina, the hen who lays eggs, and Bill, the rough chicken who can beat a rooster in a fight. This bravery is like that of the younger Dorothy in the first book. The more socialized Dorothy of this book tries to enforce various conventions and proprieties on the hen, but Billina successfully retains the self-assertion and expression of feelings that Dorothy showed in *The Wizard of Oz*.

Except for Billina, the characters on the two sides of the conflict seem unable to bring these qualities together. The Nome King is aggressive, immoral, and powerful. Ozma is proud, moral, and ostensibly powerful. But her pride and morality put her in a false and dangerous situation in which the power she should command – the army – fails her. The Nome King's furnace and fierce army are accurate reflections of his violent nature. His motives are selfish, sterile. Living in an underground kingdom, he has a low nature in contrast to Ozma's higher-principled motives. Only Billina is both aggressive and good, able to fight effectively for a cause larger than herself, willing to use low cunning to effect a high result.

Both Dorothy and Ozma take high moral ground, denying and repressing what is low, dark, and mean. But whatever is repressed uses its energy to get back at the repressor. Ozma is no match for the Nome King. Dorothy is able to respond from her less exalted position by being humble, less demanding, willing even to drop morality at the instigation of trickster Billina and steal the Nome King's belt. Brought from the underground to the daylight world of consciousness, the belt becomes a symbol of the energy released in the facing and integration of the unconscious shadow.

The yellow hen's sharp eye and clever mind permit her one more good deed as the group comes to the kingdom of Ev. Noticing that Prince Evring has a silver whistle, she discovers that he picked it up in the ornament palace. Touching the whistle, she says 'Ev,' and the Tin Woodman is suddenly with them again. Back at the palace, the people greet the royal family with enthusiasm, and the queen proclaims her eldest son king. After the rescuers journey back to Oz, Dorothy decides to rejoin the uncle from whom she was separated during the storm at sea. Ozma uses the magic belt to wish Dorothy back into our world.

While underground, Billina acted like the trickster helper in the best examples of the tale type known as the Grateful Dead.[9] This helper does his master's dirty work in the first two tests but steps aside to let the hero prove himself in the climactic test. So Billina used her secret knowledge to free the transformed captives but urged Dorothy to steal and put on the magic belt that was necessary to escape from the underground kingdom. Although Dorothy and Billina have between them earned the power of the belt, neither seems interested in claiming it permanently. The hen could not wear it, and Dorothy considers it useful only for returning to her uncle. In contrast, Billina, when given a choice rejects our 'stupid, humdrum world.' With her usual clarity of vision, she chooses to stay in the other world where her augmented nature will be appreciated. Such a destiny seems a fitting reward for her considerable accomplishments.

Yet the Dorothy who returns is not the same conventional moralizer we met early in the tale. She has benefited from Billina's assertiveness, even to the point of boldly depriving the Nome King of his belt. Dorothy's action is not only justified and successful, it represents a deepening of her nature. She has incorporated the trickster amorality of Billina and thus earned more than a mere return to our world. But like other heroes and heroines, she asks no more than such a return. In chapter 10, for instance, we shall meet a hero, Bilbo Baggins, who consciously undertakes to become a thief, who undergoes a more vigorous encounter with trickster figures than Dorothy, and who – although his moral nature evolves further as a result – is also satisfied at the end simply to return to his previous life.

# 7

# Beyond Absurdity

O MOVE FROM THE LAND of Oz to Russell Hoban's *The Mouse and His Child* is to traverse seventy years of upheaval in western culture. Although the mouse child is just as innocent as Dorothy, he deals with difficulties that challenge his innocence to a far greater extent than anything Dorothy was faced with. Deprived of the glittering world of the toy shop, he enters the seamy underside of an industrial society, which embodies cutthroat Darwinism and in which innocence is tested by existential absurdity.

The waste land into which the mechanical mice venture in chapter 3 of the book is a world governed by appetite. The relations of prey and predator so often portrayed by Kipling become a great chain of violent consumption when the title characters are captured by an army of voracious shrews. Its battle with another shrew army for hunting territory is disrupted when two weasels appear; 'smiling pleasantly,' they devour both armies.[1] But the satisfaction of these predators is soon ended. An owl swoops down and kills both. The Darwinian view of nature in this scene is made explicit by a hawk later on. It justifies its intention of eating the mouse and his child by citing the balance of nature, which is like 'a beautiful pyramid,' with 'juicy mice' below and 'a hawk up at the top.' No wonder some adults are offended by the naked violence of this merely appetitive world. It upsets all the notions that many still have about what is appropriate for children. Yet for a vulnerable predator like man, consciousness is bound to bring with it some awareness of the bottom line for our species: eat or be eaten.

When reminded of the continual violence that children are exposed to on television, some adults condemn the media and the age. But fairy-tales, which are also full of violence, have been told and enjoyed for centuries. I agree with the psychoanalytic insight that violence is not foreign to 'innocent' children. All children have experienced their own hostility over the frustrations and conflicts that are part of all their lives. Good children's literature finds ways of expressing that hostility, of suggesting that it is normal and need be neither overwhelming nor a source of guilt. How to handle it is the key question. A modern author uses tone, emphasis, and selectivity to guide a reader's reaction. The fairy-tale employs a simple style and is set in another place and another time. Its conventions reassure us that the violence directed at the hero will be ineffective, while that directed at dragons, giants, and evil magicians is justified.

Russell Hoban uses a different technique, or techniques, as we shall see. To begin with, he does not present his weasels as wicked and thus deserving a violent death. Rather he domesticates them as a couple looking for a nice, well-supplied territory. Hoban's offence lies precisely in such 'humanizing' of predators. We don't want to be reminded that the vicious killers are merely a family of meat eaters like ourselves.

Another of Hoban's means of handling violence is irony. Just before the owl kills the weasels, the female claims that this territory is the 'nicest' they have found. Earlier the two mice were forced to accompany a bumbling rat named Ralphie, who tried to rob the local Hoard and Trust Co. Alerted by the chipmunk teller, the badger guarding the vault is waiting for Ralphie. The rat 'rushed into the waiting jaws of the badger, who ate him up.' If this scene does not fill us with horror, it is because Ralphie's nastiness and ineptness have kept us from empathizing with him.

The badger would like to eat Ralphie's 'accomplices,' too, but finding they are not flesh and blood he loses interest. Although vulnerable in other ways, our protagonists, the mouse and his child, have no value in the food chain. We might argue that their immunity to this threat provides the reassurance we need to render tolerable the violence all around them. But in fact they share this ambience and its anxieties, as well as its callousness. Freed from the badger's threat, the mouse and his child begin to laugh at the irony of Ralphie's death. Surely Hoban's sense of discretion must have failed him entirely when he allowed his protagonists to take the death as comic. In fact he went on to emphasize the importance of their laughter in a passage that is the key to our understanding the version of the comic on which he constructed his world. But before looking at this passage, we need to turn to the beginning of the book and the sub-world of wind-up toys that it establishes.

*The Mouse and His Child* begins as a drawing-room comedy. The inhabitants of a dollhouse in a toy shop are carrying on their own lives after store hours. The description of a tea-party in the dollhouse lets an adult reader know that the author has a slightly satiric eye on human society, as he has the dolls speak in non-sequitur clichés. Into this pointless world come the mouse and his father. As the elephant who acts as hostess tries to indoctrinate them, one of Hoban's key themes emerges. Hers is the wisdom of received opinions, externally determined lives. 'One simply goes out into the world and does whatever one does.' The mouse child opposes her with the ignorance of limited experience. Having contrasted a glimpse of the cold dark winter outside with the bright warm surroundings inside, he doesn't want to leave. The elephant insists, 'One does what one is wound to do.' The impersonal pronouns in this sentence faithfully reflect the outlook of the elephant. She lives in the depersonalized world of 'one,' whereas the mouse child lives in the personal world of 'I.' This 'I' may seem to be ego and is certainly connected with basic desires – to have the elephant as his mother and the seal as his sister, for instance – but finally this 'I' becomes an achieved self. No more than Pooh does the mouse child intend to be held down by the difficulties of reality. But he lives in a much more complex, inhibited and threatening world than Pooh's or even Dorothy's.

The response of the mouse child to the elephant's impersonal imperatives is more revolutionary than it may at first seem: he begins to cry. The other toys are upset, and the clock reminds them of the clockwork rules that govern them: they are neither to talk nor to cry while on the job. In Hoban's clockwork world, as in an important part of our experience of our own world, social rules have been established that frustrate expression of individuality and emotion. The book is about a small creature that determines to express what he feels and search for what he desires rather than be daunted by social laws – or, when he arrives in the larger world of live animals, by natural laws.

A common sequence in fairy-tales is for a character to impose on the hero a prohibition, or what Vladimir Propp calls an interdiction.[2] As soon as we realize that he is forbidden to do something we know that the hero will do it, to his cost. What we are less likely to notice is that while the breaking of the interdiction is followed by immediate suffering or loss, in the long run its consequences are beneficial to the hero. The clock has pronounced two such interdictions on the mouse child, who will finally break both. He and his father are sold and pass four Christmases under the tree of a proper human family, doing what they are wound up to do. But on the fifth Christmas, the mouse child, seeing a new dollhouse, is reminded of the one where he began and the potential family he met there. He begins to cry; the humans don't notice, but the cat does, gets upset, and knocks over a vase, which smashes the mouse and his father.

Thrown away, they are discovered in a trash can by a tramp who fixes them, winds them, and sets them on their way. If the mouse child had not broken the interdiction, they would not have been smashed as immediate punishment, but neither would they have gained a chance to find a greater reward. To break the laws of clockwork is to move beyond the boundaries imposed by their mechanical nature. Such unruliness – refusal to be circumscribed by the rules of the species – widens the choice of what to do and to be, confers freedom. Although the mouse and his child are still limited by their need to be wound in order to move, their gaining mental freedom represents a crucial change. Their new physical mobility symbolizes this change. Earlier they had complained that they could only dance in a circle; when repaired by the tramp they can walk in a straight line, can go somewhere. Their first encounter makes them aware of the liabilities of freedom: they become the slaves of Manny Rat, foraging in the local dump. He makes them accompany the incompetent Ralphie, with the result that we have seen.

On their way to the bank, they meet a fortune-telling frog, who divines with true prescience, though oracular ambiguity, what is to happen to the mouse child. He also pronounces for Ralphie the cliché predictions whose irony subsequently tickles the mouse and his child. As they finish laughing over his fate, they come to an important realization. Hearing the clock strike seven, the father realizes it is dawn. He warns his son that they must now obey the clockwork rule of silence, but both continue laughing and talking. The frog appears to inform them that their laughter has freed them from the rules. Taking the prescient bullfrog at his word, we can infer that laughter, like crying, is a human attribute, inappropriate to mechanical creatures. They are built to be impersonal, but in reality they have human feelings. These feelings are forbidden because they threaten the performance of their mechanical task: there would be no need for a prohibition on crying if there were not a possibility of its happening.

The mouse and his child presumably laugh with relief to be out of danger from the badger, and from Ralphie and Manny, who had earlier threatened to work them over. Freud suggests that laughter is not only tension relieving, but aggressive in nature; when we were mere creatures, instead of smiling we presumably just bared our teeth. Laughter also expresses a vitality that is certainly the opposite of the self-pity exhibited earlier by the mouse child's tears. Not prohibited to clockwork, presumably because none ever expressed it, laughter becomes the means of liberation from mechanical servitude, from the laws of mechanical nature. The mouse and his child have taken another significant step on their road to selfhood.

The ability to laugh is also essential to our appreciation and understanding of Hoban's book. The mouse and his child have been fearful, but the experience with Ralphie purges that fear by making them aware how inscrutable fate must be if the attractive prediction that one will go on a long journey can immediately be fulfilled as really meaning a short life. Such a world is absurd, and that was precisely Hoban's point in constructing it as he did. The clues are plentiful for any adult who has been exposed to the theatre of the absurd. Most obvious is the Beckett-like play, *The Last Visible Dog*, performed – or at least begun – in chapter 4. The whole round of killing that I discussed earlier can also be seen as an absurd cause for laughter rather than as a grim cause for anger, pity, or depression. The tone, the plot, and the theme of Hoban's book all are informed by this absurdist approach and by the existential view of life that underlies it.

Absurdism and existentialism are all very well for intellectual adults; but isn't their introduction an error in a book ostensibly intended for children? Not at all. To the child, what we call absurd humour is just another opportunity to smile or laugh. The dog-food can in which Manny keeps spare parts is a good example. The infinite regress of its label, on which a dog holds a can, on which a smaller dog holds another can, on which etc, is described in repetitious detail. The child smiles at the silly repetition; the adult may be reminded of another infinite regress, the round sung by Vladimir at the beginning of act 2 of *Waiting for Godot*:

> A dog came in the kitchen
> And stole a crust of bread,
> Then cook up with a ladle
> And beat him till he was dead.
> Then all the dogs came running
> And dug the dog a tomb,
> And wrote upon the tombstone
> For the eyes of dogs to come:
> 'A dog came in the kitchen, etc.'

A repetitive sense of no progress characterizes both, as it does the circular dance the mouse and his child were designed to perform. The fact that it is animal food being advertised might also alert us to the infinite regress of natural appetite: Worm is eaten by shrew is eaten by weasel is eaten by owl. If owl is the top of this pyramid, it is no less bound to die and be eaten, say by worms that are eaten by shrews, etc. One school of existentialism says that this spectacle fills the viewer with anguish, which once acknowledged, frees the perceiver from biological determinism by allowing him or her to opt out of any such chain, rejecting all social dogmas. Denying past definitions of human nature, such individuals are free to choose their own natures. The mouse child is already well on the road to such a decisive point.

So far we have looked at responses to a meaningless reality: a laughing response to its absurdity and a felt response to its being void of meaning; the result in both cases is an increased freedom. But there can be a third response to a world without value. In contrast to the atheistic focus on lack of design, religious existentialism reminds us that an early church father, Turtullian, believed in Christianity *because* its basis was absurd: of course an individual must suffer anguish in a universe of which he or she is just a fragment. But this third position then suggests that a higher innocence may be built on such experience; when disenchantment gives way to enlightenment the universe is perceived as being ordered and man's spirit in harmony with it. *The Mouse and His Child* contains this level as well as the others.

Such a paradoxical state of harmony replacing disorder, of innocence confirmed by experience, is arguably the goal of any hero. To be specific, we may see it as the object of the quest undertaken by the white seal in Kipling's tale. Even though reality presented him with senseless slaughter, the negation of life, even though the trials he faced were real and disheartening, nevertheless a higher order did lie behind the brute reality he encountered. It took the form of the legend, which offered a significant pattern, an innocent sense of destiny higher than the time-worn species patterns of habit and instinct. This destiny did not assure the seal, Kotick, that he would triumph effortlessly. It only promised that *a* white seal would some day find what Kotick had been searching for. For Kotick to become that seal required not only the five years of perseverance before he heard the legend, but the determination to try again, the patience to confront dumb nature in the form of the sea cow, and the valour and stamina to swim deeply, blindly into darkness with no knowledge of what lay beyond it. We shall find essentially this pattern repeated not only in *The Mouse and His Child* but in the last two quest tales we shall be taking up.

The mouse child's quest has both an inner and an outer focus. He is most aware of the outer search for a family and a home territory in which it can live. These goals are gained late in the book. The inner quest finds fulfilment in Serpentina's pond, in chapter 6. But its inception is in chapter 2, on the night that Manny Rat inducts the mice into a life of slavery. In the heavens, the mouse child sees Sirius, the dog-star, and takes comfort in realizing that its constant light and far distance reduce the importance even of Manny, the head rat of the dump. Facing and feeling the existential void, the mouse child somehow then finds perception and vitality to carry him on. Following this insight he encounters the death of Ralphie, but before that he gains two perceptions that are more in harmony with the great world. First he observes the can of dog food with its ever-diminishing series of dogs on the label. These will be connected ultimately with the bright dog-star.

Then the mouse child has his fortune told by the bullfrog. The frog knows he is a fraud, saying to people what they want to hear. To impress the mouse child, he throws some seeds on the snow. But instead of faking the reading of their pattern, the frog finds himself caught in it. '"You have broken the circle," he said, "and a straight line of great force emerges ... *Low in the dark of summer, high in the winter light; a painful spring, a shattering fall, a scattering regathered. The enemy you flee at the beginning awaits you at the end."*' Like the legend about the white seal, this oracle builds on known information to point toward unknown future events. The circle the mouse child has broken is the one he and his father danced in until the mouse child cried and they were smashed. The line of great force is the one the tramp set them on after he fixed them. But the main prophecy is the italicized part. Here we discover that unlike a legend, a prophecy is ambiguous, filled with poetic double meanings. The enemy is and will be Manny Rat, but he will grant the mouse father's deepest wish. The shattering fall refers both to a season and to a precipitous and damaging descent. Similarly, the painful spring refers not only to a season but to the wind-up motor inside the father. (As the father says of his child, he 'fills up the empty space inside himself with foolish dreams.') Most important, the scattering regathered predicts not only the putting together of the scattered parts of father and son, but also to their being reunited with the elephant and seal of the original dollhouse to create the mouse child's dreamed of – and actively pursued – family. Yet a number of events will intervene in this picaresque tale before the mouse child sees beyond the last visible dog to his own selfhood.

During the theatrical production put on by the Caws of Art, the predators in the audience rebel against the absurdities of the play and mob the actors. When the mouse and his child are sent on to distract the audience, they voice their actual hopes and fears, which strike the audience as so absurd its members laugh until they cry. Later the father complains that they were laughed at because they were defenceless. He is correct, but instead of seeing the freedom from biological determination that their absurd condition makes possible, the father wants to correct part of that condition by becoming self-winding. In the hope of achieving that goal, they are taken to the muskrat. Meanwhile Manny Rat, after intervening in the play to retrieve his slaves, is mobbed by the predators. Although separated again from the mouse and his child, he sets out to find them, determined to destroy these symbols of his lack of complete control over his property.

Muskrat agrees to try to make the father self-winding, but he insists on being helped first in a project to impress his students with his practical ability. He spends a few days figuring out how to make a chopping machine to cut down a tree; it is left to the mouse and his child to spend the winter outside operating the contraption that slowly does the job. As the mouse child realizes, to achieve the muskrat's goal, they must literally walk in a circle again. Instead of moving them toward their true goal, this desire of the father's has caused them to regress to circular motion and lose the line of great force on which they were going. But Manny Rat changes that. Tracking them down, he completes muskrat's project, the tree falls, and the mouse child and his father are snatched away from their enemy by the line that connected them to the muskrat's primitive chopping machine. They are flung into the stream and carried to their next adventure, the climactic one of the mouse child's inner search for being.

Dropping to the bottom of another pond, stuck in its mud, they meet the author of the absurd play, C. Serpentina, a large snappping turtle whose life premiss rests on the muddy bottom of the pond. He cannot understand the desire of the mouse and his child to get on with their quest. His down-to-earth philosophy is at once 'basic' and inadequate. But its impersonality offers potential enlightenment to the mouse child. The environment provides both an object and another creature which help him toward his goal. The object is another can with a dog-food label, and the creature is Miss Mudd, with whom the mouse child becomes friends.

The strength of Serpentina's position is that by accepting where he is, valuing the bottom of the pond as deep and profound, he can let his mind loose to contemplate infinity. As it happens he had earlier found the infinite regress of dogs on the can label a convenient symbol for infinity, hence his allusion to the label in the title of his play, *The Last Visible Dog*. When the father asks for help in getting out of the pond, the turtle, in unconsciously predictive language, voices his personal philosophy. 'Each of us, sunk in the mud however deep, must rise on the propulsion of his own thought. Each of us must journey through the dogs, beyond the dots, and to the truth, alone.' This statement contains clues both to the means of their continuing their outer adventure and to the mouse child's fulfilling his inner quest. Because he can stare only at the label on the can, the mouse child develops an interest in discovering if there is anything beyond the last dog visible on it.

His intense meditation results in vision, a transcendent experience in which he feels the dogs on the label to be 'real and alive – a pack of ancient brothers through which his spirit can journey on.' Tracing them back, he sees beyond the last one to the dots and then the empty space on the label, an 'emptiness that seemed to flow back toward him.' At this point he realizes that 'Nothing is what is beyond the last visible dog.' Serpentina is pleased with this confirmation of his reductive existentialism, but the mouse child is unsatisfied. He determines to find out if there is something beyond that nothing. Over the objections of the turtle, he sets Miss Mudd, the ugly water insect, to remove that part of the label beyond the last visible dog. Under it appears the still bright tin in which the mouse child sees a reflection of his own face and his father's body. His conclusion is a revelation. 'There's nothing on the other side of nothing but us.' In the dark mud night of his spirit, the mouse child has followed his dog-star guide to a realization of the emptiness of the universe and the absurdity of existence. This acknowledgment of the void has opened him to self-awareness, a realization that he is the consciousness that perceives that nothingness. He is able to affirm himself, or more exactly the joined unit, 'us,' himself as empty dreamer, his father as motor-burdened worrier.

The mouse child comes to an affirmation of the value of being: through personal feeling and will he arrives at the position earlier stated impersonally by Serpentina. But his father, who has not had the revelation, is still stuck in the turtle's acceptance of inaction in the face of nothingness: They are all about to receive a demonstration of the falsity of this reductive apologia for stasis.

All mud is not alike, nor is it all inactive. Part has, as it were, separated itself out into a creature that calls itself Miss Mudd; although she appears 'as drab and muddy as her name,' like the mouse child she refuses to accept present appearance or mere conditions as reality. She says she feels like 'a song in the sunlight, like a sigh in the summer air.' Also like the mouse child she sees her face in the tin, and she agrees to help in his plan for escape. She places the string still attached to the mouse and his child in an advantageous position and shines up the good-luck coin given them by the frog. In the upper air for the first time, she feels exhausted, and wonders if she is dying. Then her body splits down the back and she leaves her chrysalis, a dragonfly unfolding its wings and flying away like 'a song in the sunlight, like a sigh in the summer air.' Dark winter has given way to bright summer, drab mud has been replaced by emerald green in a transformation of great impact for the reader. The mouse child, being still below the surface, will never know of her brilliant destiny, but we experience it with joy and hope.

The mouse and his child are also about to re-enter the upper world, however. A bass is attracted by the glint of the coin, swallows it and pulls away the line. This action propels the mouse and his child out of the pond onto the bank. After coaxing a bittern to wind him, the father discovers his works are broken. He is left with a tightened spring. Suddenly he and the child are seized by a hawk, who carries them aloft but drops them again upon discovering they are not edible mice. They fall to earth into Manny Rat's dump again, the impact separating them, splitting them open, and obliterating their consciousness. The earlier prophecy by the frog, of a 'painful' spring and a 'shattering fall,' has been fulfilled, sending father and son into oblivion. Their fortune, like Ralphie's, appears to have predicted death, their quest ended in a scattering instead of an integration. In contrast, Miss Mudd was also split open but as a sign of new life, a successful metamorphosis. This natural occurrence might tempt us to distinguish between the vitality and transformations of organic nature and the merely physical changes of inorganic nature. But that observation should in turn remind us to ask whether mechanical mice can die. The question is absurd.

The answer does not come immediately. Chapter 7 begins with an update on two other creatures at the pond, the frog who has been searching for the mouse and his child, and the mechanical seal from the toyshop, who is in a fishing partnership with a kingfisher. Both become aware that they have just missed the pair. The frog persuades the bittern to take him and follow the hawk. The seal and kingfisher go too. The frog finds his friends and makes the mouse child whole again. 'As his two halves came together the mouse child returned to himself.' But the new state he has entered is to be separate from his father, on his own. Standing alone for the first time, he is 'a little unsteady.' But though separate, father and child are still together, only each is autonomous now. The mouse child sees in the dump the dollhouse he had originally known in the toy shop. He claims it as his, and it thus becomes a focal point in the outer world for an integration of family and friends, comparable to the inner integration he had earlier achieved under the auspices of the dogs on the label, 'a pack of ancient brothers.' Just as his spiritual awakening, a vision of self, was preceded by an awareness of the void, so here his physical rebirth from oblivion to an independent entity is succeeded by a sensory vision of what he wants in the world.

When the father is put together, he sees the same house, and the elephant, and has the same reaction as his separate child. He even says the same words that the child has spoken: 'Ours!' The child points out the seal and the elephant as evidence of his dream coming true, but the father sees

Manny Rat as the final enemy foretold by the frog's prophecy. The dollhouse has been set on a pole and taken over by Manny. As lord of the dump he is about to have a house-warming to celebrate his dominance.

The elephant is one of the rat's slaves. She has suffered much, but both she and the seal have in their different ways become liberated from the clockwork rules. They are therefore ready to join in the battle for their house. The seal agrees to become part of the family, and the kingfisher and even the solitary bittern join with the frog to help the four meechanical creatures to win their own territory. The father spots the dog-food label on Manny's spare parts can and takes it as both a symbolic and a literal sign that they will triumph, using the wind-up parts in their battle.

Unknowingly, the mouse child comes up with a battle plan that fits in with the pattern of destiny. Much earlier the frog had prophesied – again in spite of himself – to Manny, 'A dog shall rise, a rat shall fall.' As with the frog's other prophecy, this one contains a double meaning. Although Manny remembers these lines the night of the house-warming, he does not notice that Sirius has risen in the sky. Not only is Sirius as dog-star ascending, but another dog is also about to rise. The extended family has taken Manny's spare parts can and attached the hind legs of a donkey to the father mouse. Their kicking action is used to catapult rocks at the dollhouse. Then the frog gets in the can, has it lifted by a makeshift crane, and is lofted over the house, where he calls loudly for the surrender of the rats within. Seeing the dog on the label of the can as it rises above him, Manny Rat realizes that the prophecy is coming true. With fish hooks attached to lines at the corners of the house, the can is lifted by the crane, the house tilted, and its inhabitants dumped on a passing freight train.

Only one rat escapes, Manny, who confronts them with a poisoned spear. Not understanding the father's altered physiognomy, Manny stands in front of him and receives full in the face a discharge from the father's catapult legs. The results are comically disastrous for Manny: he loses his teeth, the weapons that made him top rat in the dump. All the animals, wind-up and live, laugh at this defeat of a once-feared enemy. Released from bondage, all are able to make commitments as free creatures. The kingfisher and even the bittern join the frog as honorary uncles within the family, and the father proposes to the elephant.

The extended family repair, clean, and paint the dollhouse. Manny Rat, chastened, offers his services as handyman. He figures out how to make both the mouse and his child self-winding. But seeing this final evidence of their triumph and hearing the mouse child thank him as 'Uncle Manny' is more than rat nature can stand. Manny begins to plan revenge. While wiring the home for electricity he sets two wires in gunpowder so as to burn it down. But the tidy elephant cleans up this mess; when Manny connects his wires to the electric line, his body completes the circuit. He regains consciousness to find himself surrounded by the extended family, which is still unaware of his evil intentions. But Manny's near-death experience has caused a basic change in his nature. He rejoins them, no longer a secret enemy.

The book ends with an even larger integration. The family turns the dollhouse into a hotel named the Last Visible Dog, opens it to migrant birds and anyone else, and provides entertainment and culture, including the Caws of Art, who put on a complete version of *The Last Visible Dog*. They also offer practical courses, set up a committee to reduce conflict in the world, and bring in the profound C. Serpentina to conduct a symposium.

The only seeming let-down to this harmonious resolution is a discovery made by the mouse father. The reciprocally winding motors installed by Manny gradually run down and need rewinding. The mouse and his child appear not to have achieved full autonomy. But the frog points out that everyone needs help from a friend at some point. Once again we are reminded that the laws of nature, though rigorously enforced, can be surmounted, externally by co-operative action, internally by faith and vision, by affirmation of the spirit after facing the void on which even physics rests.

Benign though the ending is, its communal integration is less dynamic than the individual fulfilment achieved earlier by Miss Mudd and the mouse child, when both transcended limiting conditions to realize their true selves. By crying and laughing on the job, the mouse child passes the preliminary test, which gives him the mobility and confidence to face the main test. When he realizes that only they can lift themselves off the bottom of the pond, he has passed the main test, taking responsibility for his life and then persuading others to help him change it. I would therefore see the triumph of the mouse and his father in establishing a home that is a hotel as their passing the third, confirming test, in which the mouse child's internal vision is matched by external recognition.

Hoban actually ends the book with a small incident that rounds off his narrative. He reintroduces the tramp who first repaired the mouse and his child and set them on their quest with the words, 'Be tramps.' Now the tramp looks into the refurbished dollhouse at the Christmas festivities of the extended family. The last words of the book come when he speaks to the mouse and his child for the second time. "Be happy," said the tramp. This ending can be taken as the imperative version of the fairy-tale ending, 'And they lived happily ever after.' The tramp thus functions as a surrogate author, setting the figures on their quest and pronouncing a benediction on them at the end. Although he is not a writer like Charlotte the spider, I think there are good reasons for taking the tramp as in some sense the author of these adventures.

The tramp's appearances provide a frame for the narrative: his first appearance at the very beginning of the book clearly parallels the concluding scene. The story begins with the tramp during an earlier Christmas season. We first see the toy shop through his eyes as he looks in at the dollhouse, the elephant, the seal, watching the mouse and his child do their clockwork circular dance. Warned away from the window by the saleslady's disapproving stare, the tramp dances in a circle like the mouse and his child. He is then joined by a little spotted dog that follows him when he leaves. The dog, named Bonzo, is with him when he finds and fixes the smashed mouse and child, and at the end the dog is still with him. Since the can label that has been a symbol for the quest is for Bonzo dog food, this linking name invites further consideration.

If we look again at the description of the tramp at the point where the dog first joined him, we can see what its coming meant. The tramp was imitating the dance of the clockwork mice. Alienated from society, he lacked what even the mechanical figures had, a bond with another. He finds this bond with the dog, as indicated by his later sharing a meal with it. The dog becomes the tramp's point of connection with the world. Like the mouse child looking at the line of dogs on the can underwater, the tramp can be said to find in his dog something 'real and alive,' one of 'a pack of ancient brothers through which his spirit' can continue its quest. As author of the mice's quest, he makes them surrogates for himself ('Be tramps'). As their creator, he passes a final benediction on them ('Be happy'). If their adventures are really his creation, then we can say that their story is his imagining, their fantastic adventure his fantasy, its sign of constant hope (a dog-star rising) his tribute to the brute creature whose loyalty he values, and whose muteness he corrects in a tale of talking animals. His choosing the mouse and his child as the heroes of the tale can also be understood as a tribute. If he had not contrasted his unbonded condition with their connected one, he might not have attracted and accepted the dog that becomes his companion.

I have worked out this speculative reading of Hoban's use of the frame because – as I have supposed with E.B. White and will insist on again with Richard Adams – fantasy authors often put an author surrogate in their tales. They do it because a fantasy story is so overtly an artwork, an artifice, that it is as though the authors have a need to insert a version of the artificer by putting the god into the machine they have built. Hoban seems to be saying through his frame, 'Of course neither animals nor mechanical figures can talk. If I've allowed them to, it is so that human beings can see what sort of world the laws of nature provide us with, what sort of world human society imposes on us.' The answer is a mechanical world in which the tramp and the dog are 'the only two creatures on the street not *moving in a fixed direction*.' While not so bluntly the author's mouthpiece as to rob the story of excitement for the naïve reader, the Chaplinesque tramp is nevertheless there for the discerning reader, a sign of Hoban's commitment to humanity, to the outcast, to the isolated individual who may find within his imagination that spirit that is not only the source of a bond with all fellow creatures but also the centre of the self.

# 8

# Epic Integration

EN YEARS AFTER the publication in 1972 of *Watership Down*, Richard Adams collected a book of stories by his favourite childhood story-teller, Ernest Thompson Seton. His introduction provides a good sense of what Seton meant to him, growing up during a period when middle-class English parents tended to regard children 'as beautiful, innocent little creatures, passing through a golden age of infancy which ought not to be spoilt by the intrusion of anything harsh or cruel.' Although fairly realistic children's stories were available, parents favoured books that excluded 'any suspicion that pain, mortality, risk and loss are unavoidable in the human situation.' Like most children, Adams believed, he was made uneasy by such sentimentality. Thus, while praising the children's books of A.A. Milne for their 'charm and quality,' Adams contended that they need 'counter-balancing with tougher, more truthful and realistic stuff,' tales like Seton's.[1]

My own sense is that *Winnie-the-Pooh* is an appropriate book for pre-school and primary-school children, and that it does deal with the risk and pain of rudimentary human relations. Although Pooh can aptly be characterized as a 'beautiful, innocent little creature,' we have seen him coping with a number of realistic problems: the painful consequences of indulging his appetite, the outspokenness of Rabbit, the gloom of Eeyore, the evasive pedantry of Owl, and the fearfulness of Piglet. But while these portrayals of psychologically and socially realistic character interactions take the edge off Adams's criticism of *Winnie-the-Pooh* as belonging to the 'soft-centred, "sugar-candy" school of writing,'[2] they do not qualify Milne's tale for the countervailing school that Adams favoured. Milne does play down physical pain by creating a world of stuffed animals in which mortality is absent and risk consequently diminished.

Seton's Wild Animal books are thus, as Adams claimed, quite different, based on a naturalist's accurate observations of animals in their own environment. Like Kipling of his own generation and E.B. White of a later generation, Seton suggests that 'survival and death' are important concerns for humanity because we are also part of nature. This concern is also central to *Watership Down*. Death is an important part of Adams's world, even though it is much more often reported, off-stage or in the past, than directly rendered as part of the immediate action or focus of the tale. Despite this mitigation of violence, Adams's book is clearly appropriate for a somewhat older child than *Winnie-the-Pooh*. Finally, it must be said that Milne is open to criticism for writing down to his young reader; in contrast, Adams makes great demands on his reader's attention and intelligence, thus earning the compliment he paid Seton: he wrote *Watership Down* because 'a children's story' was the 'best art-form' for what he had to say.[3]

Acknowledging that Seton's tales use 'anthropomorphic fantasy,' to guide the reader to sympathize with his animal characters, Adams emphasized that Seton attributes to them 'nothing but what he knows they felt and did in reality.' Of course, the verbs 'knows' and 'felt' both beg large questions, but since Adams didn't pause over them, we need not either. Adams concluded that Seton's technique is 'natural realism,' the attempt 'to translate the animal's actual feelings and cries, without falsifying them, into terms readily comprehensible by human beings.'[4] He went on to suggest that animal tales vary from the entirely realistic to the completely fanciful and to distinguish Seton's limited anthropomorphism from both Kipling's and Adams's own more humanized fantasies: in *The Jungle Book* and *Watership Down*, Adams noted that while the animals don't 'do anything that would actually be physically impossible to' them as 'real animals,' they are given 'motives and intelligence which their real counterparts could not possess.'[5] It is also possible to distinguish Adams's animals from Kipling's. Although the animals in *The Jungle Book* all acknowledge the law of the jungle, a kind of Darwinian social structure, Adams's rabbits are more subtly anthropomorphic in their ability to learn and in the growing complexity of their social structure.

Seton's influence on *Watership Down* is evident not only in the lack of sentimentality in Adams's treatment of his rabbits but in particular incidents from Seton's tales that Adams has adopted in his own story. Seton emphasizes the importance for rabbits of the ability to deceive and trick predators, a survival mechanism that we will see Adams turn into an important theme connected with his rabbits' mythical hero, El-ahrairah. In particular, Seton has a small rabbit get the better of a large aggressive rabbit by means of a trick that Adams has Hazel use to save the burrow from the ruthless invader rabbit, General Woundwort. Raggylug, Seton's rabbit, meets a hound, which he encourages to chase him to the nest of his enemy. Unaware of the danger, the bully first threatens Raggylug, 'You miserable fool, I will kill you yet,' and then jumps into the path of the hound. 'The buck's weight and size were great advantages in a rabbit fight, but now they were fatal. He did not know many tricks' for outwitting pursuit. After a short chase, 'there was a scuffle, then loud and terrible screaming.'[6] Similarly in *Watership Down*, when Blackberry leads the 'great, black dog' among Woundwort's rabbit patrol, their first inkling of the havoc to come is 'a single high scream.'[7] The difference between Woundwort and Seton's buck is that Woundwort stands his ground, but the outcome is the same: the peaceful natives are rid of the brutal intruder.

Another Seton story, 'Little Warhorse, the History of a Jackrabbit,' also contains incidents adapted by Adams. Warhorse regularly defeats cats, is let loose from human captivity by a benign man, and while in captivity is well fed. Some captured jackrabbits are taken to a park, where they are 'turned out one by one, very gently – yes, gently; the Roman guards were careful of their prisoners, being responsible for them – the Jacks found little to complain of, a big enclosure with plenty of good food, and no enemies to annoy them.'[8] They are treated well because they are to be used in deadly greyhound races. Similarly in *Watership Down*, a farmer kills off all predators and provides fodder for a warren of rabbits that grow fat and sleek. But it is all for his own purpose, to use them for food.

There are other parallels, but these will suffice to indicate the use Adams made of Seton. These assimilations contribute to the construction of a world unified by the synthesizing ability of Adams's imagination. Beyond this convention, Adams, as we have already seen, consciously limited the actions of his animals to those of their real-life counterparts. In contrast, Hoban's animals do things animals cannot do. But such actions do not make his tale inferior to *Watership Down*; as Adams says, 'All anthropomorphic fantasies have to pick a point along' the line between human and animal. 'The genre is an illusion-game.'[9] Both authors play it well.

Adams, for instance, allows his reader to witness the growth of cognition in his rabbits soon after the formation of the small group whose experiences we share. Blackberry, the innovative one, sees how to get two small exhausted rabbits across a stream to safety. He explains to the central character, Hazel, how to use a piece of wood as a raft. But Hazel cannot understand. Fortunately, Hazel's younger sibling, Fiver, grasps Blackberry's idea and urges on the other small rabbit, Pipkin. The plan works.

Other scenes of elementary reasoning by one rabbit and incomprehension by others follow as the novel progresses.

Like Kipling in *The Jungle Book*, Adams provides his animals not only with values but also with their own culture. Whereas Grahame and Hoban put clothes on their animals and in their different ways impose a human culture on top of animal ways, Kipling and Adams provide their animals with a society that may be based on aspects of human culture but that the author and his characters insist is significantly different. Although *The Mouse and His Child* appeared five years before *Watership Down*, Hoban is self-consciously contemporary, while Adams is self-consciously classical in style, development, and theme. Both make their dialogue colloquial, and both can write straightforward description. But Adams weighs his text down with epigraphs and epic similes. His first epigraph, for instance, contains lines from Aeschylus's *Agamemnon*, in which Cassandra foretells the death of her captor: 'The house reeks of death and dripping blood.' This heavy piece of apparatus is justified by the approaching death of most of the rabbits in the warren, as well as by Fiver's Cassandra-like foretelling of it.

Adams's seriousness of purpose is always overt, whether in the epigraphs, which can easily be skipped by a child, or in his direct addresses to the reader. Chapter 23 contains in its second paragraph a more indirect form of authorial intrusion: 'As a bull, with a slight but irresistible movement, tosses its head from the grasp of a man who is leaning over the stall and idly holding its horn, so the sun entered the world in smooth, gigantic power.' With such epic similes Adams from time to time provides his text with a leisurely sense of the worth and importance of his enterprise. The contrast with Grahame's mock-heroic treatment of the battle for Toad Hall, in the chapter titled 'The Return of Ulysses,' is instructive. Grahame's pastoral comedy does not aspire to the thematic resonance or imaginative depth of *Watership Down*.

Adams's classical model may be inferred not only by the initial quotation from Aeschylus but by another epic comparison, which ends the long and didactic paragraph that opens chapter 22. Taking as his theme the rabbits' sense 'that Life is Now,' Adams underlines their ability to drop from memory dangers immediately past in favour of appetites and needs immediately present, followed by hopes of the future. 'Odysseus brings not one man to shore with him. Yet he sleeps sound beside Calypso and when he wakes thinks only of Penelope.' Such a comparison makes it quite clear that Adams's aim was to write a modern epic.

Like *The Odyssey*, *Watership Down* has a number of inset tales, tales that their author has carefully crafted to provide not only relief of tension and a sense of rabbit culture and tradition, but also a mythic model for his rabbits' actions. We shall be investigating the archetypal level of Adams's story in due course. The inset tales concern the rabbits' culture hero, El-ahrairah, some of whose adventures, the author tells us, 'are those of Brer Rabbit. For that matter, Odysseus himself might have borrowed a trick or two from the rabbit hero, for he is very old and was never at a loss for a trick to deceive his enemies.' Adams thus indicates his knowledge that Brer Rabbit is a descendant of the trickster hare, brought by slaves to North America from the ancient oral traditions of Africa. Odysseus does indeed show himself a wily trickster in his habitual unwillingness to give his true name or history, culminating in his journey in disguise to his own island and palace, a dangerous return that brings him into violent conflict with the usurping suitors. By connecting both his rabbits and Odysseus with Trickster, Adams suggests the archaic impulse behind his tale and increases the stature of his characters and their adventure.

To begin considering *Watership Down* with such an emphasis on its adult seriousness is to distort the variety both of its tone and its concerns. Not only does it offer continuous narrative tension and excitement, it appeals to children through the variety of its humour, from Bluebell's jokes to the characterization of Keehar to the comic tricks of El-ahrairah. It also provides a variety of characters, some of whom change significantly through their experiences. Since we are in Hazel's consciousness throughout most of the book, we are more aware of his development than that of any other character. Of the other two whose point of view we share for shorter periods, Bigwig also develops significantly while Fiver hardly changes in the conventional sense. Being clairvoyant, he is almost too open to the archetypal world; his relation to it grows in importance at the same time as his rarely used authority becomes evident to the other members of the group.

Fiver's first vision of the destruction of the burrow convinces his brother, Hazel, and seven others to leave it. They spend the night in a wood filled with predators. Here Hazel asks Dandelion to tell them a story to keep up their spirits. Dandelion tells a typical primitive tale, 'The Story of the Blessing of El-ahrairah,' a differentiation myth that explains how the creatures became as they are.

The tale begins with the establishment of the rabbits' version of an anthropomorphic god, Frith, who made the universe and the natural world; he also made the animals, who at first were all friends. But the rabbits multiplied so rapidly that they threatened to denude the world of grass. Frith warned their leader, El-ahrairah, that he must therefore curtail their increase, but El-ahrairah insisted it was proper and an honour to Frith: 'of all the animals they are the most responsive to his warmth and brightness.' (It is clear here and elsewhere that Frith is a sun-god.) 'Frith could have killed El-ahrairah at once, but he had a mind to keep him in the world, because he needed him to sport and jest and play tricks. So he determined to get the better of him not by means of his own great power but by means of a trick.'

Frith therefore calls all the animals together, each to receive a special present. When the fox, the stoat, and the weasel appear, they are given 'the cunning and the fierceness and the desire to hunt and slay' rabbits. This is Frith's first trick. But El-ahrairah delays out of pride and lack of reverence; as he goes to Frith for his present, he hears about the differentiation of predators. Fearful, El-ahrairah starts to dig a hole to hide in. Frith arrives when he is half in and pretends not to recognize his hindquarters. El-ahrairah in turn pretends not to be himself. Frith plays out the game: 'Then come out of that hole and I will bless you instead of him.' But El-ahrairah refuses. 'I am busy. The fox and weasel are coming. If you want to bless me you can bless my bottom, for it is sticking out of the hole.' Adams underlines the function of the tale at this point by giving the reactions of Dandelion's listeners, who identify with El-ahrairah. In fact, even Frith feels a bond with El-ahrairah because the rabbit will not give up. He blesses the bottom of El-ahrairah, especially his strong legs and flashing tail. As El-ahrairah runs off, Frith warns him that rabbits will henceforth be prey, but enunciates the qualities that will allow them to elude predators.

El-ahrairah's impudence in telling Frith to bless his bottom almost puts him on a par with his god, who made the stars from his own droppings. The rabbit's tail, next to the orifice from which the droppings come flashes 'like a star.' Between lawmaker and law-breaker there is thus a strong kinship in fecundity and energy, in creativity and trickiness. The message that the weak can be strong, the defenceless self-protected comes through to both rabbit and child listener.

Hazel's fleeing group is almost caught by a dog at the stream but, as we have seen, crosses it to safety. Not long after, Fiver sets their goal, the high down, but for quite a while he depends on Hazel to persuade the others to move toward it. Although developing as a leader, Hazel is apt, like the others, to trade long-range goals for short-term benefits. When they are invited by a strange rabbit, Cowslip, to visit his warren, they override Fiver's reservations in order to enjoy a spacious burrow and the food provided by a farmer. Adams's imagination was obviously fully engaged by this episode.

At the same time that Fiver points Hazel toward Watership Down, he warns him that they are 'in for some mysterious trouble,' though not from predators; 'it feels more like – like mist. Like being deceived and losing our way.' Not only does Cowslip deceive them and lead them away from their quest, he is portrayed as having a 'strange, *clouded* manner' (my emphasis). This deviousness is in fact characteristic of the burrow rabbits, reaching its apotheosis in Silverweed, who recites a poem about the attraction of death. Fiver rushes out of the burrow, and when upbraided by Hazel indicates his disgust with and attraction to what Silverweed offers: 'I'm not blaming you, Hazel. I felt myself moving towards him like one cloud drifting into another. But then at the last moment I drifted wide. Who knows why? ... Did I say the roof of that hall was made of bones? No! It's like a great mist of folly that covers the whole sky: and we shall never see to go by Frith's light any more.' The imagery pictures the philosophy of this warren as a fog, mist or cloud, which obscures god, takes away light, encourages a drift toward darkness.

With a more advanced culture than the newcomers, the rabbits offering hospitality look down on the simplicity of their guests. After Dandelion tells the story of El-ahrairah and the King's Lettuce, they respond with condescension to the charm of such old-fashioned tales, told by someone who actually seems to believe in El-ahrairah. Hazel answers them. 'Our stories haven't changed in generations, you know. After all, we haven't changed ourselves.' Although the question of changing ways will come up again, the point Buckthorn makes will remain a given for our rabbits. 'El-ahrairah is a trickster ... and rabbits will always need tricks.' In Dandelion's tale, El-ahrairah tricks the king, who wants to kill him, into throwing away all his lettuce so that El-ahrairah's followers may eat it. In contrast, Cowslip's warren lives on the bounty of the farmer who owns the land, a deadly trickster who daily dumps fodder conveniently close for them to eat. Sleek and large from such good nurturing, these rabbits yet believe that 'rabbits need dignity and above all, the will to accept their fate.' That fate is what the fog hides, and the visiting rabbits do not find out what it is until Bigwig experiences it.

The chapter titled 'The Shining Wire' begins with a prophetic dream, which comes not to Fiver but to Hazel. In it he sees Bigwig with red yew berries in his mouth. He says, 'Ask me where, Hazel!' In reality, the visitors have noticed that their hosts don't like to be asked 'where' any rabbit is. As this dream suggests through its cold yew berries, the answer to the question 'Where may Bigwig be running to?' is toward death. Hazel goes looking for Fiver, who has refused to sleep in the burrow. Bigwig comes, too, and after berating Fiver, runs through a hedge into a wire noose. 'The projecting point of one strand had lacerated his neck and drops of blood, dark and red as yew berries, welled one by one down his shoulder.' Frantically the other rabbits try to free him before he strangles. They manage to dig out the peg that anchors the wire. When he recovers they realize the burrow rabbits know well that the farmer traps them but have refused to warn the newcomers; in their anger they want to go back and take revenge. But Fiver exerts an almost supernatural authority to stop them. Then he explains rhapsodically how these rabbits have been corrupted by their easy life, that their warren is 'nothing but a death-hole.' He convinces his friends not to be distracted again from pursuing their original goal, the down.

The group now comes to a remote and peaceful land to found a new warren, to begin a new life, their initial quest completed. They have found a place for a burrow, but it cannot become a warren until they have some does. That will be their second quest, involving raids on Nuthanger Farm and on Efrafa. The third stage will be the defence of their Eden against invasion by rabbits from another powerful but vicious warren. These three stages correspond roughly to the three-test structure of the fairy-tale. The quest for Watership Down is the preliminary test. In finding it they gain what they need in order to pass the main test. They have earned self-confidence as well as a burrow. While there they also gain the helper who will be crucial to their undertaking the main test – the quest for the captive princess, or in their case for the does, whether caged at Nuthanger Farm or held against their will in the Efrafa burrow fortress. The third or confirming test is the one in which the fairy-tale hero proves his right to the treasure or princess he has won. In Adams's book this test is the defence of the burrow against the force that General Woundwort brings to reclaim the does.

As a prelude to discussing the helper who aids the rabbits on their second quest, we must consider how traditional a burrow Watership Down will be. In Cowslip's warren, Hazel's justification of El-ahrairah stories was that traditional tales are appropriate because 'our lives have been the same as our fathers' and their fathers' before them.' This justification seems validated by the strength the El-ahrairah tales give Hazel's group. The wild rabbits have a vitality and purpose that contrasts sharply with the decadence of the dwellers in Cowslip's warren. But in fact social evolution is one of Adams's themes. Blackberry, the innovator, voices it as they start to settle in on the down. 'There's a lot we don't know ... We're going to need some new ideas.' He goes on to point to the 'unnatural' ways of Cowslip's warren as an indication that rabbits can change. And on the immediate issue he is successful. The other rabbits have argued that they can't be expected to dig out a burrow because that is does' work. But they are finally convinced they must do so, since there are no does.

When the rabbits accept the idea of digging, they decide to include an innovative design for a meeting hall, modelled on the great burrow of Cowslip's warren. They are able to dig out such a burrow because they have with them Strawberry, one of the rabbits from the decadent warren. He asked to join them when they left, his mate having just been killed by one of the wire nooses. Instead of turning him back as a deceiver justly punished, Hazel allowed him to join. One of the qualities that make Hazel a good leader is his broad view of the group, his desire to include others in it. This desire is partly behind his helping to free the tame rabbits so they can join the warren; it is also evident in his attitude toward other creatures.

As the rabbits are settling in on Watership Down, Hazel one day sees a field-mouse exposed in the open with a hawk overhead. He offers it shelter, and it dashes into the burrow just as the hawk drops down. When he leaves them, the mouse pledges help in time of future need. Bigwig is sceptical, but Hazel's instinct is proved right. Soon after, another mouse shows them where to find good grass. And later in the book the original mouse gives advance warning of the attack on the warren.

But the most important helper that Hazel gains for the group is Keehar. His wing broken, the sea-gull has holed up in a hollow on the down. Hazel is able to persuade the reluctant rabbits to get insects for the gull and to dig a hole to protect it from predators. Hazel realizes that when Keehar is able to fly again he can do reconnaissance for them. The gull does, and returns with news of tame rabbits at Nuthanger Farm and a large warren to the south. Important as this news is, leading to the two expeditions to obtain does, Keehar's role as helper is more clearly evident at the large warren, Efrafa. There he not only carries messages between Bigwig and the others but plays a crucial role in the battle at the climax of the raid.

Hazel's accepting aliens and helping them to have a place in the group is part of an observable movement toward social integration in the book. Before Keehar's appearance, for instance, two other rabbits join the burrow. One of them is Holly, the former head of the Owsla, or burrow police, back in the original warren. In order to leave there, Hazel's group had had to fight him off. Now, half-mad with suffering, he tells the harrowing tale of the destruction of the warren by men who gassed the rabbits in their burrows – thus confirming Fiver's original vision. The other newcomer is Bluebell, who has kept Holly going by playing the fool. Taken into the group, both add their talents to it. This integration of alien members may be connected with two related themes, the process of decision making and the enlarging of the rabbits' definition of reality.

We saw earlier how Blackberry came up with the plan for rafting two weak rabbits across the stream. Most of the rabbits have a special talent. Taken together they form an entity. As Adams suggests more than once, the group experiences an unconscious, organic process of integration that transcends the individual.

The third level of integration is of the archetypal into the physical world. Fiver voices his perception and questions about the relation of the one to the other: 'There's another place – another country ... We go there when we sleep: at other times too; and when we die ... it's a wild place, and very unsafe. And where are we really – there or here?' Speculative as it may sound, this view of the connection between the two countries takes on a strong imaginative reality in the second half of the book, as does the Platonic notion that the archetypal world of dreams and visions is somehow more real than the actual world relayed to us by our five senses. (In Plato's myth of the cave, our actual world is compared to shadows thrown by God, as the sun, from models not in our world; these models, or archetypes, are ideal forms, which Plato asserted as the reality behind our evanescent actuality.) Hazel's premonitory dream about Bigwig and the red-berries-wire has already suggested a connection between the two worlds. But we shall not be surprised to discover that it is Fiver who manages to integrate the two, first after the raid on Nuthanger Farm and finally in the midst of the defence of the burrow.

The instinctive group decision-making process does not take the place of individual thought and initiative, as we have already seen with Blackberry. Thus the expedition to the farm originates in a rabbit mood that comes over Hazel. He recruits Pipkin, the most dependent of the group, and leads him down, 'secure in his mood of gay confidence.' And the expedition is a success. Placing Pipkin at the door of the barn as look-out, Hazel finds two pairs of tame rabbits in a hutch. He tells them that a larger group will come to free them and then leaves as Pipkin spots a cat. They outwit it and run back to the down.

When Fiver hears what Hazel has done without telling anyone, he is angry. But Hazel carries on organizing the raid to free the hutch rabbits. Later Fiver tells Hazel that he has had a vision of him 'all alone, sharp and clear like a dead branch against the sky.' He asks Hazel not to go; Hazel is willing to compromise but only to the extent of not entering the farmyard. The others release the hutch rabbits and bring them out, but find them slow, timid, and easily confused. When the dog begins to bark, two of them freeze. Hazel, after the rendezvous in the lane, resolves to go back for them. While he is trying to move them, the farm family drives into the yard. The headlights of their car pick up Hazel, the farmer gets his gun and finally shoots Hazel while he is acting as a decoy to enable Dandelion to lead the other hutch doe to their companions. Wounded in the leg, Hazel crawls into a drain-pipe, 'a smooth, cold tunnel' and there passes 'into a dreaming, inert stupor ... After a time, a thread of blood began to trickle over the lip of the drain into the trampled, deserted ditch.' The others return with two does and one buck from the hutch. Hazel is presumed dead by all the rabbits, except Fiver.

Fiver's prescience is evident when the last three rabbits return from the raid. He knows without being told that Hazel is not with them. In the chapter titled 'Fiver Beyond,' Adams gives us Fiver's subsequent dream. He goes through the mist to the field where he first had a vision of the original burrow destroyed by man. There he finds a man 'looking down into a deep, narrow hole sunk in the ground at his feet. The man turned to Fiver with the kind of amiability that an ogre might show to a victim ... he will kill and eat as soon as it suits him.' In the 'foggy twilight' the man shows Fiver the memorial to Hazel he has put up on a notice-board. But he admits he can't find Hazel to hang him up; the rabbit has gone down the hole. Fiver comes to peer down into it. 'It was circular, a cylinder of baked earthenware that disappeared vertically into the ground. He called, "Hazel! Hazel!" Far down in the hole, something moved and he was about to call again. Then the man bent down and hit him between the ears.' Fiver is awakened from this dream in a 'cloud of earth' caused by some of the roof falling on him. But he knows what the dream has shown him. He tells Blackberry that Hazel is not dead and asks him to go down the hill to rescue Hazel. They come to the ditch, and Fiver peers into 'the dark opening' of the horizontal drain. He sees Hazel.

The process Fiver has been through is a traditional one, as Adams signals his reader by the epigraph to the chapter, quoted from Joseph Campbell's *The Hero with a Thousand Faces*: 'On his laborious journey ... after he has wandered through dark forests and over great ranges of mountains ... [the shaman] reaches an opening in the ground. The most difficult stages of the adventure now begin when the depths of the underworld ... open before him.'[10] Adams has in fact paraphrased the beginning of Campbell's translation of Harva, substituting 'dreadful' for Campbell's 'laborious' journey. This adjusted adjective is certainly more appropriate to Fiver's experience. Campbell also quotes Harva's description of the shaman's coming 'at last to the Lord of the Underworld,' in

Fiver's case the ogre-man who clubs him at the end of the dream. Campbell subsequently comments on the hero's 'perilous journey into the darkness by descending ... into the crooked lanes of his own spiritual labyrinth[;] he soon finds himself in a landscape of symbolical figures.'[11] Remembering Bigwig caught in the wire loop and Holly's tale of rabbits dying in terror from gas underground, we can understand that man makes an appropriate symbol of all that is powerful, cruel, and destructive to a rabbit. The ogre's clubbing Fiver is also parallel to the shaman's initiation, in which he usually must suffer a painful death during his vision. As another observer has reported in *The Hero with a Thousand Faces*, the shaman, after summoning spirits, is likely to collapse 'like a dead man.' His quest in the other world is like a death to this one. In Fiver's climactic quest during the later defence of the burrow, he will follow this part of the pattern even more obviously. Writing about quest tales from all over the world, Campbell provides a general pattern that can, as I suggested earlier, be applied to several of the episodes in *Watership Down* (see appendix).

Fiver's dream quest – along with Hazel's encounter with El-ahrairah at the end of the book – represents Adams's most complete integration of the archetypal and the actual world. A more common way is one we have already noted, how important he makes the tales of El-ahrairah to the experience of the rabbits who hear them. The tales function somewhat as the legend of the white seal does in *The Jungle Book*, in influencing the conduct of Kotick.

When Holly returns from his unsuccessful expedition to Efrafa, he tells how he and his companions suffered impressment in the regimented society of General Woundwort. Fortunately the dwellers in this warren – unlike those in Cowslip's – do tell stories about El-ahrairah, and while Holly is listening to 'The King's Lettuce' he gets the seed of an escape plan from an incident in which El-ahrairah masquerades as someone else. Holly pretends to be the bearer of a message from the general summoning a captain of the Owsla. Once the officer is gone, Holly leads his companions in a race for freedom. But they are pursued by the Owsla and escape only after they cross a train track and a locomotive comes through, cutting off the enemy. Holly believes that the train is a messenger sent by Frith to save them. Since none of these rabbits knows what a locomotive is, we can understand why Holly's primitive mind should take the fortuitous appearance of the engine as a sign from another world. Being civilized and not superstitious, we may be sceptical. But when we come to the climax of the actual raid on Efrafa, we will encounter a parallel situation, for which I believe Adams asks us as readers to suspend our disbelief.

Having established the rabbits on Watership Down and noted some of Adams's key concerns, I propose in the next chapter to probe more thoroughly the archetypal level of the book by discussing both the main test and the confirming test, focusing, that is, on the Efrafa expedition and the defence of the down burrow. In addition I shall be taking a close look at the most important of the inset tales, 'The Story of El-ahrairah and the Black Rabbit of Inlé,' as a foreshadowing prelude to Bigwig's entry into Efrafa. Then, turning to the ending, I shall consider Adams's resolution of the book's archetypal motifs and his use of the *deus ex machina*.

# 9

# Archetypal Integration

ARLY IN *Watership Down*, El-ahrairah is identified with Brer Rabbit, the folk-tale hero of black-slave culture. Although more heavily anthropomorphized than Seton's tales, the Uncle Remus stories contain a similar unsentimental social realism, and a similar distrust of the dominant human society, a realism and distrust of which Adams clearly approves. But *Watership Down* differs from both these precursors in the modern tradition of the animal tale. Comparison of a story about Brer Rabbit and one about El-ahrairah will indicate one important element that Adams adds. 'How Mr Rabbit Lost His Fine Bushy Tail' is one of the few tales that appear to have originated in Europe rather than Africa.[1] In it Brer Fox turns the tables on Brer Rabbit, tricking him into thinking that the best way to catch fish is to stick the long bushy tail that the rabbit possessed at that time into the creek and to wait until he has a fine catch of fish attached to it. Brer Rabbit leaves his tail in the creek all night, the water freezes around it, and when he tries to pull it out, it breaks off. Besides being an aetiological story explaining the origin of a supposed anomaly in nature, this homy and painful tale is close to being an animal fable, cautioning against the excesses of a greedy appetite. Its tone and intent are quite different from Adams's own aetiological tale, which we looked at in the last chapter.

'The Story of the Blessing of El-ahrairah' also explains how the rabbit came to have his unique features. And it puts the explanation in a realistic context: Frith insists on a balance of nature. If rabbits won't give up their voracious appetites and their exceptional fecundity, they must be kept from dominating the earth by the creation of enemies. This creation is, however, the result not of natural law but of a god at once just and merciful. Appreciating the rabbit's trickster nature, he does not punish El-ahrairah by depriving him of a tail. Rather he rewards him, blessing 'his bottom' so that the tail grows 'shining white and flashe[s] like a star' and his back legs grow 'long and powerful.' In other words, the tone of the story is positive, celebrating the rabbits' strong points rather than suggesting their imperfection as the Uncle Remus tale does.

In most of the Uncle Remus tales, Brer Rabbit is the trickster rather than the victim; as commentators have noted, he is amoral, and responsible for some quite mean tricks. El-ahrairah can be mean, too, as in his tricks on Rowsby Woof. But usually, as in his framing of the informer, Hufsa, he is merely repaying an injury done to his followers. Hazel is even more moral in his use of tricks to liberate does who want their freedom, or to cause the death of rabbits who insist on killing or enslaving his followers. As we shall discover in this chapter, part of a leader's role is to be willing to die for the welfare of his followers. Primitive though this morality may be, it is still far beyond the comprehension of the folk-tale trickster hero. In fact, as we have seen, Adams's realism is tempered by an implicit moralism, and his portrait of his heroes informed by an enlightened optimism. His portrait of rabbit culture includes both an anthropomorphic social structure and a mystical connection with another world.

In *Watership Down* death and the other world are contiguous. Fiver and El-ahrairah leave our world and experience death in the other. More realistically, Hazel and Bigwig come close to death and realize its connection with another world. But that world is not a land of heart's desire. Fiver calls the archetypal world 'a wild place, and very unsafe.' In chapter 8, we looked at Fiver's prophetic vision about an ogre who wants to find Hazel to finish him off. We also noted Hazel's symbolic prophetic dream of Bigwig near death. Bigwig's own contact with the archetypal is not so numinous, for awe and reverence for the divine are not usually part of his make-up. Yet he does have a strong connection with the Black Rabbit, who not only brings death to rabbits but, Adams later claimed, is identical with El-ahrairah. Adams also hinted that the story of the Black Rabbit is close to being numinous.[2] In any case, Bigwig does have an actual brush with death, in the wire noose, just as Hazel does in the drain-pipe and Fiver does in his shaman's way, especially in his trance during the defence of the burrow.

Although the expedition to Efrafa is presented from Hazel's point of view, when Bigwig goes into that burrow alone the point of view shifts to him, effectively registering his efforts and anxiety. A large and powerful rabbit, Bigwig has always used his physical strength to meet any difficulty that appeared. But his experiences since leaving the original home burrow have pushed him toward broader and deeper views. He has seen a much less powerful rabbit, Hazel, become the leader of their small group instead of himself, a former member of the Owsla, the burrow constabulary. As second in command he has thus learned to trust Hazel's judgment and to modify his own over-quick, rough-and-ready response to situations. Finally, he has been caught in a wire noose, which only choked him the more when he used his strength against it. In his weakness after that experience, Bigwig finds himself 'driven to moderation and prudence.'

On the night they found Holly, Bigwig had shown a quite unexpected side of himself. In strange territory, a small group of the rabbits heard an 'unnatural ... wailing or crying.' When one suggested it might be a cat, Bigwig disagreed, insisting it was the Black Rabbit of Inlé. In rabbit folklore, this creature comes for them at death. When the voice cried out Bigwig's name, he moved toward it, 'his eyes set in a fixed, glazed stare.' All the rest were frozen with fear, but Hazel recovered in time to challenge the voice and discover that it came from Holly. This second brush with death has again tempered Bigwig, preparing him for his climactic rendez-vous in Efrafa. It also helps explain the tale he demands to be told before he leaves the others to go there.

On the trek to Efrafa, Bigwig is abstracted. This introversion in a character who was so extroverted indicates not only the change that experience has forced on Bigwig, but his gathering of inner resources for the dangerous mission ahead. As they stop for a rest near Efrafa, Dandelion tells them a tale, and then Pipkin spots a fox. Unexpectedly, Bigwig rushes out to decoy their enemy off. When he returns, Hazel is angry at him for risking himself; since Hazel has a lame leg, Bigwig is the key person in the plan to get does. After Bigwig admits that he had to let off tension, Hazel comments that he was 'Playing El-ahrairah.' Hazel is right, and because Bigwig was following his model, his action also has beneficial consequences outside himself, as we shall see later.

But Bigwig made a more important decision shortly before the fox episode. When the others were suggesting different stories they would like to hear, Bigwig demanded, 'El-ahrairah and the Black Rabbit of Inlé.' Hazel tried to veto this frightening and depressing story of El-ahrairah's expedition to the realm of death, believing it inappropriate for a group of rabbits who were themselves entering strange and dangerous territory. Fortunately, he was unsuccessful, for it is exactly the story Bigwig, with his new introspective ability, needs. Like El-ahrairah, he is going to face death, but if he can call on his hero's steadfastness he may, like El-ahrairah, emerge with the boon he entered to obtain.

'El-ahrairah and the Black Rabbit of Inlé' is the most powerful of the five inset tales in *Watership Down*. The other four are filled with humour, but this one is appropriately serious, containing emotional and philosophic depth. At the opening of the tale, El-ahrairah and his people are under siege by a powerful enemy. Food grows so short that El-ahrairah realizes he must take desperate measures. He decides to go to the Black Rabbit, the one creature he can ask that has the power to overcome the enemy. As first described the Black Rabbit is 'fear and everlasting darkness.' As subsequently portrayed he is clearly death as an impersonal force. El-ahrairah realizes he can offer the Black Rabbit only his life but decides he is willing to make this sacrifice. It is a 'dark journey' like a 'bad dream,' through mist between dark cliffs to 'a tunnel like a huge rabbit hole. In the freezing cold and silence' El-ahrairah makes out the Black Rabbit, 'cold as the stone.' When El-ahrairah offers his life, the Black Rabbit tells him he gets such offers every day but that he does not make bargains.

He treats El-ahrairah as a guest, however, and for entertainment suggests they gamble. When El-ahrairah names his people's safety as the stakes' the Black Rabbit agrees. But El-ahrairah's wits desert him and he loses. According to the agreement, El-ahrairah must give up his tail and whiskers. Next they have a story-telling contest, but the Black Rabbit's tale is so freezing that El-ahrairah can't even remember a tale. This time he loses his ears. All this while the Black Rabbit has been assuring El-ahrairah that he bears him no enmity and reminding him that he is free to leave at any time. Now El-ahrairah asks himself why the Black Rabbit is acting thus, especially why he waits before hurting El-ahrairah 'till he himself proposed a wager and lost it? The answer came to him suddenly. These shadows had no power either to send him away or to hurt him, except with his own consent.' This insight frees El-ahrairah to act, and indicates to the reader that the Black Rabbit really is fear, in one sense a subjective state that when faced will cease to impede decisive action.

No longer governed by fear of death, El-ahrairah immediately encounters his opportunity. He meets two shadowy Owsla, who are tending pits filled with diseases for the use of the Black Rabbit. El-ahrairah jumps in one pit to catch the disease so he can take it to his enemies. But on the way out he is stopped by the Black Rabbit, who reveals that this disease can be transmitted only by the fleas in a rabbit's ears, ears that El-ahrairah no longer has. At this news, El-ahrairah collapses. But the Black Rabbit, praising the courage, saves El-ahrairah's followers.

One of the Black Rabbit's Owsla refers to his master as Inlé-rah. According to the glossary Adams provided for the hardcover edition of his book, *rah* means 'prince' or 'leader,' while *Inlé* carries the primary meaning of 'moon,' but the secondary one of 'darkness, fear and death.' It is this second meaning that is most obviously appropriate to the Black Rabbit. When we remember that Frith is the sun, and that the Black Rabbit serves him, we can see how on the one hand darkness is the absence of sun, while on the other hand the moon is a cold reflection of the warm sun. Like the moon, then, the Black Rabbit is only a reflection of the fear in any rabbit. Because El-ahrairah has successfully entered and then emerged from his dark domain, it is appropriate that Frith should provide the rabbit hero with replacements for the parts he lost, including 'a little starlight' in the ears. All three beings belong to the archetypal world. Frith as sun is most creative; the Black Rabbit as darkness or moon is also powerful but subject to the sun; and El-ahrairah has earned his weaker eternal light, his immortality, through tales that give heart and wit to countless rabbits long after he has left behind the changing seasons of earth.

El-ahrairah as trickster draws his energy from what Jung calls the shadow, the normally repressed side of each individual. But in this tale he meets the archetypal shadow itself, the Black Rabbit. His self-scrutiny in that encounter tells him that fear of death – the ultimate shadow – undermines life. As much as his early encounter with Frith – the sun as creative life principle – this encounter with death tests the spirit of El-ahrairah and confirms his right to the trickster role he has made his way of life. It also ensures that release of tremendous energy that comes from facing that deepest fear that ordinary creatures spend so much of their life force trying to keep down, defending themselves against. That energy will be in evidence when Hazel meets El-ahrairah at the end of the book, and when Bigwig leads the does to freedom from Efrafa.

Like El-ahrairah, Bigwig is risking his life for the survival of his people. Also like El-ahrairah, he will face a super-rabbit, Woundwort, whose power and authority seem more than leporine, but who will accept him and offer him honour and position commensurate with his worth. Finally like El-ahrairah, Bigwig will almost lose his wits from fear in Woundwort's domain, but will maintain his courage, find tricks to make good his theft, and then will have tested his willingness to give up his life to ensure success. The differences are also noticeable. Woundwort does not do Frith's bidding impersonally as the Black Rabbit does; the contest between him and Bigwig is not open until the end; and when he confronts Bigwig over the theft of the does, he swears death instead of offering a reward for Bigwig's courage. Yet by the end of the book, Woundwort will have achieved a status very like the Black Rabbit's in rabbit folklore.

Up to the Efrafa episode, Hazel is the leader, the El-ahrairah of his group. But as Bigwig starts on his lonely quest, Hazel passes on that position to him: 'May El-ahrairah go with you. And remember you're the leader now.' Bigwig will be responsible not only for the tactics of finding and freeing the does, but for the strategy that will coordinate their escape with the help of his followers. Fortunately, he knows that under Woundwort's regimentation there is dissatisfaction in Efrafa, especially among the does, whose natural functions are distorted by the compressed living conditions. The other circumstance in his favour he does not know: the great need in Woundwort's Owsla for officers with Bigwig's qualities.

Surprisingly, this need can be traced to the rabbits from the down. The captain whom Holly tricked so he could escape has been demoted; the captain who led the pursuit of Holly was killed by the train that cut off his followers from the down rabbits; and most recently the captain of an Efrafa patrol was killed by a fox. This fox is the same one that Bigwig decoyed into the woods. Coming upon the patrol, Bigwig had warned them of the fox's pursuit, but when their captain tried to detail Bigwig, Bigwig had to knock him down, thus leaving him as prey for the following fox. The tricks of the down rabbits have thus earned them the good fortune that will give Bigwig a place and room to manoeuvre when he arrives in Efrafa.

Brought before Woundwort, he boldly states that he has heard of Efrafa and come to join the warren. He says truthfully that he has been an officer in the Owsla of a warren destroyed by men. His size and bravery help convince Woundwort, who decides to put him on trial in the Owsla under a Captain Chervil. Bigwig finds life in the burrow strictly regulated; eating, digging, and even eliminating are scheduled among the groups called Marks to which each rabbit belongs. The unnaturalness of the life is epitomized by Holly's comment that 'rabbits in Efrafa quite often go days at a time without the sight of Frith.' For rabbits to be deprived of the sun that is their lord bodes ill for the warren.

Assigned to his Mark, Bigwig meets a mutilated rabbit called Blackavar, who is under guard, kept as an example of those who rebel – he had tried to run away and been caught. Bigwig is also told of a group of dissident does, who had asked to be allowed to emigrate, and were dispersed to different Marks for their temerity. Chervil asks Bigwig to keep an eye on two of these does sent to his Mark. Bigwig complies by talking to one named Hyzenthlay. Finding her sensible, he reveals his plan to her, telling her that his 'friends have prepared a trick that El-ahrairah himself would be proud of.' But after gaining Hyzenthlay as an ally, who will initiate the process of selecting does that wish to leave, Bigwig has an anxiety dream of Woundwort looming huge and aware of his plans.

Adams matches the rhythm of Bigwig's suspense and its final release in the action of the escape, with the development of a natural phenomenon. The key chapters have titles that indicate the pattern: first 'Approaching Thunder,' then 'The Thunder Builds Up,' and finally, 'The Thunder Breaks.' In the middle chapter, Bigwig prays to El-ahrairah, 'O Lord with the starlight ears, send me a sign!' Out of 'the thundery twilight' comes Blackavar under guard. Presumably this sequence causes Bigwig to decide to include Blackavar in the escape. In any event, as they begin to flee he thinks that 'the storm was his own. The storm would defeat Efrafa.' Then, when Woundwort catches up with his group, Bigwig invokes a higher power: '"Frith sees you! ... May Frith blast you and your foul Owsla full of bullies!" At that instant a dazzling claw of lightning streaked down the length of the sky.' The connection between the desire for a blast and the descent of lightning is clear enough; the fact that it is a *claw* of lightning suggests a connection with Frith, who, besides being a sun-god is imaged as a rabbit. As the rain falls 'like a waterfall,' stupefying the rabbits, 'a small voice' speaks in Bigwig's mind. 'Your storm, Thlayli-rah. Use it.' *Thlayli* is lapine for 'Bigwig.' *Rah*, as already indicated, means 'leader.' What he hears might be an echo of Hazel's voice making Bigwig leader, or of that of El-ahrairah, to whom he prayed, or that of Frith, who has answered his plea. It is certainly also his own voice, since he has earlier thought, 'the storm was his own.'

Bigwig activates his followers. Woundwort also recovers, and is about to fight Bigwig when Keehar appears. The gull's attack confuses the enemy long enough for the does to be led to the river by Bigwig and the other down rabbits. There they play what Bigwig calls their 'magic trick' to complete the escape. They all board a small boat, Hazel gnaws through its restraining rope, and they glide downtream away from the amazed Efrafans.

Bigwig emerges from the episode with respect for Woundwort as a leader; Adams still emphasizes Woundwort's similarity to the Black Rabbit by speaking of 'how much fear Woundwort could inspire.' Like his all-knowing avatar, Woundwort lives in darkness, but unlike him he has no respect for the sun. Earlier, he has sworn on hearing of Bigwig's escape, 'Embleer Frith, I'll *blind* him when I catch him.' Putting Bigwig in permanent darkness would suit Woundwort's role; it would be a personal punishing rather than an impersonal necessity. Equally indicative is his expletive; *embleer* is lapine for 'stinking.' His swearing in this blasphemous manner is in contrast to Bigwig's 'Frith sees you.' The contrast is again of the natural against the degraded or unnatural.

With the reuniting of the down group, the point of view reverts to Hazel.

The boat the rabbits are on carries them under one bridge and lodges them athwart another. Hazel's experience with both bridges is parallel to his brush with death in the drain-pipe. In fact, before going under the second bridge, Hazel recalls the drain-pipe experience. The passage under this bridge is longer than the first, and Hazel must swim through it. But he goes into the cold dark through the passage to light and lands below the bridge. In a re-enactment of his and Fiver's earlier descent down a dark tunnel, all the rabbits on the boat must follow him. This plunging once again into the unknown is a validation of their heroic escape from Efrafa and confirmation of the special status conferred on them by the powerful forces invoked and involved in that escape. As formulated by Campbell in *The Hero with a Thousand Faces*, each has 'been swallowed and reborn. Having died to his personal ego,' he rises again 'established in the Self.'[3] Following this rite of passage from a common state to an exalted one, the rabbits must now 'return to the normal world' where they 'will be as good as reborn.' In passing this main test, the survivors are not, however, home free. They experience violence on the way back to the down. And once there they will still have to face Woundwort and a large patrol that has tracked them. The ensuing battle will be the third or confirming test, a consequence of the 'bridal theft,' which Campbell cites as one goal of the quest.

Just as the raid on Efrafa was introduced by the tale of El-ahrairah and the Black Rabbit of Inlé, so the defence of the warren on Watership Down is introduced by 'The Story of Rowsby Woof and the Fairy Wogdog.' Both inset tales feature El-ahrairah as trickster. Although the episodes that follow both represent dangerous tests of the down rabbits' ability to survive, the introductory tales are as different as they could well be. In the first El-ahrairah is paralysed with fear in a cold dark realm of death. In the second he is in complete control in a farmyard. In the first his opponent is worthy, more than a match for him. In the second his opponent is the foolish guard dog of the farm, a creature unworthy of his great abilities. These differences are mitigated by the contrast in tone between the two tales. The first has a serious tone and operates at an epic, almost tragic, level. The second has a light tone, and operates at a comic, almost farcical, level. We can thus understand that Adams's intent must be wholly different. The broad humour of the Rowsby Woof tale relaxes the tension built up again when the returning heroes are spotted by one of Woundwort's patrols; this tension will rise even higher during the defence of the warren. The tale also introduces a basic situation that is repeated in the episode that follows it. Just as El-ahrairah tricks Rowsby Woof, so Hazel will lure the farm dog into following a rabbit to the down. Another parallel is that human beings play a part in each tale. A final point of connection is that Fiver uses a quotation from the tale at a crucial point in the defence.

Warned by the mouse of the approach of Woundwort's strong patrol, the down rabbits have time to prepare their warren for attack, and Hazel has the opportunity to try to work out a peaceful settlement with Woundwort. He presents a strong case for setting up a new warren between the down and Efrafa, one that could take the overflow of Woundwort's crowded warren. Adams's report of the reaction of Woundwort, and the descriptive details in which he places it, are both highly revealing. 'At that moment, in the sunset on Watership Down, there was offered to General Woundwort the opportunity to show whether he was really the leader of vision and genius which he believed himself to be, or whether he was no more than a tyrant with the courage and cunning of a pirate. For one beat of his pulse the lame rabbit's idea shone clearly before him. He grasped it and realized what it meant. The next, he had pushed it away from him. The sun dipped into the cloud-bank and now he could see clearly the track along the ridge, leading to the beech hanger [the burrow] and the bloodshed for which he had prepared with so much energy and care.' Like Cowslip and the corrupted members of his warren, Woundwort has cut himself off from the sun. But whereas the rabbits of that warren have chosen to live with death inflicted on them, Woundwort's distortion is a fixation on inflicting death himself.

Aware how slim are their chances, the down rabbits yet prepare to defend the warren. Hazel tries to think of some trick to overcome the numbers and experience of the enemy. Fiver moves in his own inner direction. '"There's something I'm trying to hear … I'm going away, Hazel – going away." His voice grew slow and drowsy. "Falling. But it's cold. Cold." … Suddenly a terrible sound broke from Fiver; a sound at which every rabbit in the warren leapt in dreadful fear; a sound that no rabbit had ever made, that no rabbit had the power to make. It was deep and utterly unnatural … "Dirty little beasts," yelped Fiver. "How – how dare you? Get out – out! Out – out!"' Fiver is repeating the very words, and the sound of barking, that the dog, Rowsby Woof, used to frighten El-ahrairah out of his owner's vegetable garden. The sound frightens Fiver's companions, except for Hazel, to whom it recalls the 'yelping' of another dog at the beginning of their quest when they were by the stream. Suddenly Hazel sees the trick he can play. He puts Bigwig in charge and tells him, 'El-ahrairah has shown me what to do.' He takes two companions down to the farm from which they had rescued the hutch rabbits; there they will decoy the guard dog up the hill after Hazel has gnawed through its restraining rope.

He is successful, but falls off the doghouse and is pounced on by the farm cat.

Despite their fear of Keehar, whom the Efrafans do not know has migrated, the attacking rabbits dig into the main burrow, only to find it empty except for a small dead rabbit, who is in fact Fiver in his cold trance-state. The down rabbits have dug themselves into narrower tunnels. As the attackers start to work on one of the stopped-up passages, Bigwig sees how to compensate for Woundwort's superior size and strength. He digs himself in below the level of the passage through which his opponent will come. The trick works; as Woundwort plunges through the gap, Bigwig starts up from beneath him, sinking his teeth in one foreleg, seriously weakening it. Woundwort is so shaken by his subsequent inability to move Bigwig that he tries to bribe him into betraying the warren. The offer refused, Woundwort moves back and tries to get one of his subordinates to take on Bigwig. His retreat undermines the *esprit* of the attackers.

Suddenly, in the large burrow, Woundwort comes face to face with a small strange rabbit, 'wide-eyed as a kitten above ground for the first time.' It is Five, reborn from his shaman's trance. Woundwort sends one of his chief subordinates, Vervain, to kill this weak enemy, but Fiver's words demoralize him. Fiver apologizes for having to destroy the attackers. This unexpected attitude completely undoes Vervain, to whom Fiver seems a messenger from the Black Rabbit. Vervain retreats and comes outside just in time to witness the arrival of the farm dog. All the attacking rabbits bolt except Woundwort, who meets it head-on.

Meanwhile, Hazel has been rescued from the cat by Lucy, the farmer's daughter. When the doctor visits the family, she shows Hazel to him. The doctor offers to free him well away from the farm; Lucy rides in his car with him, and they both then watch Hazel run off toward the down. He returns to the warren to find the trick has worked, and the remaining Efrafans, led by Captain Campion, have departed, all but five who have surrendered and are 'allowed to join the warren' following Hazel's customary desire for integration. His offer to General Woundwort will also come about; Campion will agree to the starting of warrens between the down and Efrafa. In this way Adams provides an effective closure for his social integration theme. The rounding off of the archetypal theme is even more pronounced.

Like the shaman, Fiver has journeyed to that other country and returned, has to outward appearance died and been reborn. From there he has contributed the seed from a tale that precipitates in Hazel's mind the El-ahrairah trick that finally saves them. But before that, Fiver himself returns and offers the enlarged perspective of the other world to Vervain. His asking for pardon instead of mercy has the paradoxical effect of filling Vervain's mind with the kind of fear that is usually brought on by thoughts of the Black Rabbit. The other significant contributor to victory is Bigwig. But even his physical triumph over Woundwort has both moral and archetypal elements. The dialogue in which Bigwig refuses to betray his companions is placed in counterpoint to a tale Dandelion is telling the others to keep up their spirits. At one point it is as though the tale both speaks for Bigwig and prophesies deliverance.

[Woundwort:] 'You yourself can stop this nonsense whenever you wish.' [Dandelion:] '"No," replied El-ahrairah, "it is not fat rabbits that I see in the water, but swift hounds on the scent and my enemy flying for his life."'

The integration of the actual and the archetypal could hardly be more pronounced.

After Woundwort is presumably killed by the dog, his character begins that movement from the actual to the legendary that is an important strand in the book's ending. One day the down rabbits are discussing him when one of the former Efrafans insists Woundwort is not dead. Later we are told that his body was never found and that 'there endured the legend that somewhere, out over the Down, there lived a great and solitary rabbit, a giant who drove the elil like mice and sometimes went to silflay in the sky. If ever great danger arose, he would come back to fight for those who honoured his name. And mother rabbits would tell their kittens that if they did not do as they were told, the General would get them – the General who was first cousin to the Black Rabbit himself.' The final comparison provides effective closure for the pairing of 'The Story of El-ahrairah and the Black Rabbit of Inlé' with the raid on Efrafa in which Bigwig was El-ahrairah and Woundwort the Black Rabbit.

The same process of converting history into legend is indicated for Hazel, Fiver, and Cowslip. We hear a doe telling her litter a tale that mixes details from various incidents in the rabbits' adventures. As Hazel says, 'I seem to know this story ... but I can't remember where I've heard it.' Twice earlier a down rabbit had commented what a fine tale a particular adventure would make. But the assimilation of the actual experience to the existing archetypal figures suggests that it is less the details that matter than the form, which is epic, and the intent, which is heroic. Such tales keep the rabbits' spirit strong.

But the reality of these archetypes extends beyond the figurative power of legend and myth. In the epilogue, Adams shows us exactly how Hazel lived happily ever after. One day years later, the elderly Hazel is approached by another rabbit whom he at first does not recognize. Then he notes that the stranger's ears have a silver shine – the starlight with which the Black Rabbit honored El-ahrairah. This stranger offers Hazel a place in his Owsla. Hazel accepts and discovers that he will not be needing his body 'so he left it lying on the edge of the ditch, but stopped for a moment to watch his rabbits and to try to get used to the extraordinary feeling that strength and speed were flowing inexhaustibly out of him into their sleek young bodies.' Hazel has made good his attempt to live like El-ahrairah. Clearly the prayers to their hero and to Frith can be efficacious in more than a psychological sense. As spirit Hazel is able to infuse his strength into those who are still only physically alive.

In conclusion, I would like to note how Adams's boldness extends to a scene that I passed quickly by earlier. This is the episode in which Hazel is caught by the cat and released by human beings. The first thing to note is what the doctor says when Hazel is set free. 'He could perfectly well live for years ... Born and bred in a briar patch, Brer Fox.' Like Adams earlier in the book, the doctor is alluding to Uncle Remus, in particular to the tale in which Brer Rabbit tricks Brer Fox into throwing him into a briar patch. Hazel also has been set down where he is at home.

The second point is that this chapter is titled 'Dea ex Machina.' In rescuing Hazel from the cat, Lucy acted as the god who, in Greek tragedy, was lowered by crane to settle a human predicament beyond the power of the participants to resolve. Since Aristotle criticizes this device as violating the integrity of the drama, we might note that this episode is not essential for resolving the plot. It would have been much more economical simply to allow Hazel to escape on his own or even to let him be killed by the cat. As I see it, Adams had three reasons for structuring it as he did.

First, it allows Hazel to return with the tall tale of riding in a car, which adds to his legendary stature. Second, it is a sign of the story's originally having been told to Adams's daughters, who would have been pleased to hear of another girl who actually got to save, handle, and then release the protagonist. We know from Adams's own statements about the book that such a consideration did influence his handling of another character. 'My daughters did not want Bigwig to die.' The other reasons he gives can also be applied to Hazel. 'It would have been right artistically,' to allow Bigwig to die, 'but I could not bring myself to do it, or face up to depicting the grief of the other rabbits. Nor did I really want to attempt that most difficult of feats, a muted, half-happy ending.'[4] When Hazel finally dies, it is, as we have seen, to move to a higher plane. It is also in the epilogue, after he – like Wilbur – has lived a long life and there are apparently no friends around to mourn.

Third, this episode with the human beings allows Adams to signal his own presence as a *deus ex machina* in the book. He hints at it in the chapter title, but, as I see it, makes it quite clear in the name he gives his physician, Dr Adams. He thereby telegraphs to the alert reader his own presence in the tale as manipulator of the plot (letting Hazel go), as the latest redactor in a tradition of trickster folk-tales ('Born and bred in a briar patch'), as the trickster himself (El-ahrairah also masqueraded as a doctor in 'The King's Lettuce'), and as contemporary shaper of an epic tradition. In my opinion Adams has demonstrated his right to an honourable place in that tradition.

Old-fashioned in its adaptation of epic conventions and leisurely style, *Watership Down* also provides plenty of action and suspense, character development and humour, with incidents both various and compelling. Adams's serious purpose emerges indirectly as a contrast to the sterile sophistication of Cowslip's warren. Having lost touch with their roots, these rabbits take El-ahrairah as mythical in the derogatory sense, and can see 'traditional stories' about him as possessing only a devitalized 'charm.' Adams has put his artistry, imagination, and commitment on the line by including a covert criticism of what he is doing in the work itself. His assurance is borne out by the success not only of the main narrative but of the inset folk-tales, legends, and myths that give depth and breadth to his rabbit world. It is a world that invites the child to enter and offers not just escape and adventure, but a sense of how nature might appear to lesser creatures. By encouraging the reader to identify with its animal protagonists, the book suggests how we might cease subordinating their lives to our convenience, greed, or need for domination. *Watership Down* also suggests that there are dimensions of determination and vision as yet untapped within us all. It offers such challenges seriously and dramatically to the young reader in a supportive context that includes death and suffering but affirms life and endurance.

# 10

# Crossing the Border

ITUAL, MYTH, AND FAIRY-TALE
share a concern with the possibility of contact with a world beyond our everyday one. Developing out of an oral culture in which they helped integrate the community, they have in common a structure that emphasizes the importance of boundary crossing, a difficult movement out of this world into the other, and a consequent influx of power back into this world on the return. Many of the narratives we have been looking at contain this pattern. For instance, in *Ozma of Oz*, Dorothy crossed a number of borders: over water to land, into the underworld kingdom, out again by the power of magic, across the deadly desert to Oz, and finally back to our world. Her descent into the underworld is, of course, the most important crossing. From the Nome King's inner palace, Billina and she bring back to the upper world the Queen of Ev; her son, the heir apparent; and her nine other children – a large number suggestive of great potential vitality reclaimed.

We first met the movement into darkness when we were told of the Bandar-Log walking down Kaa's throat, and of the plunge of the White Seal into the dark tunnel under the cliff. We have since encountered it in the descent to the bottom of the pond of the mouse and his child, and in Fiver and Hazel's descent of the underground pipe. We saw it more literally, in El-ahrairah's going down into the burrow of the Black Rabbit, and Bigwig's descent into the prison of Efrafa. Similarly we shall soon accompany the hobbit, Bilbo Baggins, when he goes alone down to the very heart of two mountains to encounter first his shadow, Gollum, and finally a dragon guarding the treasure that is the objective of his quest.

Like Baum, Tolkien kept his audience in mind during the writing of *The Hobbit*, so that the tone is more child oriented than the juxtapositions of

White, the complications of Hoban, or the epic style of Adams. But even more than in the Oz books, beneath the sometimes paternal, sometimes didactic, sometimes folksy style of *The Hobbit* lies an archetypal world. Again like Baum, Tolkien has set his book in its own fantasy world, separated from ours as much by time as by space. Most of the inhabitants are familiar to us; it takes place in a world derived from northern European, pre-Christian folklore, saga, and myth. It is a world of pagan violence, of blood feuds, Viking raids, and heroic honour. *The Hobbit* has no female characters, though one is mentioned at the beginning, Belladonna Took. But she is an ancestor of Bilbo Baggins, representing a streak of adventure in the otherwise comfortable conformism of the Bagginses.

Critics have compensated for this omission by finding female symbols in the book: the ring, the barrels in the water, the various tunnels, the spiders, and even Gollum. Indeed, more has been written about *The Hobbit* than about any of the other books I have discussed. Three studies are based on an archetypal approach, all more or less helpful, and I shall be referring to them later in the chapter. It has been noted, for instance, that when Gandolf comes to Bilbo with the call to adventure Tolkien speaks of the Baggins side of him, which resists the call, and the Took side, which is attracted by it. The Bagginses are down-to-earth types who like creature comfort, while one of the Took ancestors is said to have married a fairy. This side of Bilbo responds to the magic and adventure that Gandolf brought to the Tooks.

It has also been noted that, as wizard, Gandolf is one of Jung's archetypes, the wise old man, a guide or helper with superior knowledge of the spirit. As developed by Jung in his essay on fairy-tales, the wise old man appears to the hero early in the tale to induce 'self-reflection' and the mobilizing of 'the moral forces.' The 'intervention of the old man ... would seem to be ... indispensable, since the conscious will by itself is hardly ever capable of uniting the personality.'[1] Thus we may see Gandolf's actions as aimed at breaking up the comfortable Baggins consciousness in which Bilbo has settled, stirring up the Took side and moving him across the border toward confrontation with his shadow. But Gandolf as he first appears is far from being a heavy figure of wisdom. He has a light touch and is something of a trickster, as in fact are many of the figures Bilbo encounters.

These figures all have human outlines but are technically creatures: dwarves, elves, goblins, trolls, hobbits. The latter are, of course, Tolkien's own contribution to the folklore figures he chose to work with. More human than the other creatures, each hobbit lives in a well-furnished 'hole in the ground' or 'tunnel' with a door, a stove, dishes, and lots of good food in the larder. Essentially, they are like solid, conservative farmers.

To shake Bilbo out of this dullness, Gandolf makes a direct request that the hobbit accompany him on an adventure. Through an indirect verbal chivvying, the wizard gets the hobbit enough off balance so that, although Bilbo refuses the request, he does blurt out an invitation to tea the following day. Before leaving the vicinity, Gandolf as trickster laughs and scratches a sign on Bilbo's door. As a result, before Gandolf returns the next day, Bilbo must accommodate first one, then another dwarf, then two, then five dwarves, and finally four more accompanied by Gandolf. The dwarves proceed to upset Bilbo by eating all his precious provisions. While they are washing the dishes they then tease him by singing a song of destruction.

> Chip the glasses and crack the plates!
> Blunt the knives and bend the forks!
> That's what Bilbo Baggins hates –
> Smash the bottles and burn the corks![2]

They are, in fact, careful, but the song shows they know their hobbit; the teasing I take as a sign of their tricky nature. To repay Bilbo after, their leader, Thorin, plays on his harp and sweeps Bilbo 'away into dark lands under strange moons, far over The Water.' This music and the serious song the dwarves then sing constitute Bilbo's call to adventure; the song causes 'something Tookish' to wake in him. But the Baggins side of him quickly reasserts itself. He gets up, intending to hide.

Suddenly he found that the music and the singing had stopped, and they were looking at him with eyes shining in the dark.

'Where are you going?' said Thorin, in a tone that seemed to show that he guessed both halves of the hobbit's mind.

'What about a little light?' said Bilbo apologetically.

'We like dark,' said all the dwarves. 'Dark for dark business! There are many hours before dawn.'

The dwarves had sung of 'caverns deep' and their quest is to a treasure cave. But equally they bring to Bilbo the opportunity to explore the shadow side of his own nature. Specifically the dark business they want to discuss is stealing the treasure, a business in which Bilbo's role will be that of the thief. Despite fear and misgivings, Bilbo accepts. The dwarves for their part also accept him reluctantly, not being impressed with his appearance or reactions. Gandolf, who has brought the two together, reminds the dwarves that they are thirteen, an unlucky number, and Bilbo is the best fourteenth he could find. (Gandolf will accompany them only through the first half of their adventure.) He produces a map and key to aid in the quest.

The next morning as they are leaving, Bilbo is so rushed he finds himself 'pushing his keys into Gandolf's hand.' He has a long way to go before he becomes a burglar, and keys will provide one means of judging his progress. His first test comes in camp that night when they spot a light. The dwarves insist that their burglar go reconnoitre; Bilbo discovers three huge trolls, sneaks close, and feels impelled to steal something. He gets a purse without being noticed. Unfortunately it is a magic purse, which cries out in alarm. Bilbo is caught and so are the dwarves, each stuffed in a bag. Only Gandolf stays clear, and plays ventriloquist to keep the trolls arguing until sunrise, at which time they are turned to stone. Although Bilbo has failed as a burglar on this first try, he redeems himself by finding and producing the key to the trolls' cave. On entering it, the group crosses its first overt boundary and finds elvish swords for Gandolf and Thorin, and a troll knife, which serves Bilbo as a sword.

The appetite theme that we have encountered so often in stories for younger children is quite evident in the first two chapters of *The Hobbit*. The first is titled 'An Unexpected Party,' Bilbo's for the dwarves. The second is titled 'Roast Mutton' and refers to the meal just finished by the trolls. But it should alert the reader to that other theme, which we have often encountered as a consequence of appetite – the danger of being eaten. The trolls complain that they have been too long without a 'bit of manflesh.' The first thing they think of when they see Bilbo is that he is edible. They mis-hear his species as 'rabbit,' the first of several times that he will be mistaken for that small edible animal. The appetite theme in all its violence will reappear next when the expedition encounters the goblins.

In chapter 3, Gandolf takes the party to Rivendell and its friendly elves. They are greeted by hidden voices singing a teasing song, very like the one the dwarves sang for Bilbo. The elves also make joking insults at Thorin and at Bilbo: 'Mind Bilbo doesn't eat all the cakes! ... He is too fat to get through key-holes yet!' This joke indicates that they know Bilbo's role as burglar, and realize that it conflicts with his hobbit love of ease and rich food. The image of getting through keyholes is nicely humorous, substituting the person for one of the tools of his trade. It is all the more appropriate since Bilbo's one act of successful burglary has been to supply the key to the troll cave. We will see Bilbo frequently as the expert in covert entry and exit. On Midsummer Eve Elrond, their host, is able to read some magical rune 'moon-letters' on the map: 'Stand by the grey stone when the thrush knocks ... and the setting sun with the last light of Durin's Day will shine upon the key-hole.' From the last two words we may anticipate that Bilbo will play an important part in this event, as yet far in the future.

In chapter 4, the expedition takes shelter from a storm in a cave. When they fall asleep, Bilbo dreams that the back of the cave opens, and wakes to find that it's true. He yells and out pour enough goblins to overpower him and all the dwarves. The yell has, however, given Gandolf time to make himself invisible. As the goblins march their captives down inside the mountain, they sing a third teasing song, but this one is much less playful than those sung by the dwarves and elves. It promises violence to the captives. In fact we are told that 'goblins eat horses and ponies' of which the expedition had a number, but also 'other much more dreadful things,' and that 'they are always hungry.' This ferocious appetite manifests itself when the dwarves are brought in front of the Great Goblin. He has a violent reaction to Thorin's elvish sword, which was made to kill goblins: '"Murderers and elf-friends!" the Great Goblin shouted. "Slash them! Beat them! Bite them! Gnash them! Take them away to dark holes full of snakes, and never let them see the light again!" He was in such a rage that he jumped off his seat and himself rushed at Thorin with his mouth open.' Thorin is in danger of becoming a victim if not a meal. In fact, the dwarves' introduction of Bilbo to the dark seems about to become final. The dark may hide treasure, but it also contains death. The traveller cannot find one without facing the other. Fortunately, Gandolf chooses this moment to let loose his magic. The goblin lights go out, and sparks fly, burning the goblins. Gandolf's sword pierces the Great Goblin, and the invisible wizard leads his band out. Their flight carries them 'down in the very mountain's heart.' The goblins pursue and are beaten back; Bilbo falls and is knocked unconscious.

Just as Bilbo was asleep and dreaming immediately before entering the underground kingdom of the goblins, so he wakes from unconsciousness to enter the even darker and deeper underground domain of Gollum. This double connection of the inner and outer dark suggests that Bilbo has crossed these borders in order to encounter the night side of himself, the voracious animal appetite of the goblins being the uncivilized side of his own hobbit love of good food. Now at the heart of this dark world he has entered, he is about to come face to face with his own shadow, another cannibal. This shadow is a trickster, as shown by its animal, almost amoral nature. It has a prize worth winning, though the cost of losing the struggle for the prize will, of course, be death.

Early in chapter 5, 'Riddles in the Dark,' Tolkien provides a poetic, archetypal description of Gollum: 'Deep down here by the dark water lived ... a small slimy creature ... He was Gollum – as dark as darkness,' dwelling 'down at the very roots of the mountain.' Bilbo is forced into a contest with this archaic creature without whom he cannot get out of the dark. Gollum suggests they tell each other riddles, but this is no child's game. First of all, the stakes are Bilbo's life against his safe conduct out.[3] Second, as Tolkien tells us, Bilbo is aware 'that the riddle game was sacred and of immense antiquity.' Based on an animistic belief in correspondences, the riddle is an apt vehicle for primitive religious views. One scholar has connected the rituals of asking and answering a riddle with the process of initiation.[4] The asker is the priest who knows the mysteries of the universe, and the answerer is the novice who wishes to demonstrate his competence to join the adepts. In a riddle contest, each side is trying to penetrate the dark and hidden realm of the other. If we study the differences between Bilbo's riddles and Gollum's, we can gather important insights about their natures and the realm that each represents.

Gollum offers Bilbo an opportunity to be initiated into a primeval world of elemental darkness and death. His first riddle is easy for the reader to guess because it contains the same image Tolkien himself uses to describe the realm Bilbo has entered.

> What has roots as nobody sees,
> Is taller than trees,
> Up, up it goes,
> And yet never grows?

A mountain and its roots are where the contest is taking place. Gollum's next riddle is gnomic, eerie: 'Voiceless it cries, / Wingless flutters, / Toothless bites, / Mouthless mutters.' The wind, like the mountain, is elemental, inanimate. Gollum's third riddle is the climactic one, less tangible even than the wind, primordial, and most symbolic of Gollum's nature:

> It cannot be seen, cannot be felt,
> Cannot be heard, cannot be smelt.
> It lies behind stars and under hills
>   And empty holes it fills.
> It comes first and follows after,
>   Ends life, kills laughter.

Again the answer describes where they are, in the dark. The last two lines suggest that Gollum means 'death,' which in a sense he does. The third line could indicate that he also refers to himself, since he does lie under a hill. 'Empty holes it fills,' carries a strong sense of the void; 'comes first, and follows after' suggests something not only primordial, but also inexorable, eternal, as does what 'lies behind stars.' Dark is Gollum's cosmos, the force he worships instead of light. He repels and attracts us for that reason, epitomizing the shadow side of our nature, all the black threats and dark urgings that we repudiate and keep down in our daylight lives. To confront what Gollum stands for is Bilbo's destiny – a destiny he was only marginally aware of when he agreed to go on the adventure.

Gollum's last two riddles are consonant with the first three. The fourth is the only one that speaks of something alive, but in terms of death:

> Alive without breath,
> As cold as death;
> Never thirsty, ever drinking,
> All in mail never clinking.

It happens that Gollum lives on the fish that inhabit his subterranean lake. The image in his last line, of the fish protected because 'all in mail,' suggests that appetite begets warfare, an extension of the idea behind the riddle contest: this conflict is over Bilbo's carcass, whether the hobbit can defend it from Gollum's deadly intent. The appetite theme is also evident in Gollum's last riddle, which actually stumps Bilbo; only a coincidence saves him:

> This thing all things devours:
> Birds, beasts, trees, flowers
> Gnaws iron, bites steel;
> Grinds hard stones to meal;
> Slays king, ruins town,
> And beats high mountain down.

The first three verbs in this riddle, 'devours,' 'gnaws,' and 'bites,' sound like the goblins, who also live in the mountain and are more overtly destructive in their appetites than Gollum. But the nouns on which several of the verbs act are not even animate; whatever gnaws iron, bites steel and grinds stones to meal must be not only very powerful but also more elemental than any biological force. Like the dark, time is threatening, destructive. It beats down a mountain. Since the contest is taking place under one, time can be seen as solving Bilbo's problem ('How do I get out?') though not in any useful way. Taking Tolkien at his word, that the riddle contest is sacred, I infer that Gollum has shadowed forth the forces he worships – impersonal, elemental, destructive forces that are symbolic of his nature.

Bilbo's riddles also partly expose and partly conceal his values. We cannot, however, take the first riddle he proposes as characteristic, though it does expose his anxiety and is part of Tolkien's appetite theme. Having just heard that his life will be forfeit if he loses, Bilbo is

nearly bursting his brain to think of riddles that could save him from being eaten.

> Thirty white horses on a red hill,
> First they champ,
> Then they stamp,
> Then they stand still.

That was all he could think of to ask – the idea of eating was rather on his mind.

The answer, 'teeth,' is what Gollum will use on Bilbo if he wins. After this false start, Bilbo's riddles begin to be more characteristic. The next one is elemental, like Gollum's 'air' riddle.

> An eye in a blue face
> Saw an eye in a green face.
> 'That eye is like to this eye'
> Said the first eye,
> 'But in low place,
> Not in high place.'

Gollum's getting the answer is a tribute to his memory, since it is 'ages and ages' since he lived above ground: 'Sun on the daisies it means.' There are two reasons why daisy is correct (rather than flower, say). First, the common daisy has a yellow centre and white petals – as we picture the sun and its rays; second, daisy is a word that comes to us from Anglo-Saxon, where it literally meant 'day's eye.' The sense of correspondence between high and low, small and large, biological and cosmic is appropriately primitive here. It is also counter to Gollum's cosmology. Not only is the sun opposite to dark – the answer to Gollum's next riddle – but Bilbo's riddle is creative, colourful, alive, perceptive – an eye seeing – whereas Gollum's is destructive, without colour, inanimate, blinding.

Bilbo's third riddle intensifies the themes of the second. 'A box without hinges, key, or lid, / Yet golden treasure inside is hid.' An egg contains a seed of life, is nature's answer to the destructiveness of time – the answer to Gollum's final riddle – as well as to dark and appetite. Gollum's forces cannot be overcome, but they can be circumvented. The answer to death is more life. This riddle is particularly appropriate for Bilbo and his quest. There are, of course, two ways to realize the treasure an egg holds. One Gollum would understand: crack open the egg and eat the yolk, appetite's treasure. A Baggins would also appreciate that solution. But the Took side of Bilbo is being trained to value the magic of life. The other solution is to let nature take its course and watch a fluffy golden chick pick its way out of the seamless shell. This may seem too weighted a reading of Bilbo's climactic riddle, but the idea of honouring life is borne out by his subsequent treatment of Gollum.

Bilbo's egg riddle and Billina's egg function quite similarly in *The Hobbit* and *Ozma of Oz*. And the parallels between Bilbo's present situation and Dorothy's in the Nome kingdom are even closer. Like Bilbo, Dorothy joined a group already on its quest. Like him, she went underground with them, was separated from them, and, at peril of her life, had to guess correctly the answer to what we might call the Nome King's riddle – 'Which ornament is a transformed member of the royal family of Ev?' Again like Bilbo, she affirms the value of life while underground. The gift she wins can also be compared to the magic ring Bilbo finds. He comes upon it before meeting Gollum, who has unknowingly lost it. Gollum is terribly upset when he discovers that his 'precious' is missing. Similarly the magic belt is the Nome King's prize possession, taken by Dorothy while the Nome King is unaware. Both magic objects are circular, both get their new owners out of the dangerous underground domains, and both are used to solve later important problems for the two protagonists.

Just as Gollum's fourth riddle represents a deviation from his usual concerns, so Bilbo's fourth is a definite falling off. It is asked following renewed pressure from Gollum, who is speaking of the meal Bilbo will make: 'Is it juicy? Is it crunchable?' The riddle even contains another version of the fish Gollum just asked about: 'No-legs lay on one-leg, two-legs sat near on three-legs, four-legs got some.' The answer is mundane: 'Fish on a little table, man at table sitting on a stool, the cat has the bones.' Having guessed it, Gollum returns with 'something hard and horrible,' his time riddle. Frightened, Bilbo gets the answer by accident. He asks for more time, but Gollum takes his request – 'Time! Time!' – as the answer.

By this time Bilbo is in the same demoralized situation as El-ahrairah in his contact with the Black Rabbit of Inlé. When Gollum came and sat beside him, it 'made the hobbit most dreadfully uncomfortable and scattered his wits.' Both Bilbo and El-ahrairah are in the domain of darkness and death, both desire a boon, and both are almost undone by the fear that accompanies the contest to have it granted. While El-ahrairah comes to a conscious understanding that fear is causing his difficulties, Bilbo stumbles on in the grip of fear, but is saved by luck. '"What have I got in my pocket?" he said aloud. He was talking to himself, but Gollum thought it was a riddle.' Because it is not a proper riddle, Gollum demands three guesses – and takes four, none of them correct.

The contest over, Gollum goes off to get his gold ring, since he will need its power to make him invisible while he leads Bilbo out of the mountain past the goblins. Amoral trickster that he is, Gollum then decides to use invisibility to kill Bilbo, despite having lost the contest. But the ring is not where he keeps it; Gollum becomes suspicious that Bilbo has it in his pocket. In fact, just as Bilbo had earlier accidentally found the key in the trolls' cave lying on the ground, so he by chance found the ring lying in the cavern before he met Gollum. When his antagonist returns in a rage, Bilbo turns and runs 'blindly back up the dark passage.' His hand feels for the ring, which actively slips onto his finger. Bilbo begins to understand its power when he falls and Gollum goes past without seeing him. He follows and overhears a monologue about himself: 'It doesn't know the way out ... It said so, yes; but it's tricksy.' In fact, by luck and emulation, Bilbo is gradually becoming a trickster, and a burglar.

But the hobbit has something else to gain from Gollum, something more important finally than trickiness, namely the proper use of the ring. At a crucial point, Bilbo overhears how to find his way out. At the same moment, Gollum hears and smells Bilbo behind him. Realizing that he is about to be jumped on in the narrow passage, Bilbo is 'desperate.'

He must get away, out of this horrible darkness, while he had any strength left. He must fight. He must stab the foul thing, put its eyes out, kill it. It meant to kill him. No, not a fair fight. He was invisible now. Gollum had no sword. Gollum had not actually threatened to kill him, or tried to yet. And he was miserable, alone, lost. A sudden understanding, a pity mixed with horror, welled up in Bilbo's heart: a glimpse of endless unmarked days without light or hope of betterment, hard stone, cold fish, sneaking and whispering. All these thoughts passed in a flash of a second. He trembled. And then quite suddenly in another flash, as if lifted by a new strength and resolve, he leaped. No great leap for a man, but a leap in the dark. Straight over Gollum's head he jumped.

Bilbo's safe exit is now assured. But more important is his means of obtaining it. Starting with a perception of Gollum as 'it,' a 'thing,' Bilbo by an act of empathy understands Gollum's life as a benighted fellow creature. The implications of his subsequent action are brought out by Kathryn Crabbe in religious terms: 'It is grace and luck that the ring slips on Bilbo's finger at the right moment and that he falls in the tunnel so that Gollum can pass him. But it is charity (Tolkien calls it pity) that keeps Bilbo from killing Gollum, that lets him appreciate the horror of being without grace, of living "endless unmarked days without light or hope of betterment." ... The pity he feels for Gollum calls up a "new strength and resolve," which lets Bilbo make the leap of faith.'[5]

In a contrast between Bilbo's sword and ring, Crabbe indicates another way of seeing the significance of the choice Bilbo makes. The sword has 'masculine suggestions of aggression,' while the ring is 'a symbol of the feminine, wholeness.' To kill Gollum with the sword would be to treat him as he deserved, to assert Bilbo's masculinity, but also to treat an equal as a thing. For Bilbo to abstain from killing him is to act from his feminine side, to absorb Gollum's nature sympathetically, rather than aggressively as Gollum and the goblins want to absorb Bilbo. Most important, by sparing Gollum, Bilbo adds to rather than subtracts from the microcosm of his nature. He gains wholeness by accepting his shadow.

There is solid truth as well as angry poignancy in Gollum's last words to the departing Bilbo: 'Thief, thief, thief!' By virtue of Gollum's ring, Bilbo will become a full-fledged burglar, the role to which he agreed but which was the opposite of his Baggins uprightness. Understanding Gollum rather than killing him is appreciating his own Took nature rather than denying it. Wholeness comes from such acceptance and incorporation of the rejected, the dark, the taboo.

The ring's power of invisibility has one minor flaw: whoever wears it still casts a shadow. Bilbo has difficulty recrossing the boundary between this domain of night and his own day world. When he is trying to squeeze through the exit from the mountain, the goblin guards can't see him, but one of them spots 'a shadow by the door.' With great effort Bilbo squirms through; once outside he has to keep to 'the shadow of the trees ... out of the sun.' If we remember how his third riddle affirmed the sun and Gollum's the dark, we can understand afresh what Bilbo has gained from his sojourn underground. It is not that he has exchanged light for dark; it is that he has added Gollum's dark potential to his own hobbit commitment to light. Soon he will take off the ring and enjoy the light and warmth of the sun.

Chapter 6 begins with Bilbo's impressing the dwarves as he is reunited with them; he uses the ring to sneak past their border guard and appear by a magic trick in their midst. But the group is soon attacked by wolves and must take refuge in trees; there they are threatened with a fiery death by some goblins who appear. Not only is Bilbo's new ability useless in these circumstances, he is still vulnerable physically to death and psychically to fear. Fortunately, the group is spotted by some eagles, who rescue and carry them to a mountain ledge. When they are referred to as prisoners by one eagle, Bilbo misunderstands and begins 'to think of being torn up for supper like a rabbit, when his own turn came.' In fact, the eagles mean only that the group had been prisoners of the goblins. The next day the party is again carried by eagles, to be freed. On their way, Bilbo's eagle says, 'Don't pinch ... you need not be frightened like a rabbit, even if you look rather like one.' First by the trolls, now by an eagle, and even by himself, Bilbo as possible prey is imaged as a rabbit. He soon will be again.

In chapter 7, 'Queer Lodgings,' Bilbo meets another shadow figure who will be important in his development. Gandolf recognizes the rock they are near and claims 'to know of' the 'Somebody' who 'made the steps on' it. He gradually reveals that 'the somebody I spoke of' is 'a very great person ... If you must know more, his name is Beorn. He is very strong, and he is a skin-changer ... Sometimes he is a huge black bear, sometimes a great strong black-haired man.' Whether he is 'a bear descended from the great and ancient bears' or 'a man descended from the first men' isn't known. As shape shifter, Beorn moves easily across the border that separates animal from man. In short, as Timothy O'Neill has demonstrated, he is a trickster from the Jungian shadow. In fact, he is a fuller version of the trickster than Gollum was. As Jung put it, 'Typical trickster motifs can be found ... for instance, his fondness for sly jokes and malicious pranks, his powers as a shape-shifter, his dual nature, half animal, half divine, his exposure to all kinds of tortures, and – last but not least – his approximation to the figure of a saviour.'[6] Beorn demonstrates almost all of these traits.

O'Neill places Beorn 'in the general category of self symbols because of his ... union of opposites,' transcending 'man and animal, conscious and unconscious, thought and instinct.'[7] I would like to approach this contention indirectly by noting that Bilbo's process of assimilation might allow us to claim that *he* has developed into a symbol of self, realized through a union of opposites. He differs from Gollum as shadow exactly in this, for Gollum is limited to the dark side only. The same tends to be true of Trickster in the North American Indian tales: he is undeveloped, limited. But if we look at the rabbits in *Watership Down* we could say they have, like Bilbo, become better tricksters by achieving wholeness, unifying animal instinct with 'human' consciousness. Further investigation of Beorn will reveal that he exemplifies an integration different from any such figure we have yet encountered.

Gandolf warns the company that Beorn 'can be appalling when he is angry, though he is kind enough if humoured.' He then makes them approach this Somebody a few at a time, somewhat as the dwarves approached Bilbo. The difference is that Gandolf's presence acts as mediator. He is entertaining Beorn with the story of their journey as the dwarves appear in ones and twos. Beorn takes the manner of their appearance as a joke, and they are accepted. He feeds them and puts them up for the night. But when day departs, so does he, and Gandolf warns them, 'you must not stray outside until the sun is up, on your peril.' During the night Bilbo hears 'a growling sound outside, and a noise as of some great animal scuffling at the door.' He becomes afraid that 'it could be Beorn in enchanted shape' come back 'to kill them.' When Beorn reappears the next morning, he seems aware of Bilbo's night fears. '"So here you all are still!" he said. He picked up the hobbit and laughed: "Not eaten up by ... goblins or wicked bears yet I see"; and he poked Mr. Baggins' waistcoat most disrespectfully. "Little bunny is getting nice and fat again on bread and honey," he chuckled. "Come and have some more!"' Like the Hungry Tiger, Beorn cannot resist teasing one whom he is tempted to, but will not, eat. Like the elves earlier he shows insight into Bilbo's hobbit love of food, but also into his rabbit fear of becoming prey. Since we take it he really was at the door that they were warned not to open, the joke is too close for comfort. When they go out, they find 'a goblin's head ... stuck outside the gate,' and a wolf-skin 'nailed to a tree just beyond. Beorn was a fierce enemy.' But in his bear shape he seems not able to discriminate between enemies and friends.

In his man shape Beorn agrees to help Bilbo and his companions on their way because they are fellow foes of the goblins. He lends them some of his ponies to carry their luggage as far as the path they will follow through the 'dark, dangerous and difficult' Mirkwood. As they travel toward it, Bilbo is sometimes aware 'of the shadowy form of a great bear prowling along in the same direction.' Gandolf tells them he has accompanied them 'not only to guard you and guide you, but to keep an eye on the ponies,' which 'he loves ... as his children.' Earlier, Gandolf has said that Beorn 'keeps cattle and horses which are nearly as marvellous as himself. They work for him and talk to him. He does not eat them; neither does he hunt or eat wild animals. He keeps hives and hives of great fierce bees, and lives mostly on cream and honey.' Although he kills goblins, as does Gollum, Beorn does not eat them, in contrast to Gollum. In fact, he represents the solution to the problem that has implicitly bothered Bilbo throughout the tale: how can one enjoy meat without remembering that one may also be prey? How can one escape the cycle of eat and be eaten? Bilbo figured out one answer to this problem when he used the ring to get past Gollum. This solution was the 'feminine' means of psychic rather than physical incorporation. But Beorn offers another solution. Violence against those who are violent is acceptable if one is not a meat eater. After they enter the woods, Bilbo's adaptation of this solution will be to use his 'masculine' sword to protect himself and rescue his companions.

Seen in this light, Beorn's teasing Bilbo, calling him fat rabbit prey, carries several meanings. At the most basic animal level it says he recognizes in Bilbo a good meal, but at the level of his compact with his animals (and friends; Bilbo is fat on bread and honey, not meat), it says he has voluntarily given up this kind of appetite, and has devoted the violence that sustains it to the righteous cause of attacking evil. He may thus be contrasted with the Hungry Tiger, who is never allowed an outlet for his ferocious nature. As opposed to Gollum, Beorn has enlisted his amoral animal nature in the cause of a dominant human moral personality. In later adventures, Bilbo will have important opportunities for both controlled violence and moral decision making. Beorn himself, when he appears toward the end of the tale, will demonstrate impressive archetypal qualities of the self, as he displays an attribute from a higher level of his nature than has so far emerged.

Just before Bilbo and the dwarves begin the trek through Mirkwood, Gandolf leaves them, as he had earlier warned he would. His job of unifying the group must now be taken on by Bilbo, who will have a chance to earn the dwarves' gratitude in the next stage of their adventure. Despite Gandolf's final warning not to leave the path, they are lured off by a fire and an elves' celebration. Both vanish when they approach, and Bilbo is separated from the others, 'left alone in complete silence and darkness' as he was inside the goblin mountain. Having violated a new boundary, he is about to undergo another confrontation.

Sitting and dozing, Bilbo discovers he is being wrapped in 'strong sticky string' by a great spider. With his sword he cuts the string and then attacks and kills the spider. As the author tells us, this deed accomplished 'all alone by himself in the dark' makes Bilbo feel a 'much fiercer and bolder' person, less like fearful prey. Then he discovers that the dwarves have been wrapped up by more of these giant spiders, who discuss what fine eating their victims will make. Suddenly the trickster in Bilbo emerges. To lure the spiders away, he sings his own teasing, 'can't-catch-me' song. When they have followed him off, he puts on his ring and hurries back to start freeing his comrades. Before he finishes, the spiders return, and he is forced to kill a number more. With the help of the dwarves, he and they finally get away.

The party now discovers that Thorin is missing. The wood elves have taken him prisoner for trespassing across the boundaries of their domain; they now capture the remaining dwarves. Like Gandolf earlier, Bilbo becomes invisible and thus escapes capture, but is again left with the problem of freeing the dwarves, this time from the cells in which they are locked, inside the elves' cave, with its magically sealed gates. By now an accomplished burglar and thief, Bilbo crosses this border by slipping into the cave with an elven patrol. He finds Thorin and tells him, through the keyhole of his cell, that he will reconnoitre and find a means of escape. He discovers there is another way to cross the strict bounds of the elves' stronghold; trapdoors down to the river. The elves drop empty barrels through them to ferry downstream and return to the lake town. Waiting until the chief guard is asleep, Bilbo steals his keys, lets out the dwarves, and seals them in barrels, which are soon dropped into the river by an unsuspecting work crew.

Eventually Bilbo gathers the dwarves together, and they trek down river to the lake town. Thorin assures their welcome there by singing a song, known to the townspeople, about the riches that will be revealed on the return of 'the King beneath the mountains.' They are near enough their goal so these people can tell them where the mountain with the dragon-guarded treasure is. Accepting Thorin as a rightful heir of the old dwarf king, the townspeople, in the hope of a share in the treasure, agree to outfit the travellers for the last stage of the trip.

Soon Bilbo and the dwarves come to the Lonely Mountain, from which they see steam and dark smoke rising, signs of the dragon, Smaug. Carefully they scout for an entry. Bilbo finds a flat wall, 'as smooth and upright as masons' work, but without a joint or crevice to be seen.' They are unable to cross this seemingly impenetrable boundary until, on the last day of autumn, a new moon shows before sunset. A thrush knocks a snail on a stone, and Bilbo suddenly remembers the moon-message on the map. He calls the dwarves, and they watch as a flake splits from the rock, revealing a keyhole. Bilbo cries for the key, and they enter 'a yawning mouth leading in and down.' The dwarves soon stop and send Bilbo on down the throat of the tunnel. As Tolkien emphasizes, 'Going on from there was the bravest thing he ever did ... He fought the real battle in that tunnel alone, before he ever saw the vast danger that lay in wait.' Fortunately, he finds the dragon sleeping and steals a large two-handled cup.

When Smaug wakes, he misses the cup immediately and emerges to punish the thief. The group hides in the tunnel while the dragon devours their ponies and destroys their food. Bilbo, who has become the leader, offers to go down again to see if he can find a weak spot in the dragon. There ensues a boasting exchange between the two, a contest similar to the one with Gollum. They exchange what Tolkien calls 'riddling talk,' Bilbo speaking with the authority of a self-assured adventurer.

'I come from under the hill, and under the hills and over the hills my paths led. And through the air. I am he that walks unseen.'

'So I can well believe,' said Smaug, 'but that is hardly your usual name.'

'I am the clue-finder, the web-cutter, the stinging fly. I was chosen for the lucky number.'

'Lovely titles!' sneered the dragon. 'But lucky numbers don't always come off.'

'I am he that buries his friends alive and drowns them and draws them alive again from the water. I came from the end of a bag, but no bag went over me.'

'These don't sound so creditable,' scoffed Smaug.

'I am the friend of bears and guest of eagles. I am Ringwinner and Luckwearer; and I am Barrel-rider,' went on Bilbo beginning to be pleased with his riddling.

'That's better!' said Smaug. 'But don't let your imagination run away with you!'

Fortunately or unfortunately, Bilbo's imagination already has run away with him. All that he says is accurate. (His home, for instance, is named Bag End, and he was not caught in a troll bag when the dwarves were.) But some of what he says is not well enough disguised. 'Barrel-rider' gives Smaug a clue, though not quite an accurate one. He decides the thieves are the 'tub-trading Lake-men' and shortly goes off to punish them. In the meantime, however, he cannot resist boasting back at Bilbo.

'Thief in the Shadows!' he gloated. 'My armour is like tenfold shields, my teeth are swords, my claws spears, the shock of my tail a thunderbolt, my wings a hurricane, and my breath death!'

'I have always understood,' said Bilbo in a frightened squeak, 'that dragons were softer underneath ...'

The dragon stopped short in his boasting. 'Your information is antiquated.' ...

'I might have guessed it,' said Bilbo. 'Truly there can nowhere be found the equal of Lord Smaug the Impenetrable ...'

'Yes, it is rare and wonderful, indeed,' said Smaug absurdly pleased ... The dragon rolled over. 'Look!' he said. 'What do you say to that?'

'Dazzlingly marvellous! Perfect! Flawless! Staggering!' exclaimed Bilbo aloud, but what he thought inside was: 'Old fool! Why there is a large patch in the hollow of his left breast as bare as a snail out of its shell!'

Each opponent has gained information from the other's boasting, but Bilbo has gained the most. Though cunning, Smaug is also arrogant because of his physical power. Bilbo is the better trickster, flattering his opponent into a revelation of the chink in his armour.

When Bilbo returns to the dwarves, he tells them of his discovery of this weak spot and his fear that Smaug will go to the Lake town. The thrush overhears him and flies off to warn the Lake-men. Then Smaug emerges, seals the tunnel so they are trapped in the mountain, and flies off to attack the town. His fiery breath soon has it aflame, nor can the arrows and spears of the Lake-men pierce his armour, until the thrush tells one warrior where to aim. This one is Bard, a descendant of the Lord of the Dale who had been ousted by Smaug (just as Thorin is a descendant of the 'Thror, King under the Mountain,' whose treasure had been the basis for Smaug's stolen hoard). Bard's arrow goes true and Smaug falls dead into the lake.

Some readers are disappointed that Bilbo doesn't kill Smaug. But Tolkien knew exactly what he was doing. Bilbo is not that kind of hero: as he says to the dwarves, 'I was not engaged to kill dragons, that is warrior's work, but to steal treasure.' He is the hero as thief, and trickster, but, as Dorothy Matthews demonstrates, he also exemplifies moral courage.[8] He is, in fact, about to be faced with a complex and difficult moral problem.

Realizing that Smaug has gone, the dwarves finally enter the treasure cave. Thorin is looking particularly for a 'great white gem, which the dwarves' of old 'had found beneath the roots of the Mountain, the Heart of the Mountain,' a gem called 'the Arkenstone of Thrain.' Just as Bilbo earlier gained the gold ring at the roots of the goblin mountain, so now it is he who finds the Arkenstone in the heart of Lonely Mountain. Drawn to this 'great jewel' with its 'own inner light,' he sequesters it in his deepest pocket without telling the dwarves, conscious that he is now 'a burglar indeed.'

Whatever else motivates Bilbo in this irrational deed, Tolkien is explicit that it is not the treasure fever that kindles fire in the hearts of the dwarves. Thorin particularly is caught in this 'bewitchment of the hoard,' a possessiveness little short of the dragon's. When Bard comes with a deputation of men to consult, he finds an impenetrable boundary, a wall erected by the dwarves against the elves. He reminds Thorin that he has killed the dragon and that part of the treasure originally came from his forbears, but Thorin refuses to negotiate. The men set up a siege, the dwarves send for reinforcements, and a battle looms.

Upset by the change in Thorin and the other dwarves, Bilbo decides to try to avert conflict. By night he steals out with the gem and turns it over to Bard. Just as he has earlier found the ring that was Gollum's 'precious' and used it constructively, so now with the gem that is Thorin's 'heart.' Neither 'owner' appreciates the theft, but both are tested by the separation from the object to which they are obsessively attached. Thorin at first fails the test, although in the end he outgrows his possessiveness. At the point where he repudiates Bilbo, however, a new enemy appears, a huge force of goblins and wolves. Faced with a common foe, elves, men, and dwarves band together, and 'the Battle of the Five Armies,' takes place. Having consolidated his position as moral hero, Bilbo is once again shown to be no martial hero. Shortly after the battle begins, he is knocked unconscious and misses the rest of the fighting, including the appearance of Beorn, 'in bear's shape,' seeming almost 'giant-size in his wrath.' 'The roar of his voice was like drums and guns; and he tossed wolves and goblins from his path like straws and feathers. He fell upon their rear, and broke like a clap of thunder through the ring.' In his final appearance as the trickster saviour, Beorn defeats the goblins' chief, and they flee. Bilbo awakes to find the battle over, and the elves, men, and dwarves reconciled.

Just as Bilbo faced Smaug and gained the information that allowed Bard to become a hero, so after Bilbo's steadfastness in using the Arkenstone to attempt a reconciliation of the opposing parties, events bring about that unity and provide an opportunity for another hero to emerge. In his newest manifestation, Beorn is associated with thunder. Similarly Gandolf, at the appearance of the goblin army, commanded the attention of the still-contentious men, elves, and dwarves: '"Halt!" he called in a voice like thunder and his staff blazed forth with a flash like the lightning.' The connection of both characters with thunder suggests a convergence of Gandolf and Beorn toward another Jungian archetype. In his essay on the trickster, Jung insisted that that figure was 'a primitive "cosmic" being of *divine-animal* nature ... superior to man because of his superhuman qualities.'[9] It is this side of Trickster that Beorn demonstrates in wreaking his righteous wrath on the goblins.

Although Gandolf has also shown some traits of the trickster, there is nothing of the earthly animal about him. Whereas Beorn is connected with the dark shadow side of man, Gandolf we have already seen to be connected with another archetype, the 'wise old man,' who 'symbolizes the spiritual factor.' His friendship with and rescue by the eagles allows us to elaborate Gandolf's connection with this archetype; at its highest, Jung characterized it as a 'transcendent spirit,' the 'cosmic principle of order' traditionally given 'the name of "God."'[10] As such, its affinities with thunder and lightning become clear. Jung believed that one who listens to the wise old man will be able to face his own shadow, which may in turn lead him back to the more numinous image of the wise old man. In *The Hobbit*, Gandolf as wise old man initially urges Bilbo to action; Bilbo's reluctantly positive response allows him to encounter the shadows, Gollum and Beorn; then at the climactic moment he witnesses an exalted Gandolf.

To return to the actual process of Bilbo's development, we should note that it takes place in three crucial encounters. First, with Gollum as negative shadow, Bilbo learns compassion and is rewarded with the ring that exemplifies his acquisition of dark power. Then, with Beorn as positive shadow, Bilbo learns that violence, too, can be justified by righteous anger, a lesson he acts on in the encounter with the spiders. But in his third encounter, with the dragon, he meets a foe too powerful for either compassion or violence and uses his trickster ability for information alone. He is thus prepared for his final test as intermediary between dwarves and men, in which he successfully functions as shadow thief in a moral cause. He thereby achieves autonomy as a result of the integration process begun by Gandolf, who praises him for using the Arkenstone to try to unite the conflicting factions of what should be a harmonious society.

Showing themselves unable to respond to a unifying sacrifice offered by a mortal, the contending groups are brought together only when threatened by an outside evil. The integration already achieved by Bilbo, through internal assimilation and external anger, comes to the group after the cataclysm. Men move back to Smaug's desolated territory: 'All the valley had become tilled again and rich, and the desolation was now filled with birds and blossoms in spring and fruit and feasting in autumn ... and there was friendship in those parts between elves and dwarves and men.' Bilbo meanwhile has returned home, to realize that 'prophecies in old songs' can turn out 'to be true' and to learn from Gandolf that his own 'adventures and escapes' were neither the result of 'mere luck' nor staged for his 'sole benefit.' Although Bilbo may be part of a larger impulse toward harmony, what we are guided through is much more his meeting the tests that result in his gaining integration, particularly the confrontations with Gollum, Beorn, and the dragon.

Bilbo has gladly given up his share of the treasure that was the ostensible goal of his adventure, yet after Thorin's death Bard wants to reward Bilbo 'most richly of all.' Complaining that carrying treasure on his homeward trip will only invite 'war and murder,' Bilbo finally agrees to take 'two small chests, one filled with silver, and the other with gold.' Fortunately, with Gandolf as his fellow traveller, Bilbo encounters no difficulties on his way home. Near the end he is even persuaded by Gandolf to accept more treasure, half the Trolls' gold buried for safe keeping at the beginning of their adventure. Gandolf says it may come in useful, and as usual proves correct. Bilbo finds that he has been presumed dead because of his long absence, and that most of his effects have been sold at auction. Some goods are returned, but some he must personally buy back, and much of his remaining treasure he spends on presents for relatives.

The practical problem Bilbo faces on his return represents a social difficulty: he has 'lost his reputation' and is no longer perceived as respectable by his neighbours. Bilbo has felt 'the Tookish part' of him 'getting very tired, and the Baggins ... daily getting stronger' during his return trip, but the other hobbits perceive the adventurous Took side to have left a permanent mark on his character. His dilemma is put well in the Elven King's farewell to Bilbo: 'May your shadow never grow less (or stealing would be too easy)!' To the Took side, this friendly wish says that he needs some outward sign to keep from being taken over by his newly discovered aptitude for covert activities. To the Baggins side, the wish is more the conventional one in the traditional saying: may Bilbo keep his appetite for good food and grow comfortably stout in a dignified old age. Consciously Bilbo wants the second, but in fact the balance in him has shifted irretrievably. The king's wish can be taken to suggest that the more he tries to fulfil his Baggins side through indulging his appetite, the larger his Took shadow will grow.

Bilbo's difficulty after his return to Bag-End raises an issue that is relevant to all the stories discussed in the second half of this study. All the heroes must leave home in order to grow and mature, but the conscious goal of each is ultimately to return home. Like Bilbo, Dorothy in Oz desires a literal return to home as it was when she left. Dorothy willingly leaves behind her magic slippers in *The Wizard of Oz* and her magic belt in *Ozma of Oz* to achieve this goal. She returns with no outward sign of her adventures or the gains they have brought her. At least partly because of this lack of indication of change, she is accepted without question. In contrast, the silver and gold Bilbo brings back may be taken as a sign of his altered nature. Although the solid burgher side of the other hobbits can presumably appreciate the wealth Bilbo has gained, they cannot accept the adventures and confrontations that earned it. Bilbo returns home to find it altered not only by virtue of his changed perception of it, but also as a result of its perception of his change. He has grown beyond his neighbours; similarly they, in declaring him dead, have already cut him off from the community. Even after he settles in, Bilbo is looked on by other hobbits as odd, and decides to express the Took side of himself by conspicuously displaying his sword and his coat of mail and by writing poetry and visiting the elves. 'Though few [of his neighbours] believed any of his tales, he remained very happy to the end of his days.'

In *The Mouse and His Child* and *Watership Down*, there is no question of return to the original home. The mouse child does rediscover the house and the two original inhabitants whom he had dreamed of making into a family in it. But all have changed utterly. Discarded by humanity, the elephant and the seal have been degraded, and then self-renewed to become worthy of the new home they make of the dollhouse. In *Watership Down*, just as the impossibility of return home is more drastically rendered through the destruction of the old warren, so the emphasis on a new home is most pronounced: the rabbits' quest is first to locate a new burrow, then to make a viable warren of it by finding does, and finally to defend it from attack. In line with this emphasis, some of the key auxiliary adventures also concern inadequate homes: Cowslip's decadent, death-accepting warren, the hutch rabbits' provided-for life in a cage, and Woundwort's unnatural regimentation of burrow life. Creating and defending the right kind of home emerges as the central concern of Adams's plot.

For the child who reads these books, the message is finally reassuring, in the two Oz tales perhaps too much so. Does the child really want to pretend that adventures outside the home change nothing within it? Perhaps at a certain age, and in a certain mood, the answer is yes. But I find the development in the other three stories more appealing. Without withdrawing from the hobbit community, Bilbo asserts his difference, the value of what he has experienced and learned. *Watership Down* and *The Mouse and His Child* provide even more relevant messages for the child. The mouse child learns that the desire for a home is natural but that the formal decorum of the original dollhouse must be replaced by his and his father's efforts and vision. Similarly in *Watership Down*, Hazel accepts as a given that the warren in which he and Fiver have been nurtured will soon become a place of danger to all rabbit life. Able to persuade only a few others of the danger, the two begin an odyssey that is completely focused on the finding, establishing, and protecting of a home. The theme is one with an obvious and deep appeal to the child reader.

# 11

# Conclusion

HE MOTIF OF THE RETURN home
with which the last chapter concluded leads to the theme of integration,
which has been important in most of the works considered in this book. This
theme was most noticeable in the two chapters on *Watership Down*. The
quest for a warren was a quest for a harmonious society, as exemplified by
Hazel's including not only strange rabbits but creatures such as Keehar. At
the end of his life, Hazel undergoes the ultimate archetypal experience,
transcendence of physical death to a supernatural level of integration. In
*The Hobbit* neither social nor archetypal integration is so prominent, but
Bilbo undergoes a more obvious pattern of individuation than does Hazel.
His encounters with Gollum, the spiders, and the dragon are essentially
lonely stages of self-realization.

The connection of individual and social integration is certainly prominent
in all of the tales, though none of the earlier stories goes as far as *Watership
Down* and *The Hobbit* in giving us glimpses of the deeps of the human
psyche. Both the positive and the negative forces in these two tales are
overtly male: Gandolf, Thorin, Beorn, Bard, and Bilbo vs the trolls, the
goblins, the dragon, and Gollum; Cowslip, Woundwort and Vervain vs
Hazel, Bigwig, and Fiver. In contrast, the two Oz books emphasize female
power. In *The Wizard of Oz*, a young girl instinctively gathers to herself the
powers of three different witches: a protective kiss, a pair of silver wishing
shoes, a hat to call up winged monkeys. Her quest completed by her return
home, Dorothy leaves behind an integrated world, ruled by three creatures
whom she has brought from impotence to resourceful authority: the
Cowardly Lion, who reigns as king of the beasts; the Tin Woodman, who is
emperor of the Winkies; and the Scarecrow, who is the new ruler of Oz.

Although the mouse child wants and gets a mother and a sister, and one of his helpers, Miss Mudd, is female, the action in Hoban's tale is centred on another quest involving male protagonists, antagonists, and mentors. We witness the mouse child gaining his individual identity, after which the gathering of scattered parts begins, and does not stop until all the creatures met by the mouse and his father become an extended family in the dollhouse.

In part 1, too, the goal of most of the tales was an integration achieved among the various characters, an outer harmony either based on or symbolized by the inner harmony of the protagonists. The Elephant's Child uses his newly lengthened trunk to spank the relatives who originally spanked him, but when they undergo the painful initiation of the crocodile's jaws, they become equal with him, and the spanking stops; a social balance has been achieved. This balance is more precarious in Kipling than in any author we have considered. We saw how Mowgli is evicted from both the village and the wolf-pack, choosing limited solidarity with his wolf brothers at the end. On the other hand, 'Toomai of the Elephants' and 'The White Seal,' present two quests more in line with the other tales in this study. Toomai is tried and emerges a hero, initiated into the hill tribe, and celebrated by Machua Appa, Petersen Sahib, and the elephants of the Keddah. Only after a lengthy test does the white seal find a safe haven for seals. Even then he must battle his tribe before they are willing to join him on a beach where humanity cannot disrupt their social stability.

*The Wind in the Willows* also achieves community through a final conflict. Toad's waywardness leaves a gap in the community that the stoats and weasels fill by taking over Toad Hall. They are ousted by the fearless four: Badger, Rat, Mole, and Toad. The battle brings peace, which is celebrated by a banquet at the hall. Most of the invaders having returned to the Wild Wood, the field animal community affirms its solidarity, a harmony that even includes Toad, who appears to give up his egocentric isolation.

The integration at the end of the tales is not always a result of overt conflict. A tale like *Winnie-the-Pooh* for very young children may bring an unthreatened community together several times. Always at the instigation of Christopher Robin, the animals gather first to pull Pooh out of Rabbit's burrow, then to go off on a picnic-expedition (on which Pooh wins a double distinction), and finally to celebrate Pooh's saving Piglet during the big rain, to affirm his coming of age, the integrating of his intelligence. Similarly in *Charlotte's Web*, the barnyard animals come together to help get Wilbur out of his predicament, the human plan to kill him. Also similarly, at the end of the tale Wilbur feels his harmony with the barnyard community, a sense that reflects his own integration of the mature traits of Charlotte, the creature who originally called the meeting at which the community got behind Wilbur.

Throughout these tales psychic and social integration have evolved in tandem. But to claim only so much is to fall short of justice to the stories. In order to tie their themes together more thoroughly, in the remainder of this conclusion I would like to review some of the thematic conflicts that we have encountered in considering the ten books in this study and to relate them to the animal nature of the creatures whom they affect. We can begin with appetite, a theme that at first may appear comfortable, but that we have found leads to an uncomfortable dilemma.

In Pooh, appetite is taken for granted as an accepted self-indulgence, carrying with itself the mildest of consequences: getting stung by a bee for trying to steal its honey or being read to for a week while on a crash diet, stuck in the entrance to Rabbit's hole. In *The Wind in the Willows* the appetite for food is to be indulged with more satisfaction than difficulty. The theme manifests itself not in the conflict of the plot but in a running motif of picnics, dinners, and banquets, which add to the sense of comfort in this world.

So far, we may say animals can be used as a convenient way to enjoy vicariously the appetite that we are all born with but that our family and society have taught us to regulate. It is the unsatisfied animal within us that responds to the honey-greed of Pooh and the well-stocked larders of Rat and Badger. But there is an opposite side to animal experience, and it comes out clearly in *Charlotte's Web*. The destructive implications of appetite are faced head-on by the spider in her justification of her predatory instinct. Appetite later becomes the basis for the appeal Wilbur makes to Templeton, and we are told that the rat's subsequent overeating will shorten his life. There is thus a much more realistic handling of the theme: overeating not only makes one corpulent (even Pooh does stoutness exercises); it robs one of life. Accepting this truth, one may still, like Templeton, choose that path for its satisfactions. The suspense in this story is hinged on the question whether a pig should live: taking a practical point of view, two farmers think it should die, Mr Arable because it is not worth feeding, and Mr Zuckerman because it will make up into good pork, ham, bacon, sausage. But White brings up the connection between appetite and death partly in order to transcend it. By the end Wilbur has learned to see beyond appetite, to look at nature in the barn and appreciate 'the glory of everything,' to value love and friendship over the absorption of stuffing his stomach.

*Charlotte's Web* focuses on domesticated animals whose life is both protected and threatened by human beings. Because they are animals, the child can accept the inevitability of their physical death. Because they are humanized, the reader is poignantly affected by the threat. In *The Mouse and His Child*, Hoban replaces White's perception of the life cycle in a comfortable barn by an unsettling vision of the great chain of consumption. Manny Rat epitomizes the power principle that follows from the survival of the fittest; later he loses the sharp teeth that assured his dominance, but instead of going under he is able to break free of the chain by joining the co-operative world of the mouse and his child. Nor is his shift based on enlightened self-interest; rather it is a conversion: the light floods in. As in *Charlotte's Web* it is a transcendence of the world of appetite.

If transcendence is one way, aggression offers quite another way of resolving the problem of appetite. At the beginning of *Ozma of Oz*, the chicken, Billina, and the human being, Dorothy, debate the mores of a predatory life, to the discomfiture of Dorothy. The author provides an immediate solution in the meat-growing tree, but soon counters that with the threat of the animal-like Wheelers. When their aggressiveness is revealed as a sham, they are replaced by the Hungry Tiger. His appetite may be held in check, but he makes it a constant threat. Yet his conflicted condition turns out to be a better response to nature than that of the Nomes. By denying food from above ground – considering eggs poison – they simply channel their destructiveness in another direction. The Nome King's love of artefacts, his transforming above-ground creatures into ornaments, is revealed as a sterile perversion. Billina's code of open aggressiveness and unashamed creation emerges as a much more viable, healthy response to the mixed conditions of existence.

*The Hobbit* may be fairly said to be more continuously concerned with appetite than any preceding book except *Pooh*. An ungovernable voraciousness seems to be the dominant trait of a succession of underground dwellers that Bilbo encounters. All would like to eat him, and all are foiled, the trolls and goblins by Gandolf, Gollum and the dragon by Bilbo himself. Even his allies, the dwarves, take on some of the perverted side of this appetite; once Thorin gets underground with the hoard, he becomes as possessive as the Nome King. But in Beorn, Tolkien presents us with an animal-man who has found a better use of his aggressive heritage than merely killing to consume. Having made a pact with the domestic animals he uses and protects, Beorn can satisfy appetite non-violently, channelling his angry feelings and actions toward clear enemies of life.

A character type intimately connected with appetite has appeared in various forms in most of the books considered in this study. We first met the trickster in the *Just So Stories*, as the weaker animal needing protection from the appetite of the stronger, the zebra and giraffe learning to alter their appearance so as to blend into their surroundings and escape detection by the leopard and man. But we also saw it in that book as the predator tricking the weaker animal, the crocodile luring the elephant's child closer to its jaws. And finally we saw the Big God Nqong tricking the kangaroo through a race that changed his form. All three of these kinds of trickster appear also in other tales we have considered.

Prey must use their wits. In *Charlotte's Web*, because the spider is weaker than human beings, she tricks them by writing words in her web. In *Watership Down*, because the rabbits are weaker than their enemies, they habitually use trickery to escape or hide and thus survive. Turning to predators, we might remember how in *The Jungle Book* Kaa used the same trick as the crocodile, waiting immobile like a log or stump until a suitable prey came near. Among trickster gods, we saw Frith, very much like the Big God Nqong, trick El-ahrairah by changing the rabbit's shape so he would be able to outrun his enemies. Trickster seems constantly to be escaping the appetite of his enemies or to be driven by his own appetite to try new ways of catching prey. His gods help him in these endeavours.

We have also seen the trickster appear as a response less to evolutionary transformations than to psychological pressures. Just as animals indulge appetite without moral scruples, so they resort to tricks in order to survive or remain free. The child, hemmed in by outside restrictions, appreciates such tricks as a means both of satisfying its thwarted drives and of getting even with those who enforce the rules. In *The Wind in the Willows* Toad's normally expressive personality is twice repressed by incarceration. But both times he breaks out by means of a trick, the first time feigning near-death to Rat, the second time donning a dress to impersonate a washerwoman. In *Ozma of Oz* the underground king of the Nomes is a sly trickster whose aim is to reduce to lifeless objects all who come from the world of day. In the energy behind his dark, evil design we can discern the repression of male aggressiveness that is so evident in Ozma's entourage.

Not all underground tricksters are brought into being by Freudian repression. In *The Hobbit* we encountered another dynamic, one that responded to a Jungian notion of the function of the shadow. Gollum lives in an archetypal world of darkness whose essence he distils in a chilling riddle. Yet this darkness contains a valuable prize, the ring that makes its wearer invisible except as a shadow. Gollum was tricked but not destroyed; rather his essence was to be assimilated, a shadow added to give more than physical wholeness to a plump hobbit. Similarly, Beorn the shape shifter offers trickster violence, which is acceptable precisely because its aim is not appetite satisfaction. Since Trickster is involved with that dark animal side of ourselves we have been taught to repudiate and learned to fear, he is a figure of some attraction and tremendous energy.

The animal connections of Trickster are the source of a more-than-animal potential. Beorn gives evidence at the end of *The Hobbit* of becoming what Jung calls the 'divine animal.' Gandolf, also a trickster but hardly an animal, displays this divine level as well. As we saw, in Jung's metamorphic system the shadow can easily modulate into the wise old man, a spirit archetype with a divine connection.

Paul Radin noted the same connection between appetite and creativity in his survey of North American Indian trickster tales. 'Not only does he obtain satisfaction for all his desires and impulses and appease his voracious appetite but in the course of his exploits, and never consciously willed, he creates many of the objects man needs, and fixes the customs they are to have ... a trait which we shall find throughout all North America.'[1] Trickster's adventures also demonstrate another important congruence with the tales with which we have been concerned. In discussing *Hiawatha* in the introduction to part 2, I told of the incident in which the Indian hero is swallowed by a sea monster. I noted there that this incident is found in myths around the world and mentioned that Longfellow got the tale from an Indian Trickster cycle, a nineteenth-century transcription from a Central Woodlands tribe. In the Northwest coast, this incident appears as Raven's descent into the whale. Of course he makes his escape from this darkness back into the light. In another tale Raven flies up to the realm where the 'great Chief of the Sky kept the ball of daylight or the sun.'[2] Through trickery, he steals it and brings it back down to humanity, which has lived in the dark up to that time. This shamanic adventure also contains an important transformation: the trickster transforms himself into a spruce needle floating in a spring; after the Chief's daughter goes there for a drink and swallows it, Raven is reborn as her baby, who is then given the ball of daylight to play with. Clearly there are psychological overtones in the dynamic interplay between darkness and light, appetite and creativity, being swallowed and then reborn: the animal thereby becomes human.

This dynamic of transformation struck the child therapist, D.W. Winnicott, whose investigation of the therapeutic value of play we looked into at the beginning of this study. In *Playing and Reality*, Winnicott was quite explicit about his belief that 'a sense of self' can follow only from experiencing 'an unintegrated state.' This state is equivalent to the existential void, that darkness from which a new reality may be affirmed:

'The searching can come only from desultory formless functioning, or perhaps from rudimentary playing, as if in a neutral zone. It is only here, in this unintegrated state of the personality, that that which we describe as creative can appear.' This experience is the psychological correlative of the shaman's descent and disintegration, the destruction of the neophyte's old personality in the ritual of initiation, as in Raven's descent into the whale. By entering the darkness of the womb of the chief's daughter in order to gain light, Raven gives up his old form to be created anew. Winnicott claims that this unintegrated state must be 'reflected back' to become 'part of the organized individual personality.' Such a reflection 'makes the individual to be, to be found; and eventually enables himself or herself to postulate the existence of the self.'[3]

Bilbo's encounter with Gollum follows this pattern. The hobbit descends into the dark formless underground. He meets a creature who reinforces that formlessness through 'rudimentary playing,' facing Bilbo with riddles. In order to answer correctly, Bilbo must accept the ogre time that 'all things devours,' the threatening wind that 'toothless bites, mouthless mutters,' the formless dark that 'cannot be seen, cannot be felt,' but does fill 'empty holes.' In order to answer such a riddle, Bilbo must feel his way into its constituent negations, thus opening himself to the force of disintegration. Existentially he experiences the hole that is first empty and then filled with ... dark. But following Winnicott's progression, this state is a necessary precondition. First Bilbo has gone into the dark, then he has had it reflected back by Gollum until it becomes part of him.

Finally Bilbo senses what the formless is, what it means *to be* Gollum. 'A sudden understanding, a pity mixed with horror, welled up in Bilbo's heart: a glimpse of endless unmarked days.' This acknowledgment of formlessness is immediately followed by Winnicott's next phase in which creative action is possible. 'Quite suddenly in another flash,' the hobbit is 'lifted by a new strength and resolve.' Moving beyond the defensive need to destroy Gollum, Bilbo jumps over him and returns to the sunlight having gained a sense of self. Having incorporated the formless, he carries it with him in the shadow cast by his use of Gollum's ring. He is an initiate.

Alternating with the destructiveness reflected back by Gollum's riddles is the constructive creativity of some of Bilbo's riddles. The difficulty of this integrative act is indicated by its being twice undermined when Gollum's threat of death causes Bilbo to offer his own disintegration riddles, one about teeth and the other about man and cat eating fish. But Bilbo also creates two integrating riddles, referring to the sun and the egg. In answering correctly Gollum is forced to reflect back to Bilbo the hobbit's creative act, which thus becomes part of Bilbo's 'organized individual personality' and can be said to play its part in his treatment of Gollum as another individual.

The other crucial threat of destruction comes in Bilbo's descent into Smaug's cave. 'Before him lies that great bottom-most cellar or dungeon-hole ... at the mountain's root. It is almost dark so that its vastness can only be dimly guessed.' Later Bilbo refers to his experience in the cave as being inside 'a nasty clockless, timeless hole.' Again I perceive the existential void at the centre of Tolkien's conception, as Bilbo faces another creature of formlessness. More secure than with Gollum, the invisible hobbit is able to indulge in exuberant play in his boasting riddle contest with the dragon. But Smaug is a much more active opponent than Gollum; the dragon threatens disintegration, enforces formlessness in his very definition of himself: 'My teeth are swords, my claws spears, the shock of my tail a thunderbolt, my wings a hurricane, and my breath death.' There is no empathizing with Smaug; rather Bilbo is in constant danger of falling under his 'dragon-spell': 'an unaccountable desire seized hold of him to rush out and reveal himself.' Instead Bilbo creatively manages to reflect back Smaug's sense of his omnipotence, in order to discover the secret of the dragon's vulnerability.

Bilbo's encounter with light and integration comes after Smaug has left, when he finds the Arkenstone. As he climbs the mound of treasure, a 'white gleam had shone before him and drawn his feet toward it.' Like the ring, it comes halfway to meet its destined carrier. This 'great jewel' with 'its own inner light,' the Jungian critic Dorothy Matthews suggests we should see 'as the archetype of the self, of psychic wholeness.'[4] The perspectives of Jung and Winnicott come together at this point.

With the elaboration of the darkness theme gained through Winnicott's three-stage theory – disintegration, creativity, and autonomy – I propose to take a final look at the narratives that make up this study. In the *Just So Stories*, the giraffe and the zebra go to the forest to hide in its shadows. They grow dark patches and stripes in emulation of the forest darkness and virtually disappear from the sight of their enemies. In other words, to escape destruction by these predators, they move into darkness, empathize with it until they resemble it, and create themselves with new being.

Winnie-the-Pooh's descent into darkness takes place in the Heffalump pit. As he approaches it in the pre-dawn, 'the Very Deep Pit' contains Pooh's honey jar as 'something mysterious, a shape and no more.' Pooh climbs down and immerses his head in that barely defined shape. His head takes the place of the honey that had filled the pot, and Pooh wearing that pot takes the place of the Heffalump in the pit. Seeing this dim shape and hearing its eerie cry drives Piglet to his formless verbal utterance. From the psychological perspective I am adopting here, Pooh figuratively becomes the darkness of the pot, the threatening elephant in the pit. He then breaks out of this empty darkness to have his being redefined by Christopher Robin's expression of love at the end of the episode.

Wilbur's descent into darkness comes early in *Charlotte's Web*. In chapter 4, Wilbur experiences 'the worst day of his life.' His sense of nothingness is 'reflected back' to him first by Templeton's absence, then by the lamb's rejection, and finally by Lurvy's giving him a purgative. Rejected and empty, he throws himself down and sobs. Out of this formless state comes help for his condition. 'Darkness settled over everything ... You can imagine Wilbur's surprise when, out of the darkness, came a small voice he had never heard before.' It promises to be his friend, though it refuses to identify itself right then. The voice is Charlotte's, of course, revealing herself as a part of Wilbur's mind that he never has been able to hear before. The voice is born out of the depth of his darkness and despair. It will come up with creative suggestions, and will protect him from the threat of non-being, at the same time telling him how to be. Under Charlotte's tutelage, Wilbur finally becomes a radiant self. He achieves autonomy when the voice disappears, that is, when Charlotte dies. Undone at first, he recovers to incorporate what the voice has offered him: reason, which he employs with Templeton, and unconditional love, which he offers as mentor to each new generation of spiders in the barn.

As suggested earlier, Russell Hoban consciously evoked an existential void at the centre of the universe in *The Mouse and His Child*. Empty himself, the mouse child understandably (according to his father) fills that hollow where his motor should be 'with foolish dreams.' In fact, the dreams are foolish only to those who accept their motors as the true centre of life. The mouse child's emptiness allows him to see the actual emptiness of all life. His revelation comes in the formless darkness at the bottom of the pond. There the mouse child is able to contemplate the visual regression of smaller and smaller dogs until he has a vision of the nothingness beyond life. First he sees 'emptiness that seemed to flow back toward him.' This vision of 'nothing' – the ultimate in formlessness – is 'reflected back' to him by Serpentina's ecstatic celebration of that condition. Applying Winnicott's words to the mouse child's condition, I would say this augmented message of the formless 'becomes part of the organized individual personality' of the mouse child, paradoxically allowing him 'to be, to be found, and eventually' enabling him 'to postulate the existence of the self.' Thus the mouse child insists he is mature enough to see 'the other side of nothing.'

He does, and is able to perceive his own reflection, to assert his own being and then to start doing.

In 'Toomai of the Elephants,' Kipling provided his Indian boy with two experiences of formlessness. The first takes place in the Keddah, the stockade into which the wild elephants are herded. During a mêlée there, 'after the last night's drive, the Keddah ... looked like a picture of the end of the world.' Toomai jumps from the stockade fence down into this chaos, dodging among the jostling, trumpeting elephants to catch and retrieve 'the loose end of a rope.' The boy is saved from being trampled, caught up by the trunk of Kala Nag and presented to his father, who slaps him. In the formless night, Toomai has joined the rout and has had his experience reflected back by an unsympathetic father, who realistically warns that he may be 'trampled to death in the Keddah.' Toomai's dreamlike night experience there leads to the daytime confrontation with Petersen Sahib in which the boy is again lifted by Kala Nag, not to be reprimanded but to be praised, a positive reflection of his plunge into disintegration.

Much more like a dream is Toomai's participation in the elephants' dance: it takes place at night again, and begins when Toomai is dozing by Kala Nag; he is the only human being present, and he is a passive observer of the phantasmagoria. Taking the experience as a dream, we can see its most immediate daytime stimulus as the drumming scene that precedes it, in which Toomai thumps for hours in front of Kala Nag in his happiness at being honoured by Petersen Sahib. The 'dream' of attending the dance fulfils the condition laid down by the sahib. Toomai's experience both on the way to the dance and in the dance again follows Winnicott's pattern for discovery of the self.

In darkness, nature becomes formless: 'all the mist ... seemed to be full of rolling wavy shadows.' The dance grounds themselves are nothing but 'trampled earth.' Then the elephants, their shadows 'inky black' and themselves moving 'like ghosts' begin to trample the undergrowth in the 'black darkness.' Toomai, 'all alone in the dark,' experiences this trampling as an augmentation of his own earlier drum beating: 'It sounded like a war-drum ... the booming went on' until 'it was all one gigantic jar that ran through him.' The boy resting on Kala Nag is thus reduced to formlessness in a way analogous to the earth being trampled by the elephants.

The next day, Toomai's 'dream' is honoured in real life, just as, in a primitive society, a vision resulting from a spiritual quest would be. Toomai is found to be one of the hill people and is initiated with blood from a 'newly killed jungle-cock.' He is made 'free of all the jungles,' his identity saluted by the royal 'Salaam-ut of the Keddah.' A self has been born out of the trampling to nothingness in the dark night of the elephants' dance.

Toomai, like Dorothy in *Ozma of Oz*, achieves what he does by subordinating himself to an animal. The sign of his triumph when he returns to society is the salute of the elephants. Dorothy follows Billina's lead in retrieving the key that brings the helper Tik-Tok into her life and, more important, in stealing the magic belt that allows her group of rescuers to make a successful exit from the dark underground kingdom. In both Oz books we noticed the importance of the disintegration theme. In *The Wizard of Oz*, the two creatures who function as helping animals experience an extinction of consciousness. The Scarecrow is torn to pieces and the Tin Woodman mangled into scrap by order of the Wicked Witch of the West. Subsequently, the Scarecrow becomes ruler of Oz and the Tin Woodman emperor of the Winkies. As Max Lüthi suggested, 'suffering and sacrifice – and cruelty' are a necessary step if 'lower natures are to be transformed into higher ones.'[5] In *Ozma of Oz*, all the would-be rescuers must enter the underground kingdom, and most of them suffer there an extinction of consciousness when they are transformed into art objects.

Significantly, neither Dorothy nor Billina, the actual rescuers, undergoes the experience of nothingness. Baum's unwillingness to put Dorothy through such an experience is a clear mark of the disparity between his imagination and that of Kipling, Hoban, Adams, and Tolkien. *Ozma of Oz* lacks the power of the other quest narratives. Like *Ozma*, *The Hobbit* also has a reassuring tone. In both, the protagonist goes underground and then must face a test alone. But whereas Dorothy is in a series of lighted furnished rooms, Bilbo is in the dark faced with a dangerous antagonist who plans to eat him. Although Dorothy could be turned into an ornament, neither she nor the reader experiences her situation as particularly threatening. The closest she comes to bravery is asserting her power as wearer of the magic belt, facing a Nome King rendered almost powerless by its theft. In contrast, Bilbo, despite the magic ring, is in active danger with both Gollum and the dragon. As Lüthi indicates, the encounter with the destructive dragon, like the encounter with the helpful animal, stands for a facing of 'unconscious forces within one's own self.' Both lead 'to a higher stage of development.' But the hero who opens himself to the destructive experience that the dragon represents gains more than the heroine who mainly depends on her helpful animal and is thereby spared the full experience of darkness.

In *Watership Down* the 'journey into the dark' of El-ahrairah to meet the Black Rabbit of Inlé is almost a paradigm of entering Winnicott's 'unintegrated state.' The rabbit chief is reduced to a state of witless, stammering fear, his tail, whiskers, and ears sheared away as he approaches the formlessness of death. At this point he begins to face his situation actively. A creative idea comes to him; he thinks of a trick and executes it. But it won't work, as the Black Rabbit tells him in a confrontation that reflects back El-ahrairah's powerless state. The hero gives up, aware that he has been reduced to nothing: 'His strength and courage were gone. He fell to the ground. He tried to move, but ... could not get up. He scuffled and then lay still in the silence.' But this nadir is the basis for the gift of life, and an affirmation of El-ahrairah's virtues. The Black Rabbit praises his 'warm heart' and 'brave spirit.' Then the success of the quest is proclaimed. In the final stage, Frith presents him with replacements for his sheared-away parts, including ears with 'starlight in them,' a symbolic validation of what Winnicott calls the 'organized individual personality.' Frith voices the meaning of El-ahrairah's experience: 'Wisdom is found on the desolate hillside.' El-ahrairah has been there and learned how to be.

Although I have not included each story in surveying this theme, we have already noted that they all have some version of the Black Rabbit's night realm to offer their protagonists. Most of the tales also offer some version of what Frith, the sun, may be said to stand for, the transcendent. In the *Just So Stories*, it is 'the Big God Nqong' who gives Old Man Kangaroo his distinctive appearance, or 'the Eldest Magician' who, like Frith, gives all the animals their shapes. In *The Wind in the Willows* the god is Pan, who is more than the transcendent figure of 'Awe' revealed in 'The Piper at the Gates of Dawn.' As the agent of panic, he is also immanent in Mole's terror in the Wild Wood and in the rout of the weasels in 'The Return of Ulysses.' In either case the experience connected with him is larger than life.

The transcendent in *The Jungle Book* is more integral with nature than is Grahame's Pan. I would see it in the initiation and celebration of Toomai, and as a dark force in the dance and hypnotic voice of Kaa, drawing all to disintegration. But Kaa as an archetypal initiator into death is to be compared with the Black Rabbit. There is no creator god, like Frith or 'the Eldest Magician' in *The Jungle Book*. Kipling does, however, offer another mythic means of transcendence. The legend of the White Seal provides Kotick with an archetypal contrast to his lonely actuality. He acts on the identification with a transcendent level: because he is able to see the correspondences between his history and the legend, he can move on to final success.

In *The Mouse and His Child* the archetypal breaks into the actual world through the unconsciously prophetic utterances of the frog. They correctly foretell success for the mice and defeat for Manny Rat. In *Watership Down* the transcendent is also present: first in the tales of El-ahrairah, which, like the legend of the White Seal, provide a model for those who identify with them; second in the prophetic visions and shaman dreams of Fiver; third in the actual incursions into the rabbits' everyday world of messengers from Frith – the train that saves Holly, the thunder and lightning that help Bigwig, and finally the appearance of El-ahrairah himself to escort Hazel to the archetypal world.

In *The Hobbit* the transcendent is most obviously to be seen in Gandolf as spiritual wise old man, especially when he uses thunder and lightning to unite the men, elves, and dwarves near the end of the book. If he is the divine wizard there, he is soon followed by the divine animal, Beorn as giant bear, another obvious archetypal figure whose wrath is also accompanied by thunder.

The ambivalence of divine power is thus overt in three of the tales we have considered. The daybreak figure of Pan, worshipped with awe by Mole, is contrasted to the dark panic of the night woods. The benevolent creativity of Frith as sun is contrasted to his righteous violence in the storm. Finally, Gandolf's helpful cajoling of Bilbo and the dwarves to get together can be contrasted with his violent attack on the goblins in their cave. Beorn shows the same ambivalent nature.

As entertainment, the animal fantasy tale may be turned to by readers who want to escape the pressures of actual outside demands. But fantasy as literature is precisely an area where these difficulties can be faced. We cannot question each act of our lives as it happens, but we can pull back from time to time and pay attention to some of the areas of ambivalence. Such reflection is what fantasy can provide. By lulling our ordinary sense of reality to sleep, it allows not only the demands of Freud's pleasure principle and the complaints of his repressions to be heard but also the aspirations of Jung's higher self to speak. Good fantasy writers often choose themes of basic import, such as the question of the connection between formlessness and creation. Thus love and death, creativity and destructiveness, conflict and integration, disintegration and autonomy are inextricably intertwined. The result of vicariously experiencing such difficulties is a sense of transcendence and a movement to a higher level where the dynamic of our everyday physical and psychic conflicts and resolutions still holds, but is more fully comprehended because it takes place in the clarity of that refined atmosphere.

In plumbing the psychological depths of these tales, we have inevitably shifted from a focus on the animals and other creatures that are the authors' vehicles to the broader human concern of the authors' themes. In conclusion, it is therefore appropriate to ask again, 'Why did they choose to write about animals?' The answer is both explicit and implicit in the overview we have been taking. Those stories for children have as their protagonists childlike animals or creatures, or children with animal helpers. Children, with their simplified humanity, can be easily associated with or readily represented by animals. They are closer to the animal state from which humanity evolved and can empathize with animals more readily than adults can. Specifically, as we have seen in this chapter, the undisguised dominance of appetite in children and animals leads to a theme of pleasure and its consequences, and a complementary theme, the fear of being devoured.

The restrictions children experience on their appetites and on their freedom of movement make it natural for them to respond to the indulgence of appetite and to the incarceration of domesticated and wild creatures. It also makes them sympathetic with any story in which a trickster evades such restrictions and plays tricks on those in authority. The appearance of the trickster signals the return of a natural animal energy that may be channelled but cannot be denied. Social forms that seek to repress such energy may be successful for a short time, but sooner or later it will find outlet. As the vehicle of that repressed vitality, the trickster is a protean master of disguise, who evades psychic barriers and moral rules; he, she, or it appears and reappears to the unfailing appreciation of the child, who experiences the constant pressure of life on the border between innate drives and outer restrictions.

The vulnerability of children and small animals opens up the whole question of death as an extinction and return to chaos. The child's fear of night and its dangers is answered by stories about animals and other creatures who face darkness and the threat of death, and emerge not just alive but augmented, stronger. The animal is a safe surrogate in this difficult exploration and confrontation. The mere creatures of the animal fantasy tale are thus fit vehicles for the varied impulses that flow through them and emerge in the interactions, conflicts, plots, and themes of these fictional tales that use narrative illusion to embody psychic truths.

# Appendix

**W**HAT JOSEPH CAMPBELL has called 'the monomyth' was a pattern of 'separation-initiation-return,' which he found as 'the standard path' of 'mythological adventure.'[1] At the beginning of chapter 4 of *The Hero with a Thousand Faces*, he provided a diagram of this pattern and its variants.

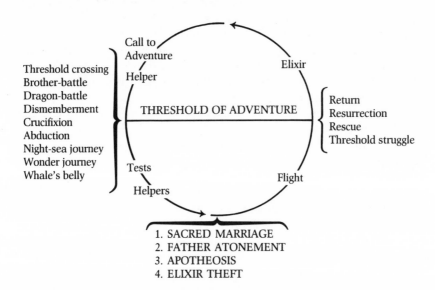

Such a schematic structure could be applied to many Greek myths and European fairy-tales. It obviously fits a 'newer wonder tale' like *Ozma of Oz* (see chapter 6): Dorothy answers the *call to adventure* represented by

Ozma's quest for the royal family of Ev. Her *helper* Tik-Tok instructs her in a successful appeal to the Nome King for entry into his kingdom – the crossing of the *threshold of adventure*. They are then *tested* by the king's guessing game, in which Dorothy is successful on her own. But the success of the venture finally rests on two other *helpers*, on Billina's trickery and the Scarecrow's accurate aim. Following Billina's instructions, Dorothy receives a magic belt and leads her comrades out of the underground kingdom. Their *flight* is harried by pursuit that she stops; the group is then free to recross the *threshold* and *return* to the upper world, bringing with them the object of the quest, the royal family (the *elixir* for the kingdom of Ev).

Since Campbell's scheme fits *Ozma of Oz*, we can expect that it would apply to *Watership Down* even if Adams, like Baum, had never heard of the monomyth. But since Adams includes a quotation from Campbell's book, we may presume he did know of the diagram; we may therefore anticipate that his tale will follow Campbell's pattern in more detail than Baum's did. Just as I applied Campbell's diagram only to the second half of *Ozma of Oz*, so we shall find it works best on discrete sections of *Watership Down*: (1) The beginning of the book, ending with the rabbits' arrival on the down; (2) the raid on Nuthanger Farm; (3) the inset tale, 'El-ahrairah and the Black Rabbit of Inlé'; (4) the final defence of the down burrow against Woundwort. I shall actually apply the diagram only to the second of these because the structure of this episode is more complex than that of the other three, and because it contains what I take to be clear authorial indications that it is based on Campbell's pattern.

The call to adventure comes to Hazel at the beginning of chapter 24 as 'a spirit of happy mischief ... He was confident and ready for adventure. But what adventure?' Unlike Fiver's vision, which was an unmistakable call, Hazel's is more personal – which is one of the reasons the adventure causes problems. Just as Adams alerts his reader with the word 'adventure' that the first stage has begun, so he provides a clue for the second stage, the appearance of a helper. Campbell says, 'Having responded to his own call, and continuing to follow courageously ... the hero finds all the forces of the unconscious at his side.' He receives a helper in 'the role' of 'the guide.'[2] Similarly, Hazel experiences one of those 'times when we know for a certainty that all is well.' Since 'there was nothing to fear ... it did not strike him as particularly lucky' to see 'a young rat scuttle' across his path. 'He had known that some *guide* or other would turn up' (my emphasis). The guide directs him to Nuthanger Farm. Then Hazel's nose guides him to a shed inside which the tame rabbits are kept. 'The door was half open and he went through it with scarcely a pause at the brick *threshold*' (my emphasis). Having now crossed Campbell's *threshold of adventure* into the human world (a threatening 'other world' to a rabbit), Hazel leaves Pipkin as a guard at the threshold to warn if the cat should appear. After he has explained to the hutch rabbits that he offers freedom and will return to rescue them, the cat does discover them, but he and Pipkin evade it and return to Watership Down. Since Hazel has planned not to bring back this time the treasure he intends ultimately to obtain, this adventure cannot be called a failure, even though it does not follow Campbell's success pattern. Rather, Adams has divided the quest into two parts: the first emphasizes the entry into the other world while the second emphasizes the difficulties the rabbits experience in later stages – in Campbell's terminology, the 'bride-theft' and 'the threshold struggle.'

The first difficulty that the augmented rescue expedition faces is actually on its re-entering the barnyard. They come upon the cat, which functions as the 'threshold guardian' and could keep them from entering the shed. But Bigwig and the others soon rout it, and they are able to cross the threshold. Inside the shed, they gnaw through the leather hinges of the hutch and free the two pairs of tame rabbits. When one pair freezes, Hazel lets the other go on while he tries to move this pair along. Pinned by the car headlights, Hazel distracts the returning farmer so the others can escape, but is shot and takes refuge in a drain pipe.

Campbell's scheme emphasizes the possible difficulty of recrossing the threshold: 'The hero may have to be brought back from his supernatural adventure by assistance from without.'[3] Of course, Hazel's has not been a supernatural adventure, though it has been a venture into a world outside of nature, an alien world of buildings, wire hutches, automobiles, bright lights, and guns. He is certainly rescued from without, that is, by rabbits who come down for that purpose from their burrow atop the escarpment. Equally important, the rescue is made possible by Fiver's dream vision, discussed in chapter 8, in which he enters the other world and confronts an ogre, who confirms that Hazel is alive and provides a clue to his whereabouts. The chapter in which Fiver has this vision is the one with an epigraph from Campbell's book.

Rather than being diminished by his lack of easy success on the quest, Hazel's reputation is enhanced by the addition of two females to the burrow and by his heroic self-sacrifice: Hazel 'had acquired, in everyone's eyes, a kind of magical quality.' In short, he has with Fiver's help brought back some of the power of the other world, as does a shaman or an initiate who has been exposed to the hardship and rewards of the supernatural. As

Campbell puts it, 'The hero is one who, while still alive, knows and represents the claims of the superconsciousness. ... The adventure of the hero represents the moment in his life when he achieved illumination' after 'a descent into unconsciousness and return.'[4] The elixir that Hazel has brought his followers is thus both the does and the aura of magic that will inspire the group, giving them not only the confidence and power but the luck to succeed.

My case has been that Adams consciously adapted Campbell's scheme from the adventure of the mythological hero, not mechanically but creatively to enhance the effectiveness of his plot. As already indicated, the pattern is more simply present in an inset tale like 'El-ahrairah and the Black Rabbit of Inlé.' Despite its more schematic plot, that tale is also very effective. We apply a different standard to a folk-tale than to *Watership Down* as a whole. The novel has more individualized characters, a more detailed environment, and a more episodic plot. But the inset tale is also more than a folk-tale; it contains a moving theme, which is close to being a moral (see chapter 9), and striking symbolic imagery. But in both cases the use of the heroic quest pattern provides an understructure of great resonance.

# Notes

PREFACE

1 D.W. Winnicott *Playing and Reality* (Harmondsworth: Penguin 1980); Bruno Bettelheim *The Uses of Enchantment* (New York: Knopf 1977); Carl Jung *The Relations between the Ego and the Unconscious* part 2, *Collected Works* vol 7. Bettelheim is concerned with integrating id, ego, and super-ego. Jung uses the term 'individuation' to mean 'coming to self-hood'; but his sense of self differs from the other two. Winnicott means by 'self' an identity based on a primary sense of 'BEING,' of 'I AM' (94 and 96); Bettelheim in a more conventional way connects 'self' with identity, something attained in the process of a child's development. Jung, in contrast to both, distinguishes between the ego, 'the subject of my consciousness' and the self, 'the subject of my totality; hence it also includes the unconscious psyche.' ('Definitions,' under *Ego*, in *Psychological Types*, *Collected Works* vol 6.) Individuation entails integrating unconscious contents into consciousness. Since integration is the more common term, I shall use it instead of individuation to describe the general process.

PART I
INTRODUCTION

1 W.R. Irwin *The Game of the Impossible* (Urbana: University of Illinois Press 1976) chap 4
2 Christine Brooke-Rose *A Rhetoric of the Unreal* (Cambridge: Cambridge University Press 1981) chap 4
3 The information and the quotation are from Ann Sieveking *The Cave Artists* (London: Thames and Hudson 1979) 19, 95, 148, and 149

4 Heinrich Zimmer *The King and the Corpse* (New York: Meridian 1960) 129
5 Florence Baer, in *Sources and Analogues of the Uncle Remus Tales* (Helsinki: Folklore Fellows Communications no 228, 1980), concludes that in Joel Chandler Harris's original collection twenty-six of the tales came from Africa and only six from Europe. I deal briefly with one of the six in chapter 9.
6 Stith Thompson *The Folktale* (Berkeley: University of California Press 1977) part 4, chap 3
7 Paul Radin *The Trickster: A Study in North American Indian Mythology* (New York: Schocken 1972) xxiii and xxiv
8 Carl Jung 'On the Psychology of the Trickster Figure' in *The Trickster* 202 and 201
9 Johan Huizinga *Homo Ludens* (Boston: Beacon 1955) 11 and 119
10 Ibid 129 and 141
11 *Playing and Reality* 15 and 60
12 Maurice Sendak *Where the Wild Things Are* (New York: Harper and Row 1963); pages are unnumbered.
13 *Playing and Reality* 61
14 Sendak was quite conscious of this threat as a child. Selma Lanes comments on the story in *The Art of Maurice Sendak* (New York: Abradale Press 1984) 77–107 and 238.
15 *Playing and Reality* 24
16 It should be noted, however, that Max's mother is never pictured and that the food has, as if by magic, simply appeared on his bedroom table at the end. In Winnicott's terms, this manifestation would be connected with an 'internal object,' since a 'transitional object is never under magical control' (11). The wild things of Max's fantasy are obviously 'internal objects' and are legitimately under the control of Max's 'magic trick' of staring. But the food actually depends on someone else. Its magical appearance is reminiscent of what Winnicott calls the infant's fantasy that it has '(magical) omnipotent control' of the mother's breast (10). See Sendak's comments on this aspect of appetite in Lanes's *The Art of Maurice Sendak* 239.
17 *Playing and Reality* 63 and 79
18 See Christopher Milne *The Enchanted Places* (Harmondsworth: Penguin 1976); Peter Green *Kenneth Grahame 1859–1932* (London: Murray 1959); Humphrey Carpenter *J.R.R. Tolkien: A Biography* (London: Allen & Unwin 1977); Richard Adams 'Some Ingredients of *Watership Down*' in *The Thorny Paradise* ed. Edward Blishen (Harmondsworth: Penguin 1975); Roger Lancelyn Green *Kipling and the Children* (London: Elek Books 1965). See also Eric Rabkin *The Fantastic in Literature* (Princeton NJ: Princeton University Press 1976) 95 and 96.

19 J.R.R. Tolkien *The Hobbit* (London: Allen & Unwin 1974) 2

CHAPTER ONE

1 Herbert Read 'Introduction' to *Just So Stories* by Rudyard Kipling (New York: Schocken 1965) xi. All quotations from the stories are from this edition, whose illustration plates are particularly clear.
2 Vladimir Propp *The Morphology of the Folktale* (Austin: University of Texas Press 1968) 39–50

CHAPTER TWO

1 A.A. Milne *Winnie-the-Pooh* (New York: Dutton 1974)
2 *Fables of Aesop* trans S.A. Handford (Harmondsworth: Penguin 1982) 3 and xiii
3 *Babrius and Phaedrus* ed and trans Ben Edwin Perry (Cambridge, Mass: Harvard University Press 1965) xxii
4 *Playing and Reality* 116 and 66
5 Sigmund Freud *Jokes and Their Relation to the Unconscious* (New York: Norton 1963) 125
6 Ibid 149
7 Ibid 103
8 A creature of gloom, Eeyore demonstrates ego consciousness each time he appears. In this chapter he shows if not his true nature, at least the motivation behind his persona of ironic gloom. Deciding that he is about to be given the present intended for Pooh, he makes a self-approving speech that exposes both his lack of social perception and his misplaced egoism (since he has done nothing to warrant receiving the gift).
9 *The Enchanted Places* 42–3

CHAPTER THREE

1 Roger Sale *Fairy Tales and After* (Cambridge, Mass: Harvard University Press 1978) 174
2 Mary Ellmann 'Introduction' to *The Wind in the Willows* by Kenneth Grahame (New York: New American Library 1969)
3 *Fairy Tales and After* 185
4 Peter Green *Kenneth Grahame*
5 Ellmann 'Introduction' xv
6 'On the Psychology of the Trickster Figure' in *The Trickster* 195

7 'The Trickster in Relation to Greek Mythology' in *The Trickster* 189 and 188

CHAPTER FOUR

1 E.B. White, *Charlotte's Web* (New York: Harper 1952)
2 The relation between Wilbur's babyhood in the Arable household and his childhood in the Zuckerman barn is perceptively discussed by Perry Nodelman in 'Text as Teacher: The Beginning of *Charlotte's Web*' *Children's Literature* 13, pp 109–27. Roger Sale also discusses the bridge between these two parts of the book in his sympathetic and helpful consideration in *Fairy Tales and After*, 258–67.
3 'The Nature and the Meaning of the Myth' in *The Trickster* 165

CHAPTER FIVE

1 Rudyard Kipling *The Jungle Book* (London: Pan 1979)
2 James Harrison 'Kipling's Jungle Eden' *Mosaic* 7, no 2 (1974) 157 and 161–2
3 Ibid 162
4 Many critics have mixed views on Kipling. Two of the authors considered in this study have expressed their attitudes toward him: Richard Adams in 'Some Ingredients of *Watership Down*' 171–2 and Russell Hoban in 'Time Slip ...' *Children's Literature in Education* 9 (1972) 35–6.
5 Eleazar Meletinsky et al make this distinction in *Soviet Structural Folkloristics* ed P. Miranda (The Hague: Mouton 1974). See also my discussion of the three-part test structure in *The World of the Irish Wonder Tale* (Toronto: University of Toronto Press 1985) chap 4.

PART II
INTRODUCTION

1 Michael Harner *The Way of the Shaman* (New York: Bantam 1982) chap 4
2 Mircea Eliade *Shamanism: Archaic Techniques of Ecstasy* (Princeton NJ: Princeton University Press 1964) 99 and 170–1
3 Ibid 214
4 Ibid 136
5 Joseph Campbell *The Hero with a Thousand Faces* (New York: Meridian 1956). See the diagram on p 245.
6 Carl Jung *Symbols of Transformation* (New York: Harper 1962) 331 and 332

CHAPTER SIX

1 L. Frank Baum *The Wizard of Oz* ed Michael Patrick Hearn (New York: Schocken 1983). In this Critical Heritage edition Hearn includes an interesting discussion of how close Baum actually came to the fairy-tale form: Brian Attebury 'Oz,' 287–9.
2 Max Lüthi *Once upon a Time: On the Nature of Fairy Tales* trans Lee Chadeayne and Paul Gottwald (Bloomington: University of Indiana Press 1976) 70
3 Zimmer *The King and the Corpse* 38 and 39
4 *Once upon a Time* 70 and 80
5 Discussed by Thompson in *The Folktale* 56–7.
6 See chapters 3, 4, and 5 of *The World of the Irish Wonder Tale.*
7 Hearn reprints a perceptive but over-determined Freudian analysis of Baum and the early Oz books: Ormond Beckwith 'The Oddness of Oz' 233–47.
8 L. Frank Baum *Ozma of Oz* (Chicago: Reilly and Lee, nd)
9 See my discussion of this figure in *The World of the Irish Wonder Tale,* chapters 8 and 9.

CHAPTER SEVEN

1 Russell Hoban *The Mouse and His Child* (New York: Avon 1974)
2 *The Morphology of the Folktale* 26–7

CHAPTER EIGHT

1 'Introduction' *The Best of Ernest Thompson Seton* (Glasgow: Fontana 1982) 7 and 8
2 'Introduction' *Seton* 7
3 Ibid 19
4 Ibid 13–15
5 Ibid 14
6 'Raggylug' *Seton* 41
7 Richard Adams *Watership Down* (Harmondsworth: Penguin 1974). Definitions come from the 'Lapine Glossary' at the back of the American edition (New York: Macmillan 1973).
8 'Little War Horse' *Seton* 109
9 Adams 'Some Ingredients of *Watership Down*' 172
10 Campbell *The Hero with a Thousand Faces* 100
11 Ibid 99–101

CHAPTER NINE

1 Joel Chandler Harris *Uncle Remus* (London: Routledge 1881) chap 25. A story with the same plot, 'How the Bear Lost His Tail,' is an ancient European folk-tale that entered literature in the Middle Ages as part of *Reynard the Fox* (see Thompson *The Folktale* 219–20).
2 'Some Ingredients of *Watership Down*' 165. He uses the word *numinous* again on 166.
3 *The Hero with a Thousand Faces* 243
4 'Some Ingredients' 170

CHAPTER TEN

1 Carl Jung 'The Phenomenology of the Spirit in Fairy Tales' *Psyche and Symbol* ed Violet S. de Laszlo (Garden City NY: Doubleday Anchor 1958) 75 and 76
2 J.R.R. Tolkien *The Hobbit*
3 In the 1937 edition, Gollum offers a present, a ring, if Bilbo wins. Although I follow the third edition (1966), I think the original exchange more appropriate; in essence, however, Bilbo still gets the ring from Gollum, as we shall see. For a discussion of Tolkien's revisions of this chapter to bring it in line with *The Lord of the Rings*, see Bonniejean Christensen 'Gollum's Character Transformation in *The Hobbit*' in *A Tolkien Compass* ed Jared Lobdell (New York: Ballantine 1980).
4 André Jolles *Einfache Formen*. See my *The World of the Irish Wonder Tale* 103 and chapter 12.
5 Kathryn Crabbe *J.R.R. Tolkien* (New York: Ungar 1981) 51–2 and 38
6 'On the Psychology of the Trickster Figure' in *The Trickster* 195
7 Timothy O'Neill *The Individuated Hobbit: Jung, Tolkien and the Archetypes of Middle-earth* (Boston: Houghton Mifflin 1979) 116 and 119
8 Dorothy Matthews 'The Psychological Journey of Bilbo Baggins' in *A Tolkien Compass* 42
9 *The Trickster* 203–4
10 'The Phenomenology of the Spirit in Fairy Tales,' 65

CHAPTER ELEVEN

1 Radin 'The Nature and the Meaning of the Myth' in *The Trickster* 156
2 'The Origin of Light' *Tsimsyan Myths* ed Marius Barbeau (Ottawa: National Museum of Canada 1961) 76. Franz Boas had earlier collected the same tale in *Tsimshian Mythology* (1916), reprinted as 'The Theft of Light' in Stith

Thompson *Tales of the North American Indians* (Bloomington: Indiana University Press 1966) 22.

3 *Playing and Reality* 71 and 75
4 In *A Tolkien Compass* 40
5 *Once upon a Time* 80

APPENDIX

1 Campbell *The Hero with a Thousand Faces* 30. The diagram is from 245.
2 Ibid 72
3 Ibid 207
4 Ibid 259

# Index

absurd. See *The Mouse and His Child.*

Adams, Richard: attempted modern epic 125; comments on *Watership Down* 146, on fantasy 124; evaluates other writers 122–3; grounds fantasy in reality 4; influenced by Seton 124; put artistry on line 147; put self in novel 146; style of 125. See also *Watership Down.*

adventure pattern 85–6, 88, 184–6

Aesop. *See* fables.

animals: and ice-age man 6–7; their evolutionary connection to man 7; in *Where the Wild Things Are* 2; their suitability in fantasy fiction 5; as protagonists 182. *See also* grateful animals, helpful animals, trickster.

animism 27

anthropomorphism 123–4, 126

appetite theme 171–2, 182; and trickster 172–4; in *The Hobbit* 150–2, 154, 156, 160–1; in *The Mouse and His Child* 108, 109, 112; in *Ozma of Oz* 98–9, 100–1, 103–4; in *Where the Wild Things Are* 13

archetype, in *Watership Down* 136, 139, 145, 146

archetypes, in *The Hobbit*: shadow 152, 158–9, 165–6, 167; trickster 149, 152, 157, 159, 165; wise old man 149, 165–6. *See also* Jung, shadow, trickster.

autonomy, development of: in Dorothy, as compared to Bilbo 179; in Elahrairah 179–80; in mouse child 177; in Oz books 179; in Pooh 176–7; in Toomai 178–9; in Wilbur 177

Badger: as shadow figure 50; in *loco parentis* 42, 47, 50

Baggins. *See* Bilbo.

Bagheera: born in captivity 65; brings out man in Mowgli 65; mesmerized by Kaa 70; punishes Mowgli 71; speaks for Mowgli 64

Baloo: speaks for Mowgli 64; teaches Mowgli 69

Bandar-log 69

Bard 164–5, 166–7

Baum, L. Frank 90

Beorn: as protector 160–1; as shadow

159, 165; as shape changer 159, 160; danger 160, 165

Bigwig: as temporary leader 140; confronts death 128–9, 137; his similarity to El-ahrairah 137, 139; matures 136–7; organizes escape 140–1; stands off Woundwort 144

Bilbo: and disintegration 175–6; and integration 175–6; and keys 151, 162; as prey 151, 154, 157, 159–61; as shadow trickster 157, 158, 159, 164; as thief 150, 151, 157, 158, 162, 164–5; development of 153, 156, 157–8, 161–2, 164, 166–7; his heritage as a Baggins and a Took 149, 150, 167, 168; in riddle contest 153–7, 163; return home of 167; teased 150, 151, 152; unconscious 152, 165; vulnerability of 15

Billina: aggressive 100, 103, 104, 105, 106; and eggs 98, 103, 104, 105; as Bill 98, 100, 105; as helper 99, 105, 106; as instinctive animal nature 98; as trickster 98, 104, 106

Black Rabbit of Inlé 137–9

boundary crossings 148, 151, 152, 158, 162. See also threshold crossing.

Brer Rabbit: as model for Adams's rabbits 135–6; as trickster 7–8

Brooke-Rose, Christine 4

Buldeo 66–7

Campbell, Joseph. See The Hero with a Thousand Faces.

cautionary tales 29–31

Charlotte: as death-dealer though helpful 54, 55; as surrogate mother 54; as trickster 55, 61–2; as writer 54, 56, 60–1; contrasted with Wilbur 54–5;

cool intelligence of 55, 60; death of 58–9

Charlotte's Web 53–62; appetite theme in 171–2; development of autonomy in 177. See also death, Templeton, Wilbur.

child reader 14–15; and The Hobbit 148–9; and Just So Stories 17–18, 21, 23; and The Wind in the Willows 47; and Winnie-the-Pooh 29–30, 41; excitement and hope stirred in 84; inducted into world 54; summary 182

Christopher Robin, supportive qualities of 30–1, 32, 36, 38, 39–41

comedy, slapstick 57

Cowardly Lion: becomes King of Beasts 95; bravery of 92, 93, 97; caged by witch 92, 94, rescued from poppy field 92; rewarded by Wizard 95; threatens Toto 91

Crabbe, Kathryn 158

creatures: as non-animal 15; defined 3. See also animals.

crying, importance of in The Mouse and His Child 110

Darwinian themes: in Just So Stories 21; in The Mouse and His Child 108

death: and life 181; in Charlotte's Web 53, 54–5, 59, 61; in The Hobbit 152, 154, 159, 160, 161, 164; in The Jungle Book 67, 70, 76–7; in The Mouse and His Child 108–9, 112, 117; in Oz books 93–4, 99, 101; in Watership Down 123, 124, 132, 133, 138–9, 140, 145. See also appetite theme, Bigwig, Black Rabbit of Inlé, Charlotte.

descent into darkness: of Bandar-log 70–1; of Dorothy 89; of Hiawatha 87; of mouse child 88; of Rikki-Tiki-Tavi 76; of shaman 85; of Toomai 74; of White Seal 77–8

disintegration. *See* autonomy.

dogs, in *The Mouse and His Child* 112, 115–16, 117, 118, 119

Dorothy: and carnivorous diet 99; and helpers 90–1, 93, 96, 97, 99–101; and quest 101, 104–5; and relation to witches 97; and three-part narrative structure 95–6; breaks interdiction 99; character traits of 97–8; gains power 104, 106; gets golden hat 94; gets silver shoes 93–4; her similarity to Gretel 94; more conventional in *Ozma of Oz* 98, 99, 100, 106

dreams 7

Eeyore 33, 189n8

ego: Christopher Robin as 31; in Piglet 36; in Toad 46, 47; Pooh as 33. *See also* self.

El-ahrairah: and Black Rabbit of Inlé 138–9, 145; and Frith 126–7; and Rowsby Woof 142; and traditional values 129; as culture hero 126–7; as trickster 128, 133, 135, 139; comes for Hazel 146; gives sign to Bigwig 141; his other-world experience 136

Eldest Magician 22–3

Eliade, Mircea: connects animals with shamans 84–5; connects shamanism with literature and religion 85

Ellmann, Mary 46, 48

evolution 7. *See also* Darwinian themes.

existentialism, in *The Mouse and His Child* 112, 113, 114, 116

fables, of Aesop 31

fantasy fiction: and play 14–15; and subjective fantasy 4; defined 3–4; psychology of 5; spiritual overtones of 6

Fern 53–4, 56, 58

Fiver: as visionary 126, 131, 132–3; his trance in burrow 143, reborn like shaman 144; sets the down as goal 127; warns against Cowslip's warren 128; warns Hazel 131

Freud, Sigmund: and structure of psyche 31, 47; on jokes 36; on laughter 35; on meaning vs enjoyment in words 34; on pleasure principle and repression 181

Frith: and wisdom 180; as benevolent god 127; as sun 127, 128, 139; insists on balance of nature 135

Gandolf: and eagles 159, 165–6; as integrator 151, 160, 161, 166; as wise old man 149, 165–6

Glinda the Good 95, 96

Gollum as Bilbo's destiny 154; asks and answers riddles 153–4, 155–7; as shadow trickster 157, 158, 166; described 153; wants to eat Bilbo 156–7

Good Witch of the North 93, 95

Grahame, Kenneth: and nature 43, 45; handles tone 42, 48; parallels characters 50

grateful animals 92. *See also* helpful animals.

Green, Peter 45, 46

Harner, Michael 84

Harris, Joel Chandler: as author of

*Brer Rabbit* 7; sources of his tales 188n5, 192 chap 9 n1

Harrison, James 64, 68

Hazel: accepts aliens 130; approached by El-ahrairah 146; as leader 127, 130; as main focus in *Watership Down* 126; enters darkness 142; leads expedition to farm 131–2; rescued and freed 144; saves warren 143–4; tries to bargain with Woundwort 143

Hedgehog 20–2

helpful animals 91–2. *See also* grateful animals.

*The Hero with a Thousand Faces*: adventure pattern in 85–6, 88, 184–6; and shaman's journey 132–3, 142

Hiawatha and shamanic motif 87; as quest hero 86–7; meets archetypes 86–7

*The Hobbit* 148–68; boundary crossings in 152, 158, 162; male and female symbols in 149, 158; male conflicts in 169; transcendence in 181. *See also* appetite theme, archetypes, Bilbo, death, Gandolf, Gollum.

hobbits: as creatures 15; humanized 149–50

Holly 130, 133

home 167–8

*Homo Ludens*. *See* Huizinga, Johan.

Huizinga, Johan 9–10

humour. *See* comedy.

Hungry Tiger 100–1

id: in Piglet 33; in Pooh 30, 33; in Toad 46

illusion, in fiction 3

impersonal vs personal 110, 111

impossible task 66, 67, 73, 77

individuation 187 pref n1. *See also* integration.

inflation/deflation 48–9, 52

initiation ritual 83; and riddles 153; incorporating the formless 175; shamanic 85

integration: discussed 187 pref n1; inner and outer 170–1; in *The Mouse and His Child* 119; in *Watership Down* 130–1; in *Winnie-the-Pooh* 40–1; male and female 169–70. *See also* autonomy.

interdiction 99, 110, 111

Irwin, W.R. 4

John of the Cross, Saint 87

Jonah 87

Jung, Carl: on anima 86–7; on concept of self 181, 187 pref n1; on personal vs collective unconscious 86; on trickster 8–9, 49; on wise old man 87; theory of archetypes of 86

*The Jungle Book*: 63–79; 'Kaa's Hunting' 69–71; 'Mowgli's Brothers' 64–6; 'Rikki-Tiki-Tavi' 76; 'Tiger, Tiger' 66–9; 'Toomai of the Elephants' 72–6, 79; 'The White Seal' 76–9. *See also* Bagheera, death, Mowgli, Shere Khan.

*Just So Stories* 17–28; illustrations in 21, 23, 24; 'The Beginning of the Armadillos' 20–2, 24–5; 'The Cat That Walked by Himself' 22, 26–8; 'The Crab That Played with the Sea' 22–3; 'The Elephant's Child' 17–18, 21, 25–6; 'How the Leopard Got His Spots' 17, 21, 23–4; 'How the Whale Got His Throat' 18–19, 24; 'The Sing-Song of Old Man Kangaroo' 19–20, 21, 25. *See also* trickster.

Kaa 70
Kala Nag 72–3, 75
Kanga and Roo 37–8
Keehar 130, 141
Kerenyi, Karl 51
Kierkegaard, Søren 87
Kipling, Rudyard: and child language 17; and power 64, 69; compared with Richard Adams 125; his imitative power 71; his need to punish 69, 71–2; his use of repetition 19–20; his use of rhythm 18–19; on freedom and law 64, 68
Kotick. See White Seal.

The Last Visible Dog 112, 115, 119
laughter 109, 111–12, 113
life: celebration of 59–60; love of 53
love: as antidote to death 53; unconditional 55
Lüthi, Max 91

magic: in Just So Stories 22; words and wishes 4
Manny Rat: as enemy 114, 118, 119; defeated 118, 119; his desire for control 111, 115
Matthews, Dorothy 176
Max 11–13
maze 23
Milne, A.A. 30. See also Winnie-the-Pooh.
Mole: and inner call 43, 45; and outer call 43, 44, 45; as trickster 50; inexperience of 48; maturing of 51
The Mouse and His Child 108–121; absurd in 112, 113, 114, 115, 117; appetite in 172; as quest narrative 88; clockwork laws in 110, 111; development of autonomy in 177–8;

drawing-room comedy in 109–10; male conflicts in 170; prophecy in 111, 114, 117, 118; social and natural laws in 110; violence in 109. See also appetite theme, death, dogs, existentialism, integration, Manny Rat.
mouse child: and dog-star 113, 118; and self 110, 111, 116, 117; cries 110; faces nothingness 114, 116; laughs 109, 111; wants family and home 110, 113
mouse father: defeats Manny Rat 118; wants family and home 117; wants to be self-winding 115, 118, 119
Mowgli as disruptive force 65; cast out 65, 67; contrasted with Fern 63; defeats Shere Khan 66–7; helps Baloo and Bagheera 70; keeps law 68; kidnapped 69; punished 71
Mudd, Miss 115–16, 117
myth 85, 86, 148, 183, 186; in Just So Stories 23; in Watership Down 123, 126, 145–6

Nome King: and magic belt 103, 104; as animal 103, 104; as non-human 101, 105; as ruler of underground 101–2, 105; as trickster 102–3, 104

Once upon a Time 191 chap 6 n2
O'Neill, Timothy 159
Owl 33, 34, 39
Ozma: excessive pride of 102–3, 105; moral quality of 105, 106; on quest 100, 101
Ozma of Oz 98–107; adventure pattern in 183–4; aggression in 172; appetite in 172; development of autonomy in 176, 179; parallel parts of 101. See also Billina, Dorothy, Nome King, power.

Pan 43, 44, 51
panic 43, 51
Perry, Ben Edwin 31
Piglet: courage of 36; fearfulness of 32–3, 35, 37; loses control of language 35; self-assertion of 37, 38
plausibility, in narrative 56
play 9–11, 14–15, 22, 28
*Playing and Reality* 11. *See also* Winnicott.
power, female vs male in Oz 96–7, 98, 101, 105–6, 169
primitive tradition, compared to civilized 83
Propp, Vladimir: on donor in fairy-tale 26; on interdiction 110
psychoanalytic theory. *See* Freud, Jung, Winnicott.
psychological reassurance, in children's tales 16

quest: elements of 6, 185; false 115; inner 113–14, 115–16, 117; origin and nature of 83–5, 88; outer 113, 117, 118, 119; in *Ozma of Oz* 105; in *Watership Down* 129, 133, 142, 184–6

Rabbit 31–2, 37
Radin, Paul, on trickster 8–9, 55, 174
Rat: as mentor 43, 44; domesticity of 45, 50; irrationality of 44–5
Rat, Manny. *See* Manny Rat.
realistic fiction 3
rebirth 85, 88, 117, 144
riddles 152, 153–6, 163

Sale, Roger 42, 45
Sartre, Jean-Paul 87
Scarecrow: as ruler of Oz 96; gets

brains 95, his initial rescue by Dorothy 92, 96, 97; plans rescue of Lion 92; protects Dorothy 94
self: Christopher Robin as 33, 40; Pooh as 33, 38. *See also* ego.
Sendak, Maurice. See *Where the Wild Things Are*.
Serpentina, C.: as author of *The Last Visible Dog* 115, 119; as deep thinker 115, 119
Seton, Ernest Thompson: anthropomorphism in 123–4; as influence on Richard Adams 123–4; realism in his animal stories 122, 123
shadow: as animal level of personality 9; as archetype 86. *See also* Jung.
shamanism. *See* Eliade.
Shere Khan: as coward 68; as disruptive force 65, 67; demands Mowgli as baby 64, 65; killed 67
Smaug 162–4
super-ego: author as 31; lack of, in Toad 47
swastika 23
*Symbols of Transformation* 86. *See also* Jung.

tame creature, in 'The Cat That Walked by Himself' 27–8; in *Where the Wild Things Are* 13
Templeton: as trickster 57; greed of 57, 59, selfishness of 57, 58–9
Thorin: accepted by men 162; and elf sword 151, 152; and treasure fever 164–5; his capture by elves 162
three-test structure: in *Watership Down* 129; in 'The White Seal' 78; in *The Wizard of Oz* 95–6
threshold crossing 184–5. *See also* boundary crossings.

Tik-Tok 100–2

Tin Woodman: as emperor of Winkies 94, 96; gets heart 95; helpfulness of 91, 92; his rescue by Dorothy 92, 96; slays enemies 94

Toad: and motor cars 46–7, 48, 49; as animal 50; as humbug 49–50; as trickster 47–9; dominated by passions 45, 46, 47, 48; his physiognomy as destiny 46, 48; his transvestism 48, 49; reformed 52; undaunted 42, 46, 48, 49

Tolkien, J.R.R.: and hobbits 15, 149–50; his tone in *The Hobbit* 148–9; nature of his fantasy world 149; unaware of Jung 88

Toomai 72–5, 178–9

Tortoise 20–2

Toto 91

tramp, in *The Mouse and His Child* 111, 119–20, 121

transcendence: archetypal 180–1; of appetite 172

trickster: and animal energy 182; and appetite 173–4; and creativity 174; and evolution 23–5; and repression 173; and shadow 173–4; and transformation 174; as spider 55; connects animal to man 8; different animal forms of 7–8; in children's stories 9; in *Just So Stories* 23–7; in popular culture 9; in *The Wind in the Willows* 48–51. *See also* Bilbo, Billina, Charlotte, El-ahrairah, Gollum, *Just So Stories*, Kaa, Radin, Toad.

*Watership Down* 122–34, 135–47, 183–6; adventure pattern in 184–6; as modern epic 125; autonomy in 179–80; male conflicts in 169; transcendence in 180; 'El-ahrairah and the Black Rabbit of Inlé 134, 137, 138–9, 145, 179–80; 'The King's Lettuce' 133; 'The Story of Rowsby Woof and the Fairy Wogdog' 142; 'The Story of the Blessing of El-ahrairah' 126–7, 135–6. *See also* archetype, Bigwig, death, El-ahrairah, Fiver, Hazel, quest, Woundwort.

*The Way of the Shaman. See* Harner.

*Where the Wild Things Are* 11–15; discussed 13–14; magic in 188n16

White Seal 76–9, 113, 180

Wicked Witches: of the East 93, 95, 97; of the West: and main test 96; captures or destroys questers 94; dissolved by Dorothy 94, 97; must be killed 94

Wilbur: appetite of 60; as baby 54; as caring friend 59; emotional 55, 58–9, 60; modesty of 57; rational 59, 60

wild creatures 12–13; in 'The Cat That Walked by Himself' 27–8; in *Ozma of Oz* 100–1; in *Where the Wild Things Are* 15–16; in *The Wind in the Willows* 50–1

the wild vs the tame 72, 75

Wild Wood, terror in 43, 44, 52

*The Wind in the Willows* 42–52, 170, 180; 'Mr. Toad' 47; 'The Open Road' 46; 'The Piper at the Gates of Dawn' 42, 44; 'The Return of Ulysses' 50–1, 125; 'Wayfarers All' 42, 44–5. *See also* Mole, Pan, Rat, Toad, trickster.

Winnicott, D.W.: on formless functioning 175; on play 11–12, 14; on self 14, 33, 174–5; on transitional objects 11; three-stage theory of 176. *See also* autonomy.

Winnie-the-Pooh: and brains 32, 34, 39, 41; and self-appreciation 32, 33, 34, 36, 38, 39; as stuffed bear 29; his indulgence of appetite 30–2, 34–5, 171

*Winnie-the-Pooh* 29–41; appetite in 171; community in 40–1, 170; contrasted with Seton's stories 122–3; development of autonomy in 176–7; fantasy and realism in 4. *See also* cautionary tales, Christopher Robin, ego, Piglet, self.

Wizard of Oz: defensiveness of 96–7; demands death of witch 94; his departure in balloon 95; rewards success on quest 94–5

*The Wizard of Oz* 90–7, 179. *See also* Cowardly Lion, Dorothy, helping animals, power, quest, Scarecrow, Tin Woodman, Wicked Witches.

Woundwort, General: accepts Bigwig 140; as super-rabbit 139; committed to violence 143; compared to the Black Rabbit of Inlé 139, 141, 145; legends about, after death 145; retreats from Bigwig 144; wins respect of Bigwig 141

Yellow Dog Dingo 19

Zimmer, Heinrich 7, 91–2